Bloom's Modern Critical Views

African American
 Poets: Wheatley–
 Tolson
African American
 Poets: Hayden–
 Dove
Edward Albee
Dante Alighieri
American and
 Canadian Women
 Poets,
 1930–present
American Women
 Poets, 1650–1950
Maya Angelou
Asian-American
 Writers
Margaret Atwood
Jane Austen
Paul Auster
James Baldwin
Honoré de Balzac
Samuel Beckett
Saul Bellow
The Bible
William Blake
Jorge Luis Borges
Ray Bradbury
The Brontës
Gwendolyn Brooks
Elizabeth Barrett
 Browning
Robert Browning
Italo Calvino
Albert Camus
Truman Capote
Lewis Carroll
Willa Cather
Cervantes
Geoffrey Chaucer
Anton Chekhov
Kate Chopin
Agatha Christie

Samuel Taylor
 Coleridge
Joseph Conrad
Contemporary Poets
Stephen Crane
Daniel Defoe
Don DeLillo
Charles Dickens
Emily Dickinson
John Donne and the
 17th-Century Poets
Fyodor Dostoevsky
W.E.B. DuBois
George Eliot
T.S. Eliot
Ralph Ellison
Ralph Waldo Emerson
William Faulkner
F. Scott Fitzgerald
Sigmund Freud
Robert Frost
William Gaddis
Johann Wolfgang von
 Goethe
George Gordon, Lord
 Byron
Graham Greene
Thomas Hardy
Nathaniel Hawthorne
Ernest Hemingway
Hermann Hesse
Hispanic-American
 Writers
Homer
Langston Hughes
Zora Neale Hurston
Aldous Huxley
Henrik Ibsen
John Irving
Henry James
James Joyce
Franz Kafka
John Keats

Jamaica Kincaid
Stephen King
Rudyard Kipling
Milan Kundera
D.H. Lawrence
Doris Lessing
Ursula K. Le Guin
Sinclair Lewis
Norman Mailer
Bernard Malamud
David Mamet
Christopher Marlowe
Gabriel García
 Márquez
Cormac McCarthy
Carson McCullers
Herman Melville
Arthur Miller
John Milton
Molière
Toni Morrison
Native-American
 Writers
Joyce Carol Oates
Flannery O'Connor
Eugene O'Neill
George Orwell
Octavio Paz
Sylvia Plath
Edgar Allan Poe
Katherine Anne
 Porter
Marcel Proust
Thomas Pynchon
Philip Roth
Salman Rushdie
J. D. Salinger
Jean-Paul Sartre
William Shakespeare
George Bernard Shaw
Mary Wollstonecraft
 Shelley
Percy Bysshe Shelley

Bloom's Modern Critical Views

Alexander
  Solzhenitsyn
Sophocles
John Steinbeck
Tom Stoppard
Jonathan Swift
Amy Tan
Alfred, Lord Tennyson
Henry David Thoreau
J.R.R. Tolkien
Leo Tolstoy

Ivan Turgenev
Mark Twain
John Updike
Kurt Vonnegut
Derek Walcott
Alice Walker
Robert Penn Warren
Eudora Welty
Edith Wharton
Walt Whitman
Oscar Wilde

Tennessee Williams
Thomas Wolfe
Tom Wolfe
Virginia Woolf
William Wordsworth
Jay Wright
Richard Wright
William Butler Yeats
Emile Zola

Bloom's Modern Critical Views

PAUL AUSTER

Edited and with an introduction by
Harold Bloom
Sterling Professor of the Humanities
Yale University

CHELSEA HOUSE
PUBLISHERS
A Haights Cross Communications Company
Philadelphia

©2004 by Chelsea House Publishers, a subsidiary of
Haights Cross Communications.

A Haights Cross Communications ✦ Company

Introduction © 2004 by Harold Bloom.

Printed and bound in the United States of America.
10 9 8 7 6 5 4 3 2 1

Library of Congress Cataloging-in-Publication Data
Paul Auster / edited and with an introduction by Harold Bloom.
     p. cm. -- (Bloom's modern critical views)
Includes bibliographical references and index.
   ISBN: 0-7910-7662-8
  1. Auster, Paul, 1947---Criticism and interpretation. I. Bloom,
Harold. II. Series.
   PS3551.U77Z7 2003
   813'.54--dc21
                                    2003011516

Chelsea House Publishers
1974 Sproul Road, Suite 400
Broomall, PA 19008-0914

http://www.chelseahouse.com

Contributing Editor: Amy Sickels

Cover designed by Terry Mallon

Cover photo by © Cardinale/CORBIS SYGMA

Layout by EJB Publishing Services

Contents

Editor's Note   vii

Introduction   1
   Harold Bloom

The Bureau of Missing Persons:
   Notes on Paul Auster's Fiction   3
   Charles Baxter

"How to Get Out of the Room That Is the Book?"
   Paul Auster and the Consequences of Confinement   7
   Stephen Fredman

Paul Auster, or The Heir Intestate   43
   Pascal Bruckner

Paul Auster's *The Invention of Solitude*: Glimmers
   in a Reach to Authenticity   51
   William Dow

The Revenge of the Author: Paul Auster's
   Challenge to Theory   63
   John Zilcosky

The Novel of Critical Engagement:
   Paul Auster's *City of Glass*   77
   William Lavender

Deconstructing *The New York Trilogy*:
   Paul Auster's Anti-Detective Fiction   97
   Alison Russell

Chance in Contemporary Narrative:
    The Example of Paul Auster   113
    Steven E. Alford

"Looking for Signs in the Air": Urban Space and
    the Postmodern in *In the Country of Last Things*   137
    Tim Woods

'The End Is Only Imaginary'   161
    Padgett Powell

A Book at the End of the World: Paul Auster's
    In the Country of Last Things   165
    Katharine Washburn

Inside *Moon Palace*   171
    Steven Weisenburger

Doubles and more doubles   183
    Bruce Bawer

Exploding Fictions   191
    Aliki Varvogli

From Metonymy to Metaphor:
    Paul Auster's *Leviathan*   207
    Linda L. Fleck

Austerity Measures: Paul Auster Goes to the Dogs   223
    Steven G. Kellman

Chronology   233

Contributors   235

Bibliography   239

Acknowledgments   243

Index   247

Editor's Note

My Introduction meditates upon *The New York Trilogy*, three distinguished short novels that both puzzle and charm me by their artful evasions.

The Austerian fear of identity loss is noted by Charles Baxter, while Stephen Fredman considers the image of (Jewish) memory in Auster's almost Kafkan sense of confinement.

Pascal Bruckner discusses Auster's stance towards his actual father, unknowable by his son, presumably in contrast to the literary fathers, Kafka and Beckett, after which William Dow adds another commentary upon *The Invention of Solitude*.

The New York Trilogy is a challenge to fashionable literary theory, according to John Zilcosky, who palpably is accurate, but now that it is 2003, the era of the Death of Theory, one can prophesy that Auster's challenge may help put the *Trilogy* into the Limbo of Period Pieces.

William Lavender also studies *City of Glass* as a conflict with French literary theory, while Alison Russell speculates upon the problematic element in Auster's "anti-detective fiction."

Chance, a crucial aspect of Auster's narratives, is the concern of Steven E. Alford, after which Tim Woods examines the ambiguous urbanity of *In the Country of Last Things*.

Padgett Powell is not persuaded by that novel, while Katharine Washburn commends it for "Swiftean guile and ferocity."

Moon Palace by Steven Weisenberger is juxtaposed both with Whitman and Emerson, after which Bruce Bawer relates this novel to *The New York Trilogy* as another interplay upon Doubles, like Poe's "William Wilson."

Aliki Varvogli, writing upon Auster's *Leviathan*, invokes the American context of the Age of Emerson, while Linda L. Fleck subjects the same book to the critical stances of Paul de Man and Frederic Jameson. Lastly, Steven G. Kellman ponders *Timbuktu*, Auster's canine narrative.

HAROLD BLOOM

Introduction

Rereading Auster's *New York Trilogy* is for me, an odd experience, if only because I never can decide how to regard these three spare, refined narratives. Auster can seem a French novelist who writes in American English, but his American literary culture is extensive and finally decisive. He acknowledges Kafka and Beckett as his masters, while finding Cervantes to be his imaginative ideal. The curious version of "detective stories" that determines the shape of the *Trilogy* is more in the mode of Borges (itself Kafkan) than in that of the hard-boiled genre of Raymond Chandler and his followers. If there is an American counter-tradition that turns the detective stories of Poe inside out, its chief practitioners are Hawthorne and Melville, the principal narrative writers of the Age of Emerson and Walt Whitman.

Auster can be said to cross Hawthorne with Kafka, as Borges did. The Argentine fabulist remarked that his favorite story was Hawthorne's "Wakefield," an altogether Austerian tale. Wakefield vanishes from home and marriage, but only to establish residence a few streets away. After a considerable interval, he returns to his life, in a reunion as inexplicable as his withdrawal. Auster, a more considerable poet in prose than in verse, is perhaps less a novelist than he is a romancer, really a pre-Cervantine kind of exposition.

Aesthetic dignity is the keynote of everything I have read by Auster. If there is a missing element in Auster's achievement, it is comedy, even of a grotesque variety. It seems fair to contrast Auster with Philip Roth, half a generation older, yet another lifelong disciple of Franz Kafka. Painful as Roth's humor tends to be, it is uproarious and heartening. Perhaps it carries the Blessing, the "more life" of Jewish tradition, though in singular form. Weirdly enough, by implication, Kafka's "The Hunger Artist" (a favorite of both Roth and Auster) also bears the Blessing. Kafka is comprehensive enough, in his extreme way, to sustain both Roth and Auster. But Kafka's

1

somber comedy remains comic: in Auster no one seems to laugh. The Jewish joke, which links Freud, Kafka, and Roth, has no presence in Auster.

What—I think—takes its place are Auster's own appearances in his fictions. In *City of Glass* the protagonist, Quinn, who writes mystery novels under the name of Poe's William Wilson, enjoys an omelette prepared for him by "Paul Auster." Quinn and Auster have an unsurprising conversation about Cervantes, and then Quinn meets Auster's wife, Siri, and son, Daniel. Again, this is unsurprising, and is charming, yet puzzling, at least to me. What does it do for *City of Glass*? Now that "French Theory" is only still hot in Peoria, the disruption of representation is hardly worth a shrug, since in no way does Auster practice an art that seeks to imitate social reality. His *Art of Hunger* celebrates Beckett, Kafka, Kanut Hamsun, and Paul Celan as seers of absence. I want to murmur: "Yes, but," and then enlarge the "but." These elliptical literary artists also manifest a richness that makes me care about *what happens next*. Auster seems to have no such concern.

Auster's creative minimalism has moved many good readers, both here and abroad. If Auster evades me, I therefore blame myself. And even so, I go back to my master, Dr. Samuel Johnson, who rightly commended Shakespeare for his just representations of general nature.

CHARLES BAXTER

The Bureau of Missing Persons: Notes on Paul Auster's Fiction

I have a friend who lives across town who fears that she is losing, not her mind, exactly, but her identity. This began about three months ago. Various foods she had once loved made her sick. Panic states like waves of fever confounded her with their inexplicable urgency. She had trouble going outside for any length of time, and her husband (who usually went off to work in the morning) rearranged his schedule so that he could be with her throughout the day. Most of the summer they stayed in their house, tired and frightened of their feelings. Nights and darkness for her managed to reclaim their traditional fright status. When she called, she would talk about the effort, really the agony at times, of being trapped inside a mind, a body, a *framework*, that she did not feel that she owned. I'd tell her about difficult episodes of my own emotional life, and she'd say, "It's funny: when people hear about this, it turns out that they all have stories, too."

Artaud—who knew as much about these states as anyone has—writes in his journals that at some moments he had no feeling of ownership over his thoughts. (He does not put it this way, exactly; I am making discursive what is essentially thought as trauma.) When ideas came into his head, he did not perceive that they had in any sense originated with him, nor could he make a claim upon them. He could not recognize them as his. Ideas, for Artaud, refused to acknowledge the mind that apparently conceived them. The

From *The Review of Contemporary Fiction* 14, no. 1 (Spring 1994). © 1994 by Charles Baxter.

homelessness of ideas is for Artaud one of the most menacing features of thought generally. This sounds abstract. Actually it is terrifying. One begins to feel the mind rising out of the body, floating just above it, suddenly susceptible to invasion by ideas that are nowhere, exactly just in the air, ownerless and, because ownerless, like starved vagrant dogs, malign.

One's selfhood, being both a cultural and personal construction, can, like thought itself, also become free of the person to whom it was once attached. Eastern philosophies talk about "hungry ghosts" that suck your identity away, and German romantic fiction is marked by devil figures who are in the business of buying shadows and souls and then hiding them in cabinets and sacks. To have a double, to see yourself mirrored in a twin, is the beginning of the feeling that something private and essential about you is being removed in a secretive and unpleasant way.

Americans tend to be very proud of their identities: the flag, the South (or any other region—in my case, the Midwest), occupation, parenthood, all the notational marks that make anyone recognizable. Tocqueville noticed the combination of wild pride and privacy in American identities, the pleasure in the recognizable that Americans took, as if in a vast empty culture identity were in fact the one genuine achievement a person could lay claim to, something earned rather than given. It's the late-Puritan myth of selfhood, and it does not go away. In this country *you've got to make yourself into something*, as my uncle, the go-getter, liked to say (to me, as a teenager). Against the genuine emptiness of things, empty because of the culture's voracious appetite for what appears at first to be improvement, one arranges these small signs of selfhood: a little trophy, a baby, an apple pie.

The achievement of Paul Auster's fiction—and it is considerable—is to combine an American obsession with gaining an identity with the European ability to ask how, and under what conditions, identity is stolen or lost. In the European intellectual tradition, every identity may be contingent and can be taken from you; in America, we tend to think of identity as unstealable, as permanent as a backyard swimming pool. In Auster's work, the small things—baseball, a bit of money, food, one's proper name, the car, one's relations and lovers—stand against the constant eroding force of ontological slippage and going under. Paul Auster's great popularity in Europe probably has to do with his refusal to share in the prideful and rather curious American faith in family as a source of identity. For him, family is more a source of *loss* of identity.

Americans have several noteworthy lyricists of identity but very few who can write at all clearly about what it is to lose a name or a self, to experience soul theft. One thinks of Nathaniel Hawthorne, Melville's confidence-man, and maybe William James in his concern for the sick soul, and then ... well, there are certainly others, but it's been a subject that makes Americans profoundly uneasy, the audible rat gnawing away in the mansion. The subject gets disguised so that it's almost unrecognizable: *Tender Is the Night*, which is probably about the pouring of one person's selfhood into the vacancy of another's, is regularly taught as a tender love story that takes place on the French Riviera.

Auster's writing, from his poems onward, has a feeling of cataclysm that has cooled somehow and become vertical, seen from above, diagrammatic. Nevertheless, it is still felt as cataclysmic, a breaking back to nothing. At its heart is a feeling for the accidents and stubborn meaninglessness of trauma. For me this mode of thinking and feeling first became apparent in *The Invention of Solitude*, which is at all points haunted by the author's father, Sam. Sam Auster is the first missing person to appear in Paul Auster's writing, and he is certainly one of the most memorable of these disappeared ones.

Having been traumatized himself by the murder of his own father, Sam is altered into a mechanical man, largely vacated of visible feelings, whose eerie emptiness is both invasive and educational. To be around such a person is to acquire a feeling for soul death. Having a person like that as a parent gives a reading of Descartes a certain urgency. Detachment under these circumstances grows into zombiehood: seeing his grandchild for the first time, Sam says, "A beautiful baby. Good luck with it." He looks and then looks away. Emotionally, this is an education in noninvolvement, self-resistance, Cartesian separations.

The Invention of Solitude is haunted by parents and children, by what parents pass on to their children, by what is *visited* upon them. In *Facing the Music*, the poet's elegy for his father is separated by two poems from an elegy for himself. It's as if an elegy for an absented father gives birth to an elegy for an absented son, who is, thanks to the words, alive in some sense, at least in the poem. In the poem for the father, "the words / have no meaning. And therefore to ask / only for words." In the author's elegy for himself, there are "so many words / lost in the wide world / within me." Emptiness, like a family contagion, can be passed on from generation to generation, and *The Invention of Solitude* is for me a book in which the author identifies an affliction he himself has suffered that he is doing his best not to pass on to anyone else. The book is haunted by the figure of Pinocchio, whose creator made him out of wood, but who wants to become non-wooden and human; at last, after a series of terrible trials, he becomes a person. No wonder the book is haunted as well by Mallarmé's poems on his dying son, Anatole, From dying, from death in life, one retrieves the words that, like clothing, once housed the spirit and are the remnants that leave the trace of the human once the spirit departs, in the shape of the clothes, the ordering of the syntax.

From here on, the project of the fiction is, at least in part, to observe the drama of lost-and-found personalities. *In the Country of Last Things* numbers among its characters a man named, almost allegorically, Sam Farr, who is loved, lost, and found again. *The New York Trilogy* gives us a set of wondrous mazes of identity, peopled with mysterious observers, authorial surrogates, mirrors facing mirrors, and persons missing to one degree or another. It's worth mentioning that, along with their conceptual rigor, these books display a real wit. I was present at a public reading of selections from these books; the audience and the author were both laughing with genuine pleasure at the subject of lost identity—as if it were both deadly serious and somehow wrenchingly funny.

Because most of Paul Auster's stories are about secrets and deception, their structures usually take the form of detection or a quest—something has to be found out. But they all have something of an aftermath feeling: the gods have done their work, someone has put some design into play, and we are here, wandering around, doing our best to construe what that design might be and how we fit into it. In *The Music of Chance* Jim Nashe runs through his inheritance, runs out of luck, and falls, along with his pal Pozzi, into the hands of the pygmy Olympians, Flower and Stone. (Auster's work is often gazing in the direction of allegory, even if it never quite arrives there.) On Flower and Stone's vast estate, following a night of terrible luck in a poker game, Nashe and Pozzi must build a giant wall to repay their debt. They do so, and very movingly. Although Nashe is x'ed out in an accident at the end of the book, his job has become him. Nashe's work and suffering give him what he has never had, something like an identity.

My description of this book has made it more schematic than it actually is—like a postmodern combination of *The Myth of Sisyphus* and *A Day in the Life of Ivan Denisovich*—but it nevertheless takes emptying out and suffering very seriously, as all of Paul Auster's work does, and it does not suggest that you can get identity anywhere anytime you please. It understands that much of what happens to us is out of our hands but that a small and even tragic possibility for selfhood is possible, given sufficient suffering, persistence, and luck. It's not a glib message, and the fiction in which it appears conveys an atmosphere of humor and disaster. All the same, like the best literature of any period, it is news that stays news, telling us with insight and grace what it's like to live in these cities of glass that all of us inhabit.

STEPHEN FREDMAN

"How to Get Out of the Room That Is the Book?" Paul Auster and the Consequences of Confinement

I.

Reading the novels of Paul Auster over the years, I find myself drawn back again and again to his first prose text, *The Invention of Solitude* (1982), especially to its second half, "The Book of Memory," a memoir-as-meditation, in which Auster confronts all of his central obsessions, obsessions that return in various forms to animate his subsequent novels.[1] One of the most resonant images from "The Book of Memory" that recurs in Auster's later work is that of "the room of the book," a place where life and writing meet in an unstable, creative, and sometimes dangerous encounter. In the present essay, I would like to examine the room of the book through three interpretive frameworks that will help to make its dimensions apprehensible. These frameworks represent dynamic issues that arise from within the room of the book, issues that account for some of the characteristic complexities of Auster's work: 1) a contest between prose and poetry that colors much of his writing; 2) a parthenogenic fantasy of masculine creativity that he constructs with great effort; and 3) a pervasive preoccupation with Holocaust imagery. In my reading of Auster's prose, the postmodern inquiry into the relationship between writing and identity metamorphoses into a confrontation with a series of gender issues, oriented

From *Postmodern Culture* 6, no. 3 (May 1996). © 1996 by Stephen Fredman.

around the father, and then metamorphoses again into an interrogation of the particularly Jewish concern with memory. Using memory to probe the ruptures in contemporary life, Auster returns ultimately to the unspeakable memories of the Holocaust, thus laying bare ways in which the postmodern is inescapably post-Holocaust.

To set the stage, we will look at an exemplary dramatization of the equation between "the room" and "the book" in *Ghosts* (1986), the second volume of Auster's *New York Trilogy*. The protagonist of *Ghosts*, Blue, has recently completed an apprenticeship to a master detective, Brown, and the novel narrates Blue's first "case," in which he hopes to establish an identity as self-sufficient "agent." Blue has been engaged by White to "keep an eye on" Black, a simple "tail job" that turns out to be much more demanding than Blue could have imagined. It's not that Black is difficult to follow; in fact, he hardly ever leaves his room. From his own room across the street, Blue, using binoculars, can see that Black spends most of his time writing in a notebook and reading. In order to record Black's activities, Blue takes out a notebook himself and begins to write, thus initiating the equation between the room and the book.

After nearly a year of tailing Black, following him on long walks and watching him read and write, Blue begins to find his lack of knowledge about Black, White, and the case unbearable. Unsuccessful in his attempt to precipitate a disclosure from the ever-elusive White, Blue realizes that his perpetual spying on the nearly sedentary Black has rendered Blue a virtual prisoner in his own room. It dawns on him that Black and White may be in collusion, and that in fact *he* may be the one under surveillance:

> If so, what are they doing to him? Nothing very terrible, finally—
> at least not in any absolute sense. They have trapped Blue into
> doing nothing, into being so inactive as to reduce his life to
> almost no life at all. Yes, says Blue to himself, that's what it feels
> like: like nothing at all. He feels like a man who has been
> condemned to sit in a room and go on reading a book for the rest
> of his life. This is strange enough—to be only half alive at best,
> seeing the world only through words, living only through the
> lives of others. But if the book were an interesting one, perhaps
> it wouldn't be so bad. He could get caught up in the story, so to
> speak, and little by little begin to forget himself. But this book
> offers him nothing. There is no story, no plot, no action—
> nothing but a man sitting alone in a room and writing a book.
> That's all there is, Blue realizes, and he no longer wants any part

of it. But how to get out? How to get out of the room that is the book that will go on being written for as long as he stays in the room? (NYT 201–2)

Not an intellectual or even much of a reader, Blue has been metamorphosed into a writer—that is, into someone who lives inside a book. Every other aspect of his life has been taken away from him—he has abandoned his fiancée, his mentor refuses to offer advice, etc.—and he realizes the terror of the writer: "There is no story, no plot, no action—nothing but a man sitting alone in a room and writing a book." This primal condition of the writer in the present age—imprisoned, facing a blank page without the structures of story, plot, or action to support him—has become Blue's life, and he begins to suspect that Black (or White?) has planned it that way, willing this monstrous metamorphosis.

Blue's suspicions that his life has been captured by a book are confirmed during two visits to Black's room. In the second, Blue crosses the street one night when Black is out and steals a pile of papers stacked on Black's desk. When he begins to read them, Blue sees that they are his own weekly reports; this means that Black and White are the same person and that, in some mysterious way, Blue and Black have been writing the same book. With these realizations, Blue collapses into vertigo and enters a state of irresolvable doubleness:

> For Blue at this point can no longer accept Black's existence, and therefore he denies it. Having penetrated Black's room and stood there alone, having been, so to speak, in the sanctum of Black's solitude, he cannot respond to the darkness of that moment except by replacing it with a solitude of his own. To enter Black, then, was the equivalent of entering himself, and once inside himself, he can no longer conceive of being anywhere else. But this is precisely where Black is, even though Blue does not know it. (226)

When Blue realizes that Black is his double, he also becomes aware that Black's room is the uncanny scene of writing, which Blue, who had never conceived of himself as a writer, had been afraid of entering all along. In confronting Black's solitude, he meets his own; in confronting Black's writing, he recovers his own and realizes that he has become a writer. When he walks across the street to Black's room one more time, Blue finds out why Black/White has hired him. Upon entering the room, Blue encounters Black

pointing a revolver at him, intending to end both of their lives. In the
ensuing dialogue, Blue, the bewildered detective, tries one more time to
understand what has been happening:

> You're supposed to tell me the story. Isn't that how it's
> supposed to end? You tell me the story, and then we say good-
> bye.
> You know it already, Blue. Don't you understand that? You
> know the story by heart.
> Then why did you bother in the first place?
> Don't ask stupid questions.
> And me—what was I there for? Comic relief?
> No, Blue, I've needed you from the beginning. If it hadn't
> been for you, I couldn't have done it.
> Needed me for what?
> To remind me of what I was supposed to be doing. Every time
> I looked up, you were there, watching me, following me, always
> in sight, boring into me with your eyes. You were the whole
> world to me, Blue, and I turned you into my death. You're the
> one thing that doesn't change, the one thing that turns everything
> inside out. (230)

Black has turned Blue into his ideal reader, for whom every moment of
Black's existence in a room writing a book has been full of unfathomable
meaning. And by allaying the writer's constant fear that the external world
will dematerialize during his residence in the space of writing, Blue's gaze has
"turn[ed] everything inside out" for Black, making his writing into a fateful,
and ultimately fatal, act. Having created this external witness to his internal
activity as writer, Black has also transformed his reader, Blue, into a double,
into a writer himself. Black has kept Blue trapped in a room, with Blue's gaze
fixed upon Black, in a successful effort to enclose himself in the space of
writing until the demands of the book are met. And because Blue is also the
writer of the book, its demands cannot be fully met until Blue comes to
understand that all along he has been author of his own fate. When Blue
achieves this recognition, the story that Black is writing ends in death—but
not quite as Black had planned. For Blue is now the author, who physically
overpowers Black and beats him, presumably to death, as though doing away
with an insufferable mirror, which has kept him confined inside the room
that is the book.

II.

For whom can it be said that entrapment within the room that is the book is intolerable? Certainly Blue, who has always thought of himself as a man of action, rather than a reader, finds it so: "He feels like a man who has been condemned to sit in a room and go on reading a book for the rest of his life" (NYT 201–2). But through the character of Blue, Auster also paints a portrait of a type of writer about whom Blue knows nothing: the modern poet. It is the modern (male) poet whose condition is most fully epitomized by the statement, "There is no story, no plot, no action—nothing but a man sitting alone in a room and writing a book" (202). In the course of explaining why he became a performance poet, David Antin has characterized this solipsism of the modern poet in derogatory terms:

> as a poet i was getting extremely tired of   what i considered
>   an unnatural language act   going into a closet so to
> speak   sitting in front of a typewriter and nothing is
>   necessary   a closet is no place to address anybody
> (Antin 56)

Although he may be perverse in Antin's terms, Auster is powerfully drawn to this "unnatural language act," for the image of the lonely poet trapped inside the room that is the book haunts his writing. On another level, though, it is not self-enclosure that constitutes an "unnatural act" in Auster's writing, but rather the intrusion of poetry into narrative prose. His fiction and memoirs have remained remarkably open to poetry and to what are thought of as poetic concerns, and this openness results in unusual pressures on the writing, pressures that account for many of its salient characteristics.

Typically, if we call a novel "poetic," we mean that it has a "lyrical" quality, like André Gide's *L'Immoraliste* or Virginia Woolf's *The Waves*, or we mean that the words have been chosen with particular relish for their sound and exactitude, as in the stories of Guy Davenport or in Michael Ondaatje's *The English Patient*. Auster's fiction, however, is not especially lyrical in its rhythm or its diction; indeed, its tone is deliberately flat, in the manner of factual statement. And although by carefully portraying dilemmas of understanding he creates characters whose driving concerns are epistemological, his exactitude is of a phenomenological or hermeneutic sort, rather than a matter of heightened verbal precision. In other words, the poetic element in Auster's fiction is not a "formal" concern. Instead, it can be located in his engagement with a range of the fundamental issues that have defined twentieth-century poetry: the materiality of language, the relations between words and objects, the commanding presence of silence, the impact of prose upon poetry, and the ways in which, as Marina Tsvetaeva puts it, "In this most Christian of worlds / all poets are Jews" (quoted by Auster, AH 114).

Just as the identity of the poet hides in the character of Blue, these poetic issues hide among the more immediately noticeable metafictional qualities of Auster's writing. Admittedly, a general description of his fiction might make it hard to differentiate Auster's work from that of any number of postmodern novelists, for whom poetry would be the least of their concerns. To give such a general description of Auster's fiction in a single sentence, you could say that his books are allegories about the impossibly difficult task of writing, in which he investigates the similarly impossible task of achieving identity—through characters plagued by a double who represents the unknowable self—and that this impossible task takes place in an irrational world, governed by chance and coincidence, whose author cannot be known. And then it would be easy to construct a map of precursors and sources as a congenial modern terrain in which to situate Auster's work: the textual entrapments of Kafka, Beckett, Borges, Calvino, Ponge, Blanchot, Jabès, Celan, and Derrida; the psychological intensities of Poe, Hawthorne, Melville, Thoreau, Dickinson, Dostoevsky, and Freud; the paranoid overdeterminations of Surrealism, magic, alchemy, and Kabbalah. This capsule description and list of affinities and affiliations slights two important features: Auster's extensive work as a poet and as a translator of French poetry and the crucial ways in which his narrative prose stages an encounter between poetry and the novel.

For many novelists at the beginning of their careers, poetry may function as a form of finger exercises, but in Auster's case there was a curiously persistent vacillation. In an interview with Larry McCaffery and Sinda Gregory, he chronicles some of the dodges he took between verse and prose, before his decisive turn to fiction: "I had always dreamed of writing novels. My first published works were poems, and for ten years or so I published only poems, but all along I spent nearly as much time writing prose. I wrote hundreds and hundreds of pages, I filled up dozens of notebooks. It's just that I wasn't satisfied with it, and I never showed it to anyone" (AH 291). Reportedly, he became so frustrated with his efforts at fiction that he stopped altogether in the mid-seventies, restricting himself to composing and translating poetry and to writing critical essays. The poems, as Auster rightly notes, initially "resembled clenched fists; they were short and dense and obscure, as compact and hermetic as Delphic oracles" (AH

293), but during the later seventies they began to open up: "The breath became somewhat longer, the propositions became somewhat more discursive" (AH 294). Finally, though, at a time of acute emotional and financial distress, he reached a profound impasse: "There were moments when I thought I was finished, when I thought I would never write another word" (AH 294). Having touched bottom, as many of his characters do, Auster was ready for a breakthrough, which he says came when he attended a dance rehearsal: "Something happened, and a whole world of possibilities suddenly opened up to me. I think it was the absolute fluidity of what I was seeing, the continual motion of the dancers as they moved around the floor. It filled me with immense happiness" (AH 294). The next day he began writing *White Spaces* (1980; D 101–110), his one work of what I would call "poet's prose," which he describes "an attempt on my part to translate the experience of that dance performance into words. It was a liberation for me, a tremendous letting go, and I look back on it now as the bridge between writing poetry and writing prose" (AH 295).[2]

Over the past two centuries, poets have attested again and again to a liberating sensation when they begin to write poetry in prose. One might expect such freedom to be a result of escaping from the rigorous demands of meter and rhyme; but instead, it's as if the poet finds him or herself on the other side of a heavily fortified wall—outside the "closet"—able for the first time to step beyond the tiny social space accorded to verse and to take command of some of the vast discursive reservoirs of prose. In Auster's case, it's as if verse (ordinarily associated metaphorically with dance) were frozen stock still, while prose (usually imagined as plodding) were free to dance; where his verse "resembled clenched fists," his poet's prose represented "a tremendous letting go." A truly generative work for Auster, *White Spaces* marks the moment when prose and poetry actually meet in his writing; out of this moment arises Auster's central poetic project in prose: the investigation of the scene of writing. It is an immense project—a kind of detective assignment that may well take him the rest of his career. In *White Spaces*, Auster records a primary investigative discovery, at once phenomenological, mystical, and social: writing takes place in a room. In the following passage, he begins to explore this room:

> I remain in the room in which I am writing this. I put one foot in front of the other. I put one word in front of the other, and for each step I take I add another word, as if for each word to be spoken there were another space to be crossed, a distance to be filled by my body as it moves through this space. It is a journey

through space, even if I get nowhere, even if I end up in the same
place I started. It is a journey through space, as if into many cities
and out of them, as if across deserts, as if to the edge of some
imaginary ocean, where each thought drowns in the relentless
waves of the real. (D 107)

In this work of poet's prose, Auster insists over and over again on the
physicality of writing. He makes this physicality graphic by welding together
three distinct spaces: the room, the space in which writing is enacted; the
interior space where writing happens in the writer; and the space on the page
the words occupy. In *White Spaces*, as later in *Ghosts*, Auster represents the
physicality of writing by an equation of the room with the book: "I remain in
the room in which I am writing this," he says, as though he were occupying
the "white spaces" of the page, the mind, and the room. Whichever way he
turns in this symbolic architecture, the writer seems to find his physical body
trapped: when he writes, it enters into the closed space of the book; when he
gets up from the book, it paces the narrow confines of the room. This
claustrophobic situation draws attention to what Antin might deplore as the
marked leaning toward solipsism in Auster's writing, a tendency that we will
look at from different vantage points in later sections of this essay. At this
point, however, it is important to note that the outside world does manage to
break through the self-inscribed mental sphere of Auster's characters,
imposing actual consequences upon their ruminations and conjectures. In
the passage above, he acknowledges at least the idea of interpenetration
between the mental and the social worlds by locating, in the manner of
Wallace Stevens or Marianne Moore, an "imaginary ocean, where each
thought drowns in the relentless waves of the real."

III.

Auster is not, of course, the first writer to figure the book as the allegorical
scene of writing. In particular, two French poets who wrote extensively in
prose, Stéphane Mallarmé and Edmond Jabès, have provided Auster with
important examples. He has translated Mallarmé's poetic fragments on the
death of his young son, *A Tomb for Anatole* (1983) (some of which appears first
in *The Invention of Solitude*), and Mallarmé's notion of a grand Book that
includes the entire world hovers in the background of Auster's explorations of
the scene of writing. But even more directly pertinent to Auster's obsessions
are those of Jabès, the Jewish Egyptian poet, whose remarkable seven volumes

of meditative and oracular poet's prose, *The Book of Questions* (1963–73), have had a shaping hand in Auster's poetic narratives.[3] Auster makes explicit the connection between Jabès and Mallarmé in an article he wrote originally in 1976 for *The New York Review of Books*, in which he links the Jewish themes of *The Book of Questions* to central issues animating modern French poetry:

> Although Jabès's imagery and sources are for the most part derived from Judaism, *The Book of Questions* is not a Jewish work in the same way that one can speak of *Paradise Lost* as a Christian work.... The Book is his central image—but it is not only the Book of the Jews (the spirals of commentary around commentary in the Midrash), but an allusion to Mallarmé's ideal Book as well (the Book that contains the world, endlessly folding in upon itself). Finally, Jabès's work must be considered as part of the on-going French poetic tradition that began in the late nineteenth century. (AH 113–14)

Although Jabès himself has no wish to deny his placement within French poetic tradition, he takes great pains, in a subsequent interview that Auster conducted with him, to differentiate his notion of the book from that of Mallarmé: "Mallarmé wanted to put all knowledge into a book. He wanted to make a great book, the book of books. But in my opinion this book would be very ephemeral, since knowledge itself is ephemeral. The book that would have a chance to survive, I think, is the book that destroys itself. That destroys itself in favor of another book that will prolong it" (AH 164). Jabès favors a midrashic approach to the book over an idealist one, a text composed of questions rather than answers, a book from which one can at least provisionally escape.[4] Like midrashic commentary upon Scripture, Jabès's *Book of Questions* proceeds by locating anomalies or paradoxes or gaps in understanding, using such questions to generate further writing—as if one first had to become lost in order to be found. Such characterizations of Jabès's work may sound like re-statements of deconstructive truisms—and one should note the profound impact Jabès's writing has had upon Derrida and other French theorists—but there is also a desire for truth and wholeness in Jabès's work (regardless of the difficulty of articulating such things) that seems at odds with deconstruction as a movement, and this desire is something Auster unashamedly espouses as well. Jabès pursues a wholeness based in fragments, and he claims to maintain an awareness of the entire book at every moment of writing, so that the whole exerts an irresistible pressure that determines the composition of the book word-by-word:

When I say there are many books in the book, it is because there
are many words in the word. Obviously, if you change the word,
the context of the sentence changes completely. In this way
another sentence is born from this word, and a completely
different book begins ... I think of this in terms of the sea, in the
image of the sea as it breaks upon the shore. It is not the wave that
comes, it is the whole sea that comes each time and the whole sea
that draws back. It is never just a wave, it is always everything that
comes and everything that goes. This is really the fundamental
movement in all my books. Everything is connected to
everything else.... At each moment, in the least question, it is the
whole book which returns and the *whole* book which draws back.
(AH 168)

His highly elaborated notion of the book as the central poetic principle
of writing—as that which holds open the space of writing—allows Jabès to
make a radical distinction between the novel and the (poetic) book. Although
The Book of Questions has characters, dialogue, and an implicit story, and
although it is classified on the jacket of the English version as "fiction," Jabès
vehemently rejects the storytelling function of the novel as undermining the
writer's fidelity to the book. For the book makes moment-to-moment
demands that Jabès believes should supersede the commitment to telling a
particular story. He complains,

The novelist's high-handed appropriation of the book has always
been unbearable to me. What makes me uneasy is his pretense of
making the *space* of the book the space of the story he tells—
making the subject of his novel the subject of the book....
Novelistic fiction, even when innovative, does not, from my point
of view, take charge of the totality of [the risk involved in
writing]. The book loses its autonomy.... A stranger to the book,
its breath, its rhythm, the novelist imposes an exterior, exclusive
speech: a life and a death, invented in the course of the story. For
him the book is only a tool. At no moment does the novelist listen
to the page, to its whiteness and silence. (Jabès *Desert* 101)

As a poet in a textual age, Jabès locates the space of poetry within the
book, which has a life of its own. Aided by the evidence that a vital Jewish
imagination has been able to survive within the book for two millennia, he
seeks to defend this space from incursions by those lesser poetic talents, the

novelists, who impose the stories of particular characters over the mysterious imperatives of the book. In his own investigations of "the space of the book," Auster takes seriously the challenge issued by Jabès, endeavoring to enter the room of the book by attending to its "whiteness and silence." Like Jabès in *The Book of Questions*, Auster writes a prose animated by the poetic issues of investigating and responding to the "white spaces" of the book. Unlike Jabès, however, Auster also has a commitment to the novel, and a deep tension arises in his prose from a confrontation between narrative and the book. At the beginning of his published prose, with *The Invention of Solitude* and *The New York Trilogy*, Auster's fidelity resides primarily with the book. This results in a flatness of characterization and in a dialogue that appears more like its surrounding descriptive prose than like the speech of discrete characters; likewise, the narrative of his early novels seems wholly governed by plot. Over the course of his four subsequent novels, *In the Country of Last Things*, *Moon Palace*, *The Music of Chance*, and *Leviathan*, Auster expands his ability to create realistic characters and begins to elaborate narratives that unfold beyond the exigencies of plot. Still, his characteristic explorations of the scene of writing take place within a palpable tension between novel and book.

Auster's first book of prose, *The Invention of Solitude*, contains a Jabèsian text, "The Book of Memory," in which he explores the space of writing through an obsessive attention to the book that nearly rivals the poetic fixation of Jabès. And yet Auster does not, like Jabès, wholly eschew narrative, for the "Book of Memory" brims with anecdotes and little stories; it is here that Auster begins to create a fiction of the book. In his article on Jabès, Auster gives a summary description of *The Book of Questions* that applies equally well to his own "Book of Memory:" "What happens in *The Book of Questions*, then, is the writing of *The Book of Questions*—or rather, the attempt to write it, a process that the reader is allowed to witness in all its gropings and hesitations" (AH 111). "The Book of Memory" begins with a literal enactment of "listen[ing] to the page, its whiteness and silence": "He lays out a piece of blank paper on the table before him and writes these words with his pen. It was. It will never be again" (IS 75). Then, we continue to "witness in all its gropings and hesitations" the further attempts to write the book:

> Later that same day he returns to his room. He finds a fresh sheet of paper and lays it out on the table before him. He writes until he has covered the entire page with words. Later, when he reads over what he has written, he has trouble deciphering the

words. Those he does manage to understand do not seem to say
what he thought he was saying. Then he goes out to eat his
dinner.

That night he tells himself that tomorrow is another day. New
words begin to clamor in his head, but he does not write them
down. He decides to refer to himself as A. He walks back and
forth between the table and the window. He turns on the radio
and then turns it off. He smokes a cigarette.

Then he writes. It was. It will never be again. (IS 75)

As in *Ghosts*, Auster creates a scene of writing that is both book and
room, and for which the question of identity is inseparable from the writing
of the book. "The Book of Memory" is an autobiography, in which the
author "decides to refer to himself as A." in order to create enough distance
to be able to see himself. He places himself at a turning point—"It was. It
will never be again."—which allows him to investigate the present in terms
of the past, utilizing memory as a kind of book that, in Jabès's terms,
"destroys itself in favor of another book that will prolong it" (AH 164): "The
Book of Memory" destroys memory by making it into a book. Likewise, the
present sense of self is an enclosure created anew over and over again by
interrogating the past. In other words, the question that Blue asks in *Ghosts*,
"How to get out of the room that is the book that will go on being written
for as long as he stays in the room?" (NYT 201–2), animates "The Book of
Memory" as well. The room and the book are thematized in many ways in
"The Book of Memory:" A. describes the room in which he lives and writes
(as well as a number of significant rooms in his past) in obsessive detail; as in
the old art of memory, he portrays memory in architectural terms, comprised
of rooms in which contiguous impressions are stored; in addition, A. explores
the principles that determine such contiguity—chance, coincidence, free
association.

Like Thoreau, whose *Walden* he plays with in *Ghosts*, Auster is
fascinated by solitude; many of the images that recur throughout "The Book
of Memory" evoke solitary enclosure, such as the references to Jonah in the
whale, to Pinocchio in the shark, to Anne Frank in hiding, and to George
Oppen's phrase "the shipwreck of the singular." Regardless of the imagery
with which it is portrayed, enclosure within the room of writing invokes not
just a sense of aloneness but an actual claustrophobia in Auster's characters:
"It is as if he were being forced to watch his own disappearance, as if, by
crossing the threshold of this room, he were entering another dimension,

taking up residence inside a black hole" (IS 77). Ultimately, what we have been considering as a poetic anxiety about the room of writing is revealed as a fear of death, a fear so acute that A. tries to evacuate his life out of the present in order to observe it safely, albeit in a disembodied fashion, from the future:

> Christmas Eve, 1979. His life no longer seemed to dwell in the present. Whenever he turned on his radio and listened to the news of the world, he would find himself imagining the words to be describing things that had happened long ago. Even as he stood in the present, he felt himself to be looking at it from the future, and this present-as-past was so antiquated that even the horrors of the day, which ordinarily would have filled him with outrage, seemed remote to him, as if the voice in the radio were reading from a chronicle of some lost civilization. Later, in a time of greater clarity, he would refer to this sensation as "nostalgia for the present." (IS 76)

In this passage, Auster employs four different methods of displacing the present: by portraying A. as bouncing between the past and the future, hearing first a report of present events as though it were referring to the distant past, and next trying to imagine himself looking at the present from the future; then, in the last sentence, by having a narrator locate himself at a future point, "Later," looking back upon A. in the "present" moment; and finally, by giving this alienated condition the label "nostalgia for the present," which further congeals and reifies it. There is, of course, a long genealogy behind the enactment of extreme alienation in modern literature—especially, for this text of Auster's, in Jewish writers: Kafka, Freud, Scholem, Benjamin, Celan, Jabès, Barthes, Anne Frank, George Oppen, Charles Reznikoff, Henry Roth, etc. But in "The Book of Memory" Auster deploys the effects of alienation in a particularly active way that he shares with a smaller circle of writers, like Samuel Beckett and the John Ashbery of *Three Poems*. These writers create what I have called elsewhere a translative prose, which is always engaged simultaneously in investigating identity and writing, bringing forth a tenuous fiction from the ever-new exigencies of the book.[5] At one point in "The Book of Memory," Auster invokes translation as an image for what occurs when one enters the room of the book:

> For most of his adult life, he has earned his living by translating the books of other writers. He sits at his desk reading the book in

French and then picks up his pen and writes the same book in English. It is both the same book and not the same book, and the strangeness of this activity has never failed to impress him. Every book is an image of solitude.... A. sits down in his own room to translate another man's book, and it is as though he were entering that man's solitude and making it his own. (IS 136)

In the act of translation, identity is both found and lost: rewriting the words of another writer is a profoundly intimate form of relationship, in which the translator finds identities melting, mingling, or repelling one another. The translator invades the solitude of the space of writing, and the intruder never knows whether he or she will leave that violated solitude with a sense of self fortified or weakened by the encounter. For Blue, in *Ghosts*, this penetration into another's solitude results in a terrifying *mise en abime*: "Having penetrated Black's room and stood there alone, having been, so to speak, in the sanctum of Black's solitude, he cannot respond to the darkness of that moment except by replacing it with a solitude of his own" (NYT 226). Like the later fictional character Blue, "A. imagines himself as a kind of ghost of that other man, who is both there and not there, and whose book is both the same and not the same as the one he is translating" (IS 136).

Out of this meditation upon translation, though, A. achieves a realization that gives the ghostly existence of translation a new sort of life: "it dawns on him that everything he is trying to record in "The Book of Memory," everything he has written so far, is no more than the translation of a moment or two of his life—those moments he lived through on Christmas Eve, 1979, in his room at 6 Varick Street" (IS 136). Translation not only renders the writer a ghost enclosed in the room that is the book; it is also a way out. For the moment that inaugurates "The Book of Memory"—the recognition that A.'s life and his writing have been on a collision course that has finally eventuated in their complete merging, a recognition provoked when he sits down at his desk and writes, "It was. It will never be again." (IS 75)—also begins a translation of that moment out of itself. The only way to get out of the room that is the book is by writing the book, for writing translates the moment that inaugurates the book into an ongoing present that opens out of the memory of that moment. Auster makes explicit the notion of escape through the translation of memory by citing the example of Pascal's "Memorial," an ecstatic testimony that was sewn into the lining of the philosopher's clothes as a constant reminder of his moment of mystical illumination, on the night of November 23, 1654 (137). The memory of such a moment illuminates the space of writing, so that as the writer dives into the memory he can see a way of moving beyond his solitude and out into the world and, ultimately, into history:

> As he writes, he feels that he is moving inward (through himself) and at the same time moving outward (towards the world). What he experienced, perhaps, during those few moments on Christmas Eve, 1979, as he sat alone in his room on Varick Street, was this: the sudden knowledge that came over him that even alone, in the deepest solitude of his room, he was not alone, or, more precisely, that the moment he began to try to speak of that solitude, he had become more than just himself. Memory, therefore, not simply as the resurrection of one's private past, but an immersion in the past of others, which is to say: history— which one both participates in and is a witness to, is a part of and apart from. (139)

The poet is trapped in narrative prose, the writer is trapped in the book, the "agent" is trapped in the room: can these figures use memory to come out into the world, into history? One way of looking at this conundrum would be to notice that for both Pascal and A., memory already includes simultaneously an inside and an outside: when Pascal writes his memory and then sews it into his clothing, he gives it a double exteriority, which matches the way that A. moves both inward and outward by writing about what he remembers of Christmas Eve, 1979. But thinking of memory in this way offers too easy a solution to Auster's dilemma. We can complicate the notion of memory by seeing it not only as a matter of interiority and exteriority, but also as an interplay of remembering and forgetting. From the latter perspective, we will have to hold off deciding whether to accept Auster's affirmation that memory leads out of the room and into history, until we have looked at what his text actively forgets.

IV.

In order to think about what is repressed in "The Book of Memory," I would like to bring a second framework into play, which is that of the parthenogenic fantasy of masculine creativity embedded in the text. "The Book of Memory" is ostensibly a book of mourning, for A.'s father has just died and his grandfather dies during its composition. The previous half of *The Invention of Solitude*, "Portrait of an Invisible Man," treats the death of Auster's father and his subsequent discovery that his paternal grandfather was murdered by his grandmother. Throughout "The Book of Memory," Auster reflects upon the relations of fathers and sons, brooding particularly on his feelings toward his own young son in the midst of his reflections upon the traumas and losses inscribed within the continuity of generations.[6] The mood of the text is one of melancholy, veering between hopelessness, nostalgia, and obsessive self-regard, but its desperately sought goal seems to be the regeneration of a life through writing. In this context, the room of the book receives a different set of figurative equivalents from those found in *Ghosts*. In the latter, the room of the book is a place where Blue is trapped, and where he is forcibly initiated into the brotherhood of writers. In "The Book of Memory," the room of the book is figured as a void, a place of nothingness or meaninglessness, a site for the confrontation with death. Auster makes explicit a metonymic chain of rhyming words that underlies this particular figuration of the room as scene of writing: "Room and tomb, tomb and womb, womb and room" (IS 159–60).

The implication of this chain of equivalents is that the room of the book is a place where death can be transformed into rebirth. But this can only happen, Auster asserts, if we take meaninglessness as a first principle. By meaninglessness, Auster has a specific denial in mind, that of the motivated connection between any two factors:

> Like everyone else, he craves a meaning. Like everyone else, his life is so fragmented that each time he sees a connection between two fragments he is tempted to look for a meaning in that connection. The connection exists. But to give it a meaning, to look beyond the bare fact of its existence, would be to build an imaginary world inside the real world, and he knows it would not stand. At his bravest moments, he embraces meaninglessness as the first principle .... (147)

By enshrining meaninglessness as first principle, Auster seems to be striking a blow against the conventions of the novel, which rest upon the assumption that a meaningful connection between events can be constructed; without this assumption, the ideological work of the novel as creator of identity within a social world would collapse. Auster undermines the ideological basis of the novel by telling a series of stories in which coincidences and connections are never sufficient to ensure identity.

Auster asserts the "principle" of meaninglessness several times in "The Book of Memory," particularly when discussing coincidence or chance. After telling a story about M., a friend who finds himself living in Paris in the exact same attic room where his father had hidden from the Nazis twenty years before, A. notes the further coincidence that he, too, lived in such a *chambre de bonne* and that it was where his own father had come to see him. These thoughts cause A. to "remember his father's death. And beyond that, to understand—this most important of all—that M.'s story has no meaning" (81). In this passage, the principle of meaninglessness is associated directly with A.'s father's death, and beyond that with the equation of the room of the book with the tomb. From this void, however, comes A.'s impulse to write, to make of his memorializing book a site of regeneration, to find himself anew within the act of mourning. Recognizing that M.'s story is meaningless, A. counters,

> Nevertheless, this is where it begins. The first word appears only at a moment when nothing can be explained anymore, at some instant of experience that defies all sense. To be reduced to saying nothing. Or else, to say to himself: this is what haunts me. And then to realize, almost in the same breath, that this is what he haunts. (81)

But what does haunt Auster and his character in this experience of nothingness? He offers a clue to his haunting in the equations quoted earlier: "Room and tomb, tomb and womb, womb and room." These equations take us beyond the ostensible subject of mourning into a repressed but highly significant motivation of the writing; to tie the room and the tomb with the feminine image of the womb brings in gender considerations to a narrative that is otherwise almost exclusively masculine. It seems to me that in this text terms like "nothingness" and "meaninglessness" are gendered feminine, and that based upon this equation women are rendered as void and men are imagined as self-generating. Having projected so many desires upon the notion of nothingness, it's as though Auster then takes the Buddhist image of the "pregnant void" and splits it in half, assigning the void to women and pregnancy to men. In "The Book of Memory," Auster attempts a kind of parthenogenesis, using the room as a womb to give birth to the book, without the intervention of the feminine. Let me offer some illustrations to make this assertion convincing.

In a discussion of Paris and of a composer he meets there, S., who becomes a father figure to him, A. gives a striking description of the room as a place at once claustrophobic (to the body) and infinitely generative (to the mind)—a masculine womb. He begins the description by noting, "These are his earliest memories of the city, where so much of his life would later be spent, and they are inescapably bound up with the idea of the room" (89). Having highlighted the room's significance, A. goes on to describe first its claustrophobic quality: "S. lived in a space so small that at first it seemed to defy you, to resist being entered. The presence of one person crowded the room, two people choked it. It was impossible to move inside it without contracting your body to its smallest dimensions, without contracting your mind to some infinitely small point within itself." Here, the claustrophobia seems to affect both the body and the mind, as though the room were attempting to squeeze both down to nothingness. For the mind, however, this extreme form of contraction results in its opposite, a sudden expansion, inaugurated by becoming aware of the contents of the room:

> For there was an entire universe in that room, a miniature cosmology that contained all that is most vast, most distant, most unknowable. It was a shrine, hardly bigger than a body, in praise of all that exists beyond the body: the representation of one man's inner world, even to the slightest detail. S. had literally managed to surround himself with the things that were inside him. The room he lived in was a dream space, and its walls were like the skin of some second body around him, as if his own body had been transformed into a mind, a breathing instrument of pure thought. This was the womb, the belly of the whale, the original site of the imagination. (89)

In this masculinist fantasy of self-generative creativity, the enwombing room is "like the skin of some second body around him," capable of giving birth to the solitary artist's works of art, without the intervention of woman, or even of the body. This is a kind of male "hysteria," in which the wandering womb of the room takes on the generative qualities of the composer's inner life.[7] The most fully realized image of masculine birth in "The Book of Memory" is that of Pinocchio, who is sculpted into being by his father, and this image, as I shall later demonstrate, runs as a leitmotif throughout the text. Another major image of masculinist self-generation, Leibniz's monadology, recurs at several points in the text and also partakes of the psychological disturbance of male birth. For instance, further on in the same meditation that produces the equation of room with tomb and womb, A. imagines that language is a kind of monadology, a matrix of rhyming words that "functions as a kind of bridge that joins opposite and contrasting aspects of the world with each other:"

Language, then, not simply as a list of separate things to be added up and whose sum total is equal to the world. Rather, language as it is laid out in the dictionary: an infinitely complex organism, all of whose elements—cells and sinews, corpuscles and bones, digits and fluids—are present in the world simultaneously, none of which can exist on its own. For each word is defined by other words, which means that to enter any part of language is to enter the whole of it. (160)

A. ascribes tremendous potency to language, imagining it as the matrix of being, as the genetic matter of the world. He sums up this apotheosis of language by invoking Leibniz: "Language, then, as monadology, to echo the term used by Leibniz" (160). The monadology is the interconnected network of the "monads" that compose the universe, each of which is affected by the motion of all the others. After a long quote from Leibniz, Auster concludes, "Playing with words in the way A. did as a schoolboy, then, was not so much a search for the truth as a search for the world as it appears in language. Language is not truth. It is the way we exist in the world" (161). This seemingly Heideggerean recognition, that language "is the way we exist in the world," is given a particular twist, though, by A.'s fantasy that "language ... is an infinitely complex organism" with "cells and sinews, corpuscles and bones, digits and fluids," as though language were not just a mode of existence *in the world* but a replacement for life *in the body*; for, when "it is possible for events in one's life to rhyme as well" (161), the monadology of language has taken over everything. At the end of this three-page meditation on the power of language, A. arrives at the mysterious recognition that, in fact, everything is beginning to rhyme for him:

What A. is struggling to express, perhaps, is that for some time now none of the terms has been missing for him. Wherever his eye or mind seems to stop, he discovers another connection, another bridge to carry him to yet another place, and even in the solitude of his room, the world has been rushing in on him at a dizzying speed, as if it were all suddenly converging in him and happening to him at once. Coincidence: to fall on with; to occupy the same place in time or space. The mind, therefore, as that which contains more than itself. As in the phrase from Augustine: "But where is the part of it which it does not itself contain?" (162)

To see interconnections can be a result of a visionary heightening of consciousness, or, with the sense that "the world has been rushing in on him at a dizzying speed," it may well be that A. is experiencing a moment of sheer paranoia. If this is a moment of paranoia, it must have a causal connection to A.'s masculinist notion of self-generation, of mind outside body in a room. In fact, A.'s imagining of the human mind as the entire monadology goes far beyond Leibniz, whom Auster quotes as cautioning that "A soul, however, can read in itself only what is directly represented in it; it is unable to unfold all at once all its folds; for these go on into infinity" (161). In his more paranoid rendition of a monadology, A. has taken something like Robert Duncan's poetic conceit about "the structure of rime" and inflated it into the fantasy of a wrinkle-free existence, in which all interconnections are apparent to the mind.[8]

The gender implications of this fantasy of disembodiment are most disturbingly represented in an earlier scene in the text, in which A., "for no particular reason," wanders into a topless bar in Manhattan. In a completely detached tone of voice, Auster describes how A. "found himself sitting next to a voluptuously naked young woman," who invites him into the back room. "There was something so openly humorous and matter-of-fact about her approach, that he finally agreed to her proposition. The best thing, they decided, would be for her to suck his penis, since she claimed an extraordinary talent for this activity." At the moment of ejaculation, the Leibnizean monad is revealed as an image of masculine parthenogenesis:

As he came in her mouth a few moments later, with a long and throbbing flood of semen, he had this vision, at just that second, which has continued to radiate inside him: that each ejaculation contains several billion sperm cells—or roughly the same number as there are people in the world—which means that, in himself, each man holds the potential of an entire world. And what would happen, could it happen, is the full range of possibilities: a spawn of idiots and geniuses, of the beautiful and the deformed, of saints, catatonics, thieves, stock brokers, and high-wire artists. Each man, therefore, is the entire world, bearing within his genes a memory of all mankind. Or, as Leibniz put it: "Every living substance is a perpetual living mirror of the universe." For the fact is, we are of the same stuff that came into being with the first explosion of the first spark in the infinite emptiness of space. Or so he said to himself, at that moment, as his penis exploded into the mouth of that naked woman, whose name he has now forgotten. (114)

In this passage the conjunction of woman as nothingness with masculine parthenogenesis is made explicit. The sexual function of the woman is located in the mouth, not in the womb, and absolutely no connection, aside from mechanical friction, is made between the woman and the man. Not only is the woman nameless, but her name is actively erased by A.'s seemingly unnecessary final qualification: "that naked woman, whose name he has now forgotten." There is a barb in that statement, which we will have to look at momentarily. In the meantime, note the careful working out of a parthenogenic procreation: the emotionless ejaculation is converted into a purely mental reverie—as though the phallus were the mind, capable of generating the entire world by its explosive satisfaction. The woman's role in this fantasy of masculine self-generation is "effaced" (that is, she is rendered faceless), and as recipient of the exploding penis she becomes mute.

A few pages further on in "The Book of Memory," A. makes a seemingly technical reference to "Solitude," a song recorded by Billie Holiday (whose heart-wrenching vocal style registers unforgettably the effects of masculine aggression). Following the technical reference, A. notices that the mention of Billie Holiday and an immediately prior description of Emily Dickinson's room ("it was the room that was present in the poems and not the reverse" [123]) constitute "First allusions to a woman's voice. To be followed by specific reference to several" (123). But he does not deliver on this promise. Instead, he launches into an odd speculation: "For it is his belief that if there is a voice of truth—assuming there is such a thing as truth, and assuming this truth can speak—it comes from the mouth of a woman" (123). This conjectured truth never arrives in the text, where, ironically, the only thing that "comes from the mouth of a woman" is A.'s penis. It's as though Billie Holiday and Emily Dickinson are invoked only to be silenced. The question arises, then, why this desire to erase the woman's voice?

A clue to answering this question appears in a passage describing A.'s relationship to the one other character in "The Book of Memory" who is denied a name—also a woman. A. is telling a story about his two-year-old son's sudden illness and resultant stay in the hospital. The fearful parents spend every waking hour with him:

> His wife, however, began to show the strain. At one point she walked out to A., who was in the adult sitting room, and said, "I give up, I can't handle him anymore"—and there was such resentment in her voice against the boy, such an anger of exasperation, that something inside A. fell to pieces. Stupidly,

> cruelly, he wanted to punish his wife for such selfishness, and in
> that one instant all the newly won harmony that had been
> growing between them for the past month vanished: for the first
> time in all their years together, he had turned against her. He
> stormed out of the room and went to his son's bedside. (108)

The woman-without-a-name in "The Book of Memory" is A.'s wife. In the
passage above, his repressed anger begins to leak out. Her statement, "I give
up, I can't handle him anymore," is something one expects to hear from the
mother of a two-year-old at least daily. But its effect upon A., who has
transferred the force of his anger at his wife to an excessive doting upon his
son (which appears in many passages of "The Book of Memory"), is to break
through the shell of his repression. Rather than commiserate with her, "A.
fell to pieces," that is, he became angry: "stupidly, cruelly, he wanted to
punish his wife for such selfishness." What is "stupid" and "cruel" in the
context of a marriage, though, is not the anger itself but the reported
repression of it for so many years: "for the first time in all their years
together, he had turned against her." If these two characters have suppressed
conflict for so many years, it's no wonder that their marriage is falling apart
and that A.'s anger toward women has reached a bizarre climax in his attempt
to exclude them completely from the room of the book. The parthenogenic
fantasy running through "The Book of Memory" and the masculine
genealogy of fathers and sons that Auster constructs in the entire *Invention of
Solitude* must arise, at least in part, from the unacceptably explosive potential
that resides in a bottled-up anger toward women. One important facet of this
psychic economy is A.'s transforming his anger and sense of betrayal into a
smothering identification with his son: in the passage quoted above, for
instance, A. "stormed out of the room and went to his son's bedside," shifting
his affection and allegiance from wife to son. In his identification with the
son, Auster writes the mother out of the family romance; he effects this
erasure by portraying A.'s wife as her son's betrayer and by shifting the focus
of the divorce drama onto the relationship of the parents to the son.

If this is a book of mourning, a book of confrontation with death, then
the fatality that looms largest within it but is given least expression is the
death of a marriage. At one "ghostly" level, this is a book of divorce, a book
of memory born from the almost total suppression of the memories of a
marriage. A. allows his nameless wife very few appearances, and in none of
them does she represent any of the positive creative qualities of regeneration
that A. so desperately seeks. For instance, he figures their marriage as
hopelessly unproductive from its outset: "He remembers returning home

from his wedding party in 1974, his wife beside him in her white dress, and taking the front door key out of his pocket, inserting the key in the lock, and then, as he turned his wrist, feeling the blade of the key snap off inside the lock" (145). Rather than explore the interior landscape of his marriage in order to understand how what we might interpret as a symbolic castration took place, A. retreats to a room and writes a book of self-regeneration, in which he invents a masculine genealogy of creativity that will substitute for his father's emotional distance and will also mourn the father's recent death. From the perspective of this fundamental inability to confront the breakdown of his marriage and his feelings about women, it's the connection between death and divorce that makes the most striking "coincidence" in the book: "Two months after his father's death (January 1979), A.'s marriage collapsed" (101). In his desperate attempt to deny the true consequences of his divorce—the collapse of his ability to relate to women in a mutually beneficial manner—A. turns, as we have noted, to his son: "it was quite another thing for him to swallow the consequences it entailed: to be separated from his son. The thought of it was intolerable to him" (101).

V.

Within the masculine genealogy of this text, all of A.'s hopes for regeneration are transferred to his son. His feelings toward his son are not just those of the understandably protective father in such potentially damaging circumstances, but they also partake of a messianic desire for deliverance that the son is imagined as fulfilling. Throughout *The Invention of Solitude* Auster cultivates a fantasy, most fully represented by the Pinocchio story, that the son will rescue the father.[9] Like Gepetto, A. as father hides in the room of the book, creating his own son parthenogenically as his savior. Given the depiction in "Portrait of an Invisible Man," the first half of *The Invention of Solitude*, of Auster's own desperately wounded father (who witnessed his father's murder at the hands of his mother), the provenance of this desire for the son to rescue the father is painfully apparent as a patrimony Auster inherits. This desire is not, however, only a feature of Auster's psychological makeup, a response to his father's maddening emotional distance; it also corresponds to the desire to rescue their parents experienced by children of Holocaust victims and survivors. The connection between Auster's personal history and a post-Holocaust sensibility runs throughout "The Book of Memory." Of all the scenes of hiding in a room rehearsed in the text, the most central thematically is that of Anne Frank, writing her own identity in a book while hiding from the Nazis. To consider further the relationship of a masculine redemptive genealogy to hiding within the room of the book, we must begin investigating the third framework, which is the post-Holocaust imagery pervading "The Book of Memory."

I say "post-Holocaust" because, although he includes a number of scenes from the Holocaust itself, Auster is a Jewish writer born after the war, and so what's pertinent, both in his recounting of Holocaust material and throughout the text, is the way his imagination has been infected by the Holocaust. Although his secularity and his close reliance upon Protestant American writers like Poe, Hawthorne, Thoreau, and Melville may inadvertently hide the pervasiveness of the Jewish context for his writing, Auster provides a significant gauge of this context in his essays, collected in *The Art of Hunger*. Of the nineteen essays, eleven discuss secular Jewish writers, all of whom have had telling influences upon Auster's writing: Laura Riding (2), Franz Kafka (2), Louis Wolfson, Charles Reznikoff, Paul Celan, Edmond Jabès (2), George Oppen, and Carl Rakosi. For Jews like Auster, born after World War II, two paramount realities demand attention: the Holocaust and the State of Israel. Auster makes mention of Israel in "The Book of Questions" only by reproducing an encyclopedia entry about a relative, Daniel Auster, who became the first mayor of Jerusalem after independence (85). Daniel is also the name of A.'s son (who is the only character given a full name in the text), so that this coincidence ties his Israeli relative into the genealogy A. is constructing. The invocation of Israel takes place, significantly enough, within the context of an extended meditation upon and identification with Anne Frank. During this meditation, Auster identifies Anne Frank's room directly with the room of the book, setting forth the post-Holocaust thematics of his text.

On a short trip to Amsterdam, ostensibly to look at art, A. finds himself confronted by the traces of Anne Frank. As in his entry into the topless bar, A. goes to Anne Frank's house "for no particular reason." By this point in the narrative, it is clear that this phrase indicates not chance but overdetermined motives:

> For no particular reason (idly looking through a guide book he found in his hotel room) he decided to go to Anne Frank's house, which has been preserved as a museum. It was a Sunday morning, gray with rain, and the streets along the canal were deserted. He climbed the steep and narrow staircase inside the house and entered the secret annex. As he stood in Anne Frank's room, the room in which the diary was written, now bare, with the faded

pictures of Hollywood movie stars she had collected still pasted to the walls, he suddenly found himself crying. Not sobbing, as might happen in response to deep inner pain, but crying without sound, the tears streaming down his cheeks, as if purely in response to the world. It was at that moment, he later realized, that the Book of Memory began. As in the phrase: "she wrote her diary in this room." (82–3)

Anne Frank's room of the book, in which she wrote her diary, supplies an originary moment for "The Book of Memory." Entering this room, A. experiences not just a psychological but an ontological pain, as if the condition of hiding imposed upon Anne Frank by the threat of the Holocaust had now become the condition of being in the world. Two paragraphs later, A. imagines this claustrophobic ontology as "a solitude so crushing, so unconsolable, that one stops breathing for hundreds of years" (83)—as though every post-Holocaust experience of solitude, every self-encounter, were haunted by Anne Frank's absolute isolation. Looking out her window at children's toys in a yard, A. wonders "what it would be like to grow up in the shadow of Anne Frank's room" (83), in the shadow of that breath-stopping solitude. In a figurative sense, all Jews after the war grow up within this shadow. Whenever Auster enters the room of the book, he seems to find it enveloped by this shadow, as if his writing were a repetition-compulsion brought about by the trauma of the Holocaust. In an ironic juxtaposition, A. quotes a famous saying of Pascal, "All the unhappiness of man stems from one thing only: that he is incapable of staying quietly in his room" (83), as though Anne Frank's life in the room of the book were a reproach to the monastic psychology of hiding and self-incarceration as a freely chosen way of life. Growing up figuratively in the shadow of Anne Frank's room, A. feels trapped inside the room of the book; he *chooses* not his location but his identification with Anne Frank as writer, as though his overwhelming task of mourning were given concretion and containment by her room and her book.

Not only does A. identify himself with Anne Frank, but he also notes that "Anne Frank's birthday is the same as his son's" (83), thus placing her into the genealogical chain of fathers and children, rather than opening up for her occupation the closed space of the feminine. Following this recognition of a kind of post-Holocaust kinship between Anne Frank and himself, A. quotes from an extraordinary document of familial trauma: "Israel Lichtenstein's Last Testament. Warsaw; July 31, 1942," in which one of the resistance fighters of the Warsaw Ghetto, knowing he is about to die, asks not "for gratitude, any monument, any praise. I want only a remembrance" (84). Lichtenstein asks for remembrance of himself, of his wife, and especially of his preternaturally gifted daughter: "Margalit, 20 months old today. Has mastered Yiddish perfectly, speaks a pure Yiddish.... In intelligence she is on a par with 3- or 4-year old children. I don't want to brag about her.... I am not sorry about my life and that of my wife. But I am sorry for the gifted little girl. She deserves to be remembered also" (84). Traumas of this magnitude—involving the obliteration of individuals, of communities, and, most poignantly for A., of marvelous children—are suffered not only by those who experience them; they are passed on to future generations as unfinished projects of mourning. At the family level (in traumas such as Auster's father's witnessing of his father's murder) and at the societal level (in traumas such as the Holocaust or American slavery), unbearable memories are braided within the continuity of generations, so that the trauma maintains a virulent force, which has the ability to yank a member of a succeeding generation out of the present and into its secret room. When A. imagines the continuity of generations, he cannot call up a biblical plenitude within which to reside; instead, the trauma displaces him into a realm of isolation, in which the generations are squeezed into an individual body—itself incapable of inhabiting the present:

> When the father dies, he writes, the son becomes his own father and his own son. He looks at his son and sees himself in the face of the boy. He imagines what the boy sees when he looks at him and finds himself becoming his own father. Inexplicably, he is moved by this. It is not just the sight of the boy that moves him, nor even the thought of standing inside his father, but what he sees in the boy of his own vanished past. It is a nostalgia for his own life that he feels .... Inexplicably, he finds himself shaking at that moment with both happiness and sorrow, if this is possible, as if he were going both forward and backward, into the future and into the past. And there are times, often there are times, when these feelings are so strong that his life no longer seems to dwell in the present. (81–2)

When he is transported out of the present by trauma, A. lives in a genealogical world in which time is speeded up and fathers and children subsume one another: "Each time he saw a child, he would try to imagine what it would look like as a grown-up. Each time he saw an old person, he would try to imagine what that person had looked like as a child" (87). This

Blakean vision of the "mental traveller," whose "life no longer seems to dwell in the present," takes on a possibly misogynist twist when A. gazes at women:

> It was worst with women, especially if the woman was young and beautiful. He could not help looking through the skin of her face and imagining the anonymous skull behind it. And the more lovely the face, the more ardent his attempt to seek in it the encroaching signs of the future: incipient wrinkles, the later-to-be-sagging chin, the glaze of disappointment in the eyes. He would put one face on top of another: this woman at forty; this woman at sixty; this woman at eighty; as if, even as he stood in the present, he felt compelled to hunt out the future, to track down the death that lives in each one of us. (87)

The post-Holocaust haunting by death dovetails with A.'s inability to imagine regeneration through the feminine, such that fertility and fecundity are replaced by dissolution and decay. A. ends this passage with a dispiriting quotation from Flaubert: "The sight of a naked woman makes me imagine her skeleton" (87).

Casting aside the feminine as a source of regeneration, A. turns to the hope that the son can rescue the father. When the father has suffered an unbearable trauma, it is natural for the son to entertain the fantasy of rescuing the father. An impulse of this sort must be at work, for instance, in *Maus*, Art Spiegelman's remarkable Holocaust narrative. By foregrounding his difficult relationship with his father during his telling of the father's tale of survival, Spiegelman subtly inscribes the son's desire to rescue the father into the narrative. In "Portrait of an Invisible Man," Auster presents himself as trapped within trauma, incapable both of rescuing his father and of mourning him satisfactorily, for complete mourning would require exorcising the trauma, and this he is unable to do: "There has been a wound, and I realize now that it is very deep. Instead of healing me as I thought it would, the act of writing has kept this wound open. At times I have even felt the pain of it concentrated in my right hand, as if each time I picked up the pen and pressed it against the page, my hand were being torn apart. Instead of burying my father for me, these words have kept him alive, perhaps more so than ever" (32).

To attempt the rescue of his unburied father, A. goes into the room of the book and begins to write, seeking through writing to find his way back to the present: "The world has shrunk to the size of this room for him, and for as long as it takes him to understand it, he must stay where he is. Only one thing is certain: he cannot be anywhere until he is here. And if he does not manage to find this place, it would be absurd for him to think of looking for another" (79). It sounds as though A. is setting himself a phenomenological project of learning to inhabit the room, as in the saying by Heidegger, "But we do not want to get anywhere. We would like only, for once, to get just where we are already" (Heidegger 190). But instead of proceeding to register his sense of location in phenomenological terms, A. turns figurative immediately and begins to remember stories: "Life inside the whale. A gloss on Jonah, and what it means to refuse to speak. Parallel text: Gepetto in the belly of the shark (whale in the Disney version), and the story of how Pinocchio rescues him. Is it true that one must dive to the depths of the sea and save one's father to become a real boy?" (79). Through the intertwined stories of Jonah and Pinocchio A. tries to understand what it means to live in the room of the book and how such dwelling might result in a rescue of the father. Thinking about Jonah's residence inside the whale, A. notes that the whale "is by no means an agent of destruction. The fish is what saves him from drowning in the sea" (125). Such confinement represents incarceration as salvation, a kind of symbolic death that is "a preparation for new life, a life that has passed through death, and therefore a life that can at last speak" (125).

The room of the book is an alchemical site, in which Auster hopes to make death speak life through the regeneration of the father by the son. In "The Book of Memory," this alchemy makes its fullest appearance when A. meditates upon *Pinocchio* as he reads the story to his young son. Noting how "the little boy never tired of hearing the chapter about the storm at sea, which tells of how Pinocchio finds Gepetto in the belly of the Terrible Shark" (130), A. quotes Pinocchio's charged exclamation, "Oh, Father, dear Father! Have I found you at last? Now I shall never, never leave you again!" (131). On one level, this exclamation gives direct expression to the feelings of these particular readers: "For A. and his son, so often separated from each other during the past year, there was something deeply satisfying in this passage of reunion" (131). On another level, this exclamation reiterates A.'s desire to recover his own father and, beyond that, to recover a patrilineal power from the dead that will enable him to speak. In his own life, as in the story of Pinocchio, the reunion with the father has become essential for the son's regeneration: as A. notes, the bulk of *Pinocchio* "tells the story of Pinocchio's search for his father—and Gepetto's search for his son. At some point, Pinocchio realizes that he wants to become a real boy. But it also becomes clear that this will not happen until he is reunited with his father" (132).

When this reunion happens, however, the story is far from over. For regeneration to take place, for Pinocchio to become a "real boy," for A. to redeem his traumatized father, the boy must emerge from the belly of the shark with his father upon his back. The parthenogenically created boy must give birth to himself out of the womb/tomb. This image resides at the core of Auster's fantasy of regeneration through the room of the book, and he has A. meditate upon it intensively:

> The father on the son's back: the image evoked here is so clearly that of Aeneas bearing Anchises on his back from the ruins of Troy that each time A. reads the story aloud to his son, he cannot help seeing ... certain clusters of other images, spinning outward from the core of his preoccupations: Cassandra, for example, predicting the ruin of Troy, and thereafter loss, as in the wanderings of Aeneas that precede the founding of Rome, and in that wandering the image of another wandering: the Jews in the desert, which, in its turn, yields further clusters of images: "Next year in Jerusalem," and with it the photograph in the Jewish Encyclopedia of his relative, who bore the name of his son. (133)

In this swirling series of associations, the Greco-Roman "master"-civilization is brought into conjunction with the "wandering" Jewish culture and with A.'s own family. Here, the Jewish son carries his tradition upon his back, redeeming "Hebraism" in the face "Hellenism." The story of Pinocchio is so seductive for A. because of the redemption of the fathers (and, proleptically, of the son) that it promises.

For A.'s son, who spends an entire summer dressed as Superman, this fantasy of omnipotence and salvation is as irresistible as it is for his father:

> And for the little boy to see Pinocchio, that same foolish puppet who has stumbled his way from one misfortune to the next, who has wanted to be "good" and could not help being "bad," for this same incompetent little marionette, who is not even a real boy, to become a figure of redemption, the very being who saves his father from the grip of death, is a sublime moment of revelation. The son saves the father. This must be fully imagined from the perspective of the little boy. And this, in the mind of the father who was once a little boy, a son, that is, to his own father, must be fully imagined. *Puer aeternus*. The son saves the father. (134)

Through the regenerative figure of the *Puer aeternus*, the son gives birth to the father—and thus to himself as "a real boy." This represents the son's wish-fulfillment of the overcoming of the father's trauma, as well as the post-War Jew's fantasy of saving the victims of the Holocaust. Through the agency of the "incompetent little marionette," a mere simulacrum of a boy, the world of the fathers is to be redeemed. At the same time, however, A. as father remains only too aware of his own son's vulnerability. In a meditation upon sons who die before their fathers, A. muses upon an imaginary stack of photographs: "Mallarmé's son, Anatole; Anne Frank ('This is a photo that shows me as I should always like to look. Then I would surely have a chance to go to Hollywood. But now, unfortunately, I usually look different').... The dead children. The children who will vanish, the children who are dead. Himmler: 'I have made the decision to annihilate every Jewish child from the face of the earth'" (97–8). These are the children whose fathers were unable to rescue them; their fate is encompassed by Himmler's chilling anti-redemptive vow: for if there are no children, then there is no one to rescue and no one to do the rescuing.

VI.

It is time to return for a final look at the central question of this essay: what happens, then, inside the room of the book? Answer: a Book of Memory is being written. By engaging in such writing, Auster follows a central command reiterated throughout the Jewish scriptures: Remember! The Jewish historian, Y. H. Yerushalmi, notes that "the verb *zakhar* [to remember] appears in its various declensions in the Bible no less than one hundred and sixty-nine times, usually with Israel or God as the subject, for memory is incumbent upon both" (Yerushalmi 5). Remembering is a central activity of Jewish culture, a form of commemoration that takes the place of priestly rituals, sanctifying the present through linking it to the past. In the Passover seder, for instance, the celebrants are enjoined to place themselves directly into the biblical scenes of deliverance, in order to understand that they are celebrating not something done by God for their ancestors but something done for themselves. As A. writes himself deeper and deeper into the room of the book, his relationship to memory undergoes a change: memory, when made active, need not be only a means of hiding from the present by residing in the past; instead, it can be a way of allowing the past, with all its traumas, to inform a more fully lived in present. "As he writes, he feels that he is moving inward (through himself) and at the same time moving outward (towards the world)" (139).

By claiming that writing effects a dual movement—both inward and outward—A. posits a way for memory to lead him at least partially outside his confinement in the room of the book. To the extent that the memory of trauma can function as restorative—as, in Kabbalistic terms, *tikkun* (a mending of the broken vessels of creation)—there is an opportunity for the writing that occurs in the room of the book to re-imagine not only individual experience but also history. From this perspective, A. begins to realize that his initial entry into the room of the book ("He lays out a piece of blank paper on the table before him and writes these words with his pen. It was. It will never be again" [75].) contained a far greater potential than he was aware of at the time:

> What he experienced, perhaps, during those few moments on Christmas Eve, 1979, as he sat alone in his room on Varick Street, was this: the sudden knowledge that came over him that even alone, in the deepest solitude of his room, he was not alone, or, more precisely, that the moment he began to try to speak of that solitude, he had become more than just himself. Memory, therefore, not simply as the resurrection of one's private past, but an immersion in the past of others, which is to say: history— which one both participates in and is a witness to, is a part of and apart from.... If there is any reason for him to be in this room now, it is because there is something inside him hungering to see it all at once, to savor the chaos of it in all its raw and urgent simultaneity. (139)

A. believes that memory will never "make sense" of the past, but that it is instead a necessary form of vision that keeps the past alive in the present. When he is inhabiting the room of the book in this way, A. seems to be writing as though his very life depended upon it, for the traumatic world of the fathers represents a burden this latter-day Pinocchio must carry in order to become "a real boy."

As a post-Holocaust narrative, *The Invention of Solitude* takes the memory of trauma as the groundless ground from which writing and life begin. The past cannot be possessed or made whole, but trauma and memory can become generative forces. Thinking about Jabès's poetry as a response to the Holocaust, Auster speaks of the writer's duties with regard to such memories: "What he must do, in effect, is create a poetics of absence. The dead cannot be brought back to life. But they can be heard, and their voices live in the Book" (AH 114). When the survivors emerged from the camps after World War II, their nearly uniform reaction to the Holocaust was expressed in two words: "Never again!" This meant, we must remember so that the moral revulsion created by these memories will prevent such situations from ever recurring. The last line of "The Book of Memory" seems to allude to this resolution: "It was. It will never be again. Remember" (172). These words bring "The Book of Memory" full circle, repeating the inaugural statements of the book and adding to them the command, "Remember." Can this injunction to remember trauma create the conditions for understanding history? In his famous image of the Angel in the "Theses on the Philosophy of History," Walter Benjamin gives us a figure for history who stands open-mouthed at the traumatic wreckage of history piling up at his feet without cessation (Benjamin 259). This gesture bears a family resemblance to the "crying without sound" that overcomes A. in Anne Frank's room, a reaction that arises not only "in response to deep inner pain," but also "purely in response to the world. It was at that moment, he later realized, that the Book of Memory began" (82–3).

As a writer, Auster has made use of the room of the book as a way to interrogate the relationship of writing to history, through an invocation of memory. With respect to "The Book of Memory," the question that needs asking is whether memory makes it possible for Auster to witness the world in such a way that he succeeds in releasing himself from the confining quality of the room of the book. On balance, I think we would have to answer that question in the negative, particularly in light of his refusal to remember the issue of divorce and of his unacknowledged anger toward women. But I would like to applaud the seriousness of Auster's attempt to place issues of writing at the center of issues of living. Confronting head-on the situation of "a man sitting alone in a room and writing a book" (NYT 202), Auster makes of that situation an incredibly rich field of meditation, in which profound intellectual, historical, and personal issues arise and ask to be heard. As we have seen, Auster's room of the book houses a fascinating struggle between the absolutizing qualities of poetry and the narrative investment in fictional characters; it functions for the male writer both as a site of retreat from engagement with women and as an alchemical retort in which a parthenogenic theory of creativity can be proposed; and it becomes a space of hiding and torment, in which the irresolvable problems of writing with reference to the Holocaust can be embodied. Within the room of the book, Auster stages with compelling expertise central dilemmas of the writer, dilemmas that will not go away. To Blue's question, "How to get out of the room that is the book that will go on being written for as long as he stays in the room?" (NYT 202), the only decisive answer would be to walk out of the room that is the book. But for the writer, infinitely vulnerable to accusations of not living up to the moral claims enunciated in the writing, to walk out of the room of the book would be impossible: it would mean to stop writing.[10]

NOTES

1. In "Paul Auster, or the Heir Intestate," an excellent short essay on *The Invention of Solitude*, Pascal Bruckner also makes a strong case for the centrality of this book in Auster's oeuvre.

2. For a definition of poet's prose, see Fredman xiii, 1–2.

3. On the back cover of *From the Book to the Book: An Edmond Jabès Reader*, Auster writes: "I first read *The Book of Questions* twenty years ago, and my life was permanently changed. I can no longer think about the possibilities of literature without thinking of the example of Edmond Jabès. He is one of the great spirits of our time, a torch in the darkness."

See Finkelstein for a short consideration of Auster's relationship to Jabès (48–9); for more extended discussions of Jewish elements in Auster's work, see Finkelstein (48–53) and Rubin (60–70).

4. When Jabès speaks of a "book that would have a chance to survive," he means also a book whose reader would have a chance of surviving *it*. See Marc-Alain Ouaknin's *The Burnt Book* for a fascinating meditation, via Jabès and Levinas, on the creative necessity of an escape from the book.

5. Perloff argues strongly for the contribution of Beckett to contemporary poet's prose. There is a discussion of Ashbery's "translative prose" in Fredman, 101–35.

6. For a useful application of notions of genealogy to Auster's *Moon Palace*, see Weisenburg.

7. In many ways, Auster's fantasy of masculine self-generation is similar to Melville's in *Moby-Dick*—an analogy quite appropriate in light of A.'s characterization of S.'s room as "the womb, the belly of the whale." In Chapter 95 of *Moby-Dick* (350–51), a character also wears "the skin of some second body around him," namely the "pelt," or outer covering, of the whale's penis. Having skinned and dried it, the "mincer" wears the sheath to protect himself from boiling blubber. Melville presents this investiture as a form of primitive phallus-worship (and then, as he does so often in *Moby-Dick*, compares jeeringly the "primitive" with the Christian: "what a candidate for an archbishoprick, what a lad for a Pope were this mincer!" [351]); but interestingly, by turning the phallus into a sheath, the mincer has, in effect, invaginated it.

8. "The Structure of Rime," one of Duncan's two open-ended poetic sequences, first appears in *The Opening of the Field*. Although Duncan calls the Structure of Rime "an absolute scale of resemblance and disresemblance [that] establishes measures that are music in the actual world" (13), he does not allow the mind to imagine itself as privy to this "absolute scale." He ascribes this knowledge, instead, to a feminine presence, whom he designates in "Often I Am Permitted to Return to a Meadow" as the "Queen Under the Hill / whose hosts are a disturbance

of words within words / that is a field folded" (7). As in Leibniz, interconnectedness
remains for Duncan "folded within all thought" (7).

9. It is interesting to note how Auster, in crafting a Jewish interpretation of the
Pinocchio story, makes nothing of the puppet's embarrassingly prominent nose. See
Gilman, especially Chapter 7, "The Jewish Nose," for reflections on the stigma of the
nose and the history of the "nose job."

10. Auster was recently given the opportunity to walk out of the room and yet
continue writing. In the midst of shooting a film, *Smoke*, for which Auster wrote the
screenplay, the director, Wayne Wang, Auster, and one of the actors, Harvey Keitel,
were having so much fun they decided to improvise another film. Auster outlined the
screenplay on the fly and even directed *Blue in the Face* for two days when Wang took
sick. After describing the joys of working with actors like Keitel, Michael J. Fox,
Roseanne, Lou Reed, Jim Jarmusch, Lily Tomlin, and Madonna, Auster was asked by
a journalist if he plans to direct or write screenplays again. He answered in the
negative, but noted a signal benefit from the endeavor: "It was a great experience, it
got me out of my room" (Chanko 15).

Works Cited

Antin, David. *Talking at the Boundaries*. New York: New Directions, 1976.
Auster, Paul. *The Art of Hunger*. New York: Penguin, 1993. Abbreviated AH.
———. *Disappearances: Selected Poems*. Woodstock, NY: Overlook Press, 1988.
    Abbreviated D.
———. *The Invention of Solitude*. 1982. New York: Penguin, 1988. Abbreviated IS.
———. *The New York Trilogy*. 1985, 1986, 1986. New York: Penguin, 1990.
    Abbreviated NYT.
———, ed. *The Random House Book of Twentieth-Century French Poetry*. New York:
    Random, 1982.
Barone, Dennis, ed. *Beyond the Red Notebook: Essays on Paul Auster*. Philadelphia: U of
    Pennsylvania P, 1995.
Bruckner, Pascal. "Paul Auster, or the Heir Intestate." Barone 27–33.
Benjamin, Walter. *Illuminations*. Trans. Harry Zohn. New York: Harcourt, 1968.
Chanko, Kenneth. "'Smoke' Gets in Their Eyes." *Entertainment Weekly* 281/282
    (June 30/July 7, 1995): 14–15.
Duncan, Robert. *The Opening of the Field*. New York: Grove, 1960.
Finkelstein, Norman. "In the Realm of the Naked Eye: The Poetry of Paul Auster."
    Barone 44–59.
Fredman, Stephen. *Poet's Prose: The Crisis in American Verse*. 2nd. ed. Cambridge:
    Cambridge UP, 1990.
Gilman, Sander. *The Jew's Body*. New York: Routledge, 1991.
Heidegger, Martin. *Poetry, Language, Thought*. Trans. Albert Hostadter. New York:
    Harper, 1971.
Jabès, Edmond. *From the Book to the Book: An Edmond Jabès Reader*. Trans. Rosmarie
    Waldrop. Hanover, NH: Wesleyan UP, 1991.

————. *From the Desert to the Book: Dialogues with Marcel Cohen*. Trans. Pierre Joris. Barrytown, NY: Station Hill, 1990.

Melville, Herman. *Moby-Dick*. Norton Critical Edition. Ed. Harrison Hayford and Hershel Parker. New York: Norton, 1967.

Oppen, George. "Of Being Numerous." *Collected Poems*. New York: New Directions, 1975. 147–179.

Ouaknin, Marc-Alain. *The Burnt Book: Reading the Talmud*. 1986. Trans. Llewellyn Brown. Princeton: Princeton UP, 1995.

Perloff, Marjorie. "Between Verse and Prose: Beckett and the New Poetry." *The Dance of the Intellect: Studies in the Poetry of the Pound Tradition*. Cambridge: Cambridge UP, 1985. 135–54.

Rubin, Derek. "'The Hunger Must Be Preserved at All Cost': A Reading of *The Invention of Solitude*." Barone 60–70.

Spiegelman, Art. *Maus: A Survivor's Tale I and II*. New York: Random, 1986, 1991.

Weisenburg, Steven. "Inside *Moon Palace*." Barone 130–42.

Yerushalmi, Yosef Hayim. *Zakhor: Jewish History and Jewish Memory*. 1982. New York: Schocken, 1989.

PASCAL BRUCKNER

Paul Auster,
or The Heir Intestate

*T*he *Invention of Solitude* is both the *ars poetica* and the seminal work of Paul Auster. To understand him we must start here; all his books lead us back to this one. Novel-manifesto in two parts, "Portrait of an Invisible Man" and "The Book of Memory," this work immediately sounds the theme of remorse.

Paul Auster was able to become a writer because his father left him a small inheritance that spared him a life of poverty. The father's death not only liberated his son's writing but literally saved his life. The son would never stop repaying this debt, would never finish reimbursing the deceased, in prose, for his fearsome gift. As payment Auster seeks to revive the image of this man he barely knew. The elder Auster, landlord by profession, was an absent character, "a block of impenetrable space in the form of a man" (7), an invisible being, "tourist of his own life" (9). One had the feeling that he never could be located, and he masked this evanescence with perpetual chatter. How could you be yourself in a world where your father was disengaged? This father remained a stranger to Auster, and made Auster a stranger to himself. His father had denied him the usual outlet of youth: rebellion, because one can't rebel against a phantom. And the author, who had to lose his father in order to find him, would respond by filling his novels with figures of weak, colorless, pitiful parents, overwhelmed by their

From *Beyond the Red Notebook: Essays on Paul Auster,* edited by Dennis Barone. © 1995 by the University of Pennsylvania Press.

offspring and incapable of assuming fatherhood. Like Pinocchio snatching Geppetto from the jaws of the shark, Paul Auster would save his father from oblivion and, by giving him new life, justify his own existence.

As the story unfolds, sketching an increasingly more complex image of the deceased, one truth becomes evident: reaching one's father requires work. By giving birth to his own parent through words, the author repairs a broken communication and makes it possible for himself, in turn, to become a father. In short, a subtle dialectic directs this plot. According to Auster, proximity is deceptive, and anonymity is not only the misfortune of the masses, or of the cities, but also a cancer gnawing away at the family and marital unit. Human contact often masks a gulf that only death or distance can bridge. We are separated from others by those very things that also connect us; we are separated from ourselves by the illusion of self-knowledge. just as we must forget ourselves in order to reach a certain level of self-truth, we must also leave others in order to find them in the prism of memory or separation. That which is closest is often the most enigmatic, and distance, like mourning and wandering, is also an instrument of redemption.

In the beginning, therefore, are sin and dispossession. Only an accident, a rupture, will shake the self from its apathy, from the pseudo-intimacy it maintains with itself. It is here that Auster's series of staggering paradoxes begins.

For Auster, confinement is a form of exile. *The Invention of Solitude* can be read as a celebration of rooms and closed spaces. This enclosure has nothing to do with the so-called panegyric of private life, or "cocooning." There is neither public nor private in this novelistic universe since the individual does not own himself. His center is located outside himself. This penchant for narrow spaces, where the spirit can project itself against the walls (the examination of this theme in Hölderlin, Anne Frank, Collodi, Van Gogh, or Vermeer is fascinating) makes the room a kind of mental uterus, site of a second birth. In this enclosure the subject gives birth, in essence, to himself. From mere biological existence he now attains spiritual life. This confinement transforms him into a voluntary castaway, a Robinson Crusoe run aground in the middle of the city, wedged into a tiny fissure of the urban habitat. This shipwreck is necessary, even if it resembles a deferred suicide. The self must die, Auster seems to say, in order to live; there is a redemptive sense to annulment; hence Auster's heroes push themselves to the limit of hunger and physical deprivation. This self-destructive passion, which barely avoids total annihilation (in a way similar to that analyzed by Auster in Knut Hamsun's *Hunger*), transforms this confinement in one's room into a sort of secular asceticism without transcendence, without God. As if the fathers' actual death required the fictitious death of their sons, Auster's character is always ready to offer himself in sacrifice. The only valid existence is that which has experienced extinction.

Auster's work explores a second paradox: death is the first step toward resurrection. Since this life given us by another is invalid, descent into hell is the only way to reclaim an authentic existence, to kill the old man within. Our room is a prison that opens the gates of freedom; the self is a dungeon we must voluntarily enter in order to find escape. If confinement leads to nomadism, the latter in turn will guide the protagonists toward self-reconciliation.

Auster also examines a third paradox: wandering is intimacy's helpmate. In his work, it is fate, ironic and mischievous providence, that breaks down the false barrier between the near and the far, between mine and yours, ours and theirs. No matter how far he roams, the individual will ultimately meet himself; he is inclined to be at home everywhere, since he is not at home in his own house:

> During the, war, M.'s father had hidden out from the Nazis for several months in a Paris *chambre de bonne*. Eventually, he managed to escape, made his way to America, and began a new life. Years passed, more than twenty years. M. had been born, had grown up, and now was going off to study in Paris. Once there he spent several difficult weeks looking for a place to live. Just when he was about to give up in despair, he found a small *chambre de bonne*. Immediately upon moving in, he wrote a letter to his father to tell him the good news. A week or so later he received a reply: your address, wrote M.'s father, that is the same building I hid out in during the war. He then went on to describe the details of the room. It turned out to be the same room his son had rented. (80)

All of Auster is there in this love of coincidences that rhyme the most remote, improbable events. He excels at sprinkling his characters' adventures with correlations, which have no a priori meaning, but to which the story gives unexpected consequences. Noting the signs that fate strews along our path is the only way to combat the arbitrary: suddenly, in the randomness of existence, a certain order appears just below the surface, an order which seems mysteriously to control its. There is meaning in the world, but this meaning is only suggested, never clearly expressed. Therefore, everything in Paul Auster's work occurs by chance; and what better image of chance than an inheritance—an event as harmful as it is beneficial. It is as if money of the deceased were an oppressive gift that could drag us, with its donor, beyond the grave. The novelist's challenge here is to endow this image of the unexpected with the weight of necessity, to continue converting the improbable into the inevitable, to avoid gratuitousness. The novelist must also be a bit of an acrobat: plunging his characters into confusing situations, then weaving among them a fabric of dense analogies, linking the episodes together in such an inevitable manner that the reader cannot imagine the story occurring any other way. This penchant for reversals, for sudden about-faces, also places Paul Auster in the picaresque tradition, at the opposite extreme from his avowed masters, Kafka and Beckett.

Wandering, in Auster, has this original aspect: rather than pitting the individual against a cold, hostile world, it forces him to confront himself and the scattered fragments of his existence. Everything relates back to the self, and, while the closed room serves as a microcosm, the outer world itself becomes an enclosure, which speaks in veiled tones. "Home" is everywhere since the self is not at home with itself. *The Invention of Solitude* announces a theme that Paul Auster will raise to the level of a true obsession: nomadism as a means of cloistering oneself; introspection as a means of escape. (Hence the appeal of pseudonyms and non-places in *City of Glass*, the characters' capacity to take on other identities, the kaleidoscope of doubles, of contingent selves, the suspended moments when a person almost chooses to become someone else, illusions that bathe this trilogy in a kind of subdued Platonism.) "Exiling himself in order to find out where he was" (16). This formula that Auster applies to Thoreau suits Auster perfectly. He is able to reverse the language of mobility and immobility, of the wanderer and the sedentary. Through escape, we experience intimacy; through confrontation, estrangement. And this reversal may be rooted in the experience of a young boy who, in the presence of his father, felt total absence and solitude.

It is easy to see what distinguishes Paul Auster from other contemporary writers and to see why he is so successful. There is no one less narcissistic than this novelist obsessed with the self. This is because he challenges two attitudes that are common today: the proud, in-control self with no ties and no past, and the traditionalist or minority, proud of his identity, his roots, his people. Auster's point of view is different: he recognizes his connection to a family, a tradition, a culture, but he also realizes that this is a highly problematic link. In short, to paraphrase the famous verse of René Char, the legacy is ambiguous: the will is missing. Since nothing has a priori meaning—this, the very curse of modernity—the self, like solitude and tradition, must literally be invented and recreated. Auster is not an advocate of difference; he claims no particular status, does not ghettoize himself in any group. He does not seek what separates people, but, rather, what brings them together; and what they have in common is a similar confusion about their identity. But he has also avoided what has been killing French literature for the past twenty years: the invasive proliferation of autobiography, of the diary, of self-preoccupation as a genre in and of itself. This literature, which tends to narrow rather than broaden experience, is most frequently reduced to a bitter whine, since it conveys above all the impossibility of escaping the self. And it is the unfortunate irony of these books, devoted to revealing the individual's most intimate essence, their subjectivity unparalleled, that they all end up resembling each other, as if written by the same person. With these publications writing becomes an isolating activity, which contradicts its intended universality. And its fanatical celebration of the writer's uniqueness or interiority repels the reader, who is reluctant to let himself be trapped or fascinated. Instead of creating a world where all might live together, the writer takes from the community its common tool, language, which he then uses to distance himself from the group and to express his own uniqueness. All these voices raised in soliloquy, detailing their petty problems, create a universe of mutual deafness where each person, talking about himself, no longer has the time to listen to others.

Unlike this orgy of egotism, Auster's *The Invention of Solitude* is a story whose strength lies in its very simplicity. Through this apparent banality the reader finds himself, and the novel regains its true identity. It is once again a homeland open to all without distinction, a place of welcome: "I don't feel that I was telling the story of my life so much as using myself to explore certain questions that are common to us all" (292), Auster says in an interview. Auster's hero is not someone who prefers himself, to repeat Brecht's definition of the bourgeois, but someone who doubts and communicates this doubt to the reader. Readers identify less with the protagonists' adventures than with the strangeness they feel about themselves—for whom being or becoming someone constitutes the ultimate difficulty. Auster does not condemn, like classical writers, the self's wretchedness in the face of God's grandeur. He does worse: he dissolves this self, declares it a nonentity. Uncertainty eats into the core of our being; our heart is empty or cluttered with so much static that it seems to hold nothing.

This work clearly also expresses the genealogical passion of the uprooted, and it is not insignificant that Auster is an American entirely oriented toward Europe. But this proximity is misleading. A reading of Auster produces a double sensation of familiarity and disorientation, for Auster, deeply anchored in the New World, does not write European books in America; he enriches the American novel with European themes. *The*

Invention of Solitude, a tribute to Auster's departed father, continues in the second part with a warm greeting to all those poets and thinkers who have influenced the author. Through writing we can choose other fathers to compensate for our own, discover a spiritual link, go beyond ourselves. Memory is immersion in the past of all those others who comprise us. The narrator distinguishes, one by one, these voices that speak through him that must be quieted before his true inner voice can be heard. But this goal is impossible to attain: the palimpsest self, like an ever-unpeeling onion, resists categorization. This peregrination through the continents of memory may be a marvelous journey, but it does not succeed in easing the pain. No matter how far it roams, the self is always haunted and tortured by the others; it is a room full of strangers and intruders who speak in his place. Auster's approach is not, of course, the same as Proust's anamnesis, an attempt to compensate for life's imperfections by fixing the flight of time in a work of art. It is an eternal quest, without guaranteed results, which can never achieve closure. A detective of the self, Paul Auster applies an uncompromising narrative skill to a metaphysical quest: Why is there a self rather than nothing? To facilitate this task, he presents his fiction in the protective guise of the detective novel. In the end, however, nothing is resolved. Each book is a collective work, the tribute of a writer to all those, past and present, who have helped him create. But this courtesy toward the dead, calling them to his bedside, inviting them to a vast, cross-century symposium, does not expunge the debt. Just as a son can never stop paying for the death of the father who gave him life, so, too, the self can never stop paying its due. It could even define itself this way: the eternal debtor always under obligation to others. That is why this literature must tirelessly rewrite its missing testament. And if, as the famous saying goes, a prophet is someone who remembers the future, the writer, according to Auster, is someone who predicts the past in order first to capture and then to free himself from it. But memory's archives are both chaotic and infinite, and the clerk who attempts to record them will soon get lost in the maze.

Paul Auster completely renews the coming-of-age novel. With unusual talent he reveals how painful it is to be an individual today thrust out from the protective shell of a belief or tradition. After these extensive investigations he offers no final wisdom. Each of his novels outlines the beginning of a redemption, which it subsequently rejects. The lack of response, or of comfort, the stubborn refusal to abandon the pain of this issue, that is the strength of these works. As each plot is unraveled an increasingly more obscure enigma is resealed. His literature is like a brief burst of sunshine between a hidden and an exposed mystery, a glimmer between two shades of darkness." Just because you wander in the desert, it does not mean there is a promised land" (*Solitude* 32). All his characters—vagabonds, gamblers, semi-tramps, magnificent losers, failed writers—are under way. Like Marco Stanley Fogg at the end of *Moon Palace*, facing the ocean in the hazy moonlight, these characters are more serene at the end of the day, but they are never sovereign. Their chaotic odyssey never ends in peace, and they always fail to regain their lost innocence. Writing never removes the agony, but, rather, alters and deepens it. Writing is futility because it fails to express the experience of loss and renunciation. Perhaps Paul Auster's rich works already prefigure what certain historians foresee as the religion of the future: Christian-Buddhism, that is, a concern with personal salvation linked to an acute awareness of uncertainty and the void.

—Translated by Karen Palmunen

WORKS CITED

Auster, Paul. "Interview with Larry McCaffery and Sinda Gregory." In *The Art of Hunger: Essays, Prefaces, Interviews*. Los Angeles: Sun & Moon Press, 1992. Pp. 269–312.

———. *The Invention of Solitude*. New York: Penguin, 1988.

WILLIAM DOW

Paul Auster's The Invention of Solitude: *Glimmers in a Reach to Authenticity*

Paul Auster's *The Invention of Solitude* uses and questions the validity of postmodern typologies and thus properly can be read in light of recent postmodernist theory. At the same time, *Invention* challenges the idea that autobiography issues from a pre-existing self or a unique and autonomous self. Auster's "autobiography," consequently, constructs a self that requires negotiation, complicity, and collusion (terms that refer not to single individuals but to relationships) as it shapes the materials of the past "to serve the needs of the present consciousness" (Gergen 100, Eakin 55). As G. Thomas Couser remarks:

> With the undermining of the referential theory of language
> and the consequent emphasis on the self-reflexive nature of
> all texts, the writing of autobiography has been declared to
> be, on the one hand, problematic—if not impossible—and,
> on the other, a paradigm for all writing. (26)

For Auster's fiction, *Invention* provides a consistent angle of vision, signals the problematic and paradigm of his later work, and represents, in its dialogic potential, new possibilities for twentieth-century autobiographical structures. Imagining literary forms decisively in accord with the rhythms of

From *Critique: Studies in Contemporary Fiction* 39, no. 3 (Spring 1998). © 1998 by the Helen Dwight Reid Educational Foundation.

individual perception, Auster has extended the postmodernist topos to include the power of contingency in his narrative emphasis on ambiguity and coincidence. In a world made of glimmers and sudden intuitions, Invention moves through the postmodern domains of decreation, disappearance, and other forms of "unmaking" to demonstrate how the novel genre can interpret and criticize itself.

But Auster goes against the postmodernist topos as well. His attempt to give language to the glimpses points to its own epistemology and theory of literary expression. Found abundantly in the early reviews and criticism of *Invention* the word *postmodern*, though "undoubtedly a part of the modern" (Lyotard, "Answering" 44), is increasingly used to describe an oppositional stance to modernist thought. If Jean-François Lyotard is right in concluding that "enlightenment" values (truth, progress, virtue, homogeneity) are no longer applicable in a postmodern epoch (19),[1] *Invention*, in its reflection on the human condition and emphasis on the ethical component of the intellect, is at once a postmodernist extension and contravention.

The current debate on postmodernism as an operative cultural paradigm involves, in such theories as Charles Jencks's "sublation" and Ihab Hassan's "hybridization"[2] postmodernism's dialectical *opposition* to the modern. As Karlis Racevskis has argued,

> Although the debate centers around the terms defined by Jean-François Lyotard in his epoch-making book *La condition postmoderne: rapport sur le savoir*, published in 1979, it involves, generally speaking the whole structuralist and poststructuralist phenomenon and its effects on the world of intellect. Briefly, it is alleged that the so-called structuralists (often called post-structuralists [in the United States]), the thinkers whose intellectual ascendancy goes back to the mid-sixties, have more or less discredited the ideological and metaphysical foundations of the modern age: they have rendered inoperative the values inherited from the Enlightenment and made humanism obsolete. (276)

Racevskis adds,

> What is deplorable about the current situation, from the perspective of the defenders of modernism, is that no new system of values has been found to replace the old one, no new ethical *modus vivendi* has been defined; rationality and order have been

replaced by the irrationality and disorder spawned by an irresponsible relativism. (276)

We are left, it is claimed, with a state of affairs that has given license to the cynical and unscrupulous "who are no longer held in check by a universally applicable and rationally justifiable set of principles" (276). Generally speaking, the poststructuralist thought—particularly in its postmodernist manifestations—has been reproached for discrediting any version of a geographically and historically grounded depiction of humanity; for its "counter-productiveness" in bringing reason to the point where it reveals its dependency on factors beyond conscious control; and for failing to provide an ethical basis for writing (Racevskis 278).[3] Christopher Norris, for example, essentially adopts this position, lamenting the "'deconstruction' of the humanist subject as a locus of ethical choices, conflicts, and responsibilities" (7).

But as a postmodernist text, Invention does emphasize the ethical component of a private intellectual activity and subverts this commonly cited postmodernist paradigm. Invention, moreover, questions the postmodernist topos of demonstrating that the discourse of humanism and rationalism serve only to hide irreconcilable and indeterminant meanings. Although Invention stresses the end of a single world view, and wages its own war on "totality,"[4] it gives, at the same time, value to the "partial, glimpsed achievements" (Rowen 232) of the novel's narrators.

In the beginning of "Portrait of an Invisible Man," for example, Auster, shortly after the death of his father, comes across several hundred family photographs stashed and scattered about in his father's bedroom closet (13). Auster subsequently discovers a large, gold-stamped album, entitled "This is Our Life: The Austers," totally blank inside, which Auster must "arrange," losing nothing, until all the "images" become part of him (14). The realization that his "father had left no traces" (6) spurs him to "fill the album," to make his father "visible" to himself and the reader. While accepting the fragmentation and pluralism of the postmodern condition (suggested by the scattered photographs), Auster continues to "look for the father who was not there," feeling that he must "go on looking for him" (7). Thus he begins his attempt to "put forward," as Lyotard argues in another context, "the unpresentable in presentation itself" (Lyotard, "Answering" 46): in Auster's case, the creation of a realizable system of images, glimmers.

But the reconstitution of his father's character and Auster's memories of his father do not take the form of a conventional totality, a definitive portrait. Rather, Auster's own meaning and deductions defer and accrete from one linguistic (and epistemological) interpretation to another. When, for example, Auster's father tells him the story of "his prospecting days in South America," Auster (the narrator) concludes:

> Not only was he telling me new things about himself, unveiling to me the world of his distant past, but he was telling it with new and strange words. This language was just as important as the story itself. It belonged to it, and in some sense was indistinguishable from it. Its very strangeness was proof of authenticity. (22)

But the narrator says nothing more about this "strangeness"; he simply defers his discussion of language and quickly goes on to the next anecdote (his desire, as a Little League star, to do "something extraordinary" to impress his father [23]). Nevertheless, before commenting (in his memory of the Memorial Day game) on his father's reversion to an automatic, decorous language and "abstracted tone of voice" (23), Auster receives from his father a glimmer of language's "authenticity." Auster's reliance on deferral in his narrative construction of his father's "portrait" evinces a trust in knowledge as a slow accretion, a series of emotional and intellectual proximities.

When Auster returns to his thoughts on the "authentic language" he applies them to his sense of failure to express "the truly important thing": "the story I am trying to tell is somehow incompatible with language ... the degree to which it resists language is an exact measure of how closely I have come to saying something important" (32). Paradoxically, Auster uses deferral to get at the connections language can supply. At the beginning of the "Book of Memory," he comes back to the connection, this time under the mnemotechnic notion that Giordano Bruno posits: "[T]he structure of human thought corresponds to the structure of nature. And therefore ... everything, in some sense, is connected to everything else" (76). Through his use of deferral, Auster thus points to—however temporary or "invisible"—a conceivable "authenticity" that memory and language can provide.

To that end, he employs in both parts of *Invention* a diaristic and anecdotal structure, relying on "found" or "cut-up" life experiences. Although that structure underlines the postmodern opprobrium of "totalisation" or any synthesis, Auster does construct a coherent and continuous identity of his father and himself. In his retrospective diaristic form Auster sees not a day-to-day pattern, but a lifetime pattern characterized by a tension of linguistic resistance and silences.

Auster points out the consistent pattern of his father's gestures, behaviors, "absences," and language. In fact, his father's language is perhaps the most important determinant of their relationship. When Auster's father sees for the first time Auster's two-week-old son, his father indifferently remarks, "A beautiful baby. Good luck with it" (19). That cliché is first repeated when Auster compares it to a cliché his father had used twenty years before (after Auster's worst performance in a childhood baseball game). "Well you did your best," his father tells him. "You can't do well every time" (23). The third time Auster uses the cliché, he does so in the context of a most explicit interpretation:

> Reliance on fixed routines freed him from the necessity of looking into himself when decisions had to be made; the cliché was always quick to come to his lips ("A beautiful baby. Good luck with it") instead of words he had gone out and looked for. (31)

Auster constructs his father (and himself) as a subject through language, to which he can only adopt positions or responses—as in condemning his father's use of cliché—at any given moment. The self (i.e., Auster's self) then is defined in the diaristic form of *Invention* as a position, a locus where the discourse between Auster and his father intersect.[5]

Invention echoes Auster's belief that as a novelist, he is "morally obligated," as he states in the McCaffery–Gregory interview, to incorporate events contingent on "chance" and "destiny" into his books. One of the epistemological premises of *Invention* therefore is that "our lives really don't belong to us ... they belong to the world, and in spite of our efforts to make sense of it, the world is a place beyond our understanding" (*Art* 279). But *Invention*'s notative form, although denying a self-evident center, emphasizes the notion that the self is not one self but many selves formed as a collection of moments of conscious glimmers, transcending, subverting, or feeding our understanding.

The linguistic deferrals and accretions, and the diaristic devices of *Invention* do not simply fizzle into a fragmentary stasis and relativism. *Invention* does not follow the diaristic pattern of recording the self (Auster, his father) as being significantly different today or tomorrow from yesterday. Indeed, the general characters of Auster and his father appear to have been established (oppositionally) *before* the recording of *Invention* begins. *Invention* becomes, therefore, not a diurnal chronicle of Auster's life but an evocation of his existence.

What then is the "unpostmodernist-postmodernist" epistemology of *Invention*? What has Auster accomplished in "vacating" the traditional diaristic self? How do *Invention's* postmodernist devices go beyond, for instances, Ihab Hassan's postmodernist *definien* in which "we undecide, relativise," a world in which "indeter-minancies pervade our actions" (196)?

Auster transcends such facile categories by anchoring his narrative in a double-voiced discourse of tragic optimism, leaving the narrators in both parts of *Invention* free to defer and accrete meaning. Auster's discourse, although emphasizing the unknowable nature of the world, continually points to the importance of fragmented or partial knowledge. Toward the end of "Portrait of an Invisible Man," Auster evokes these contradictory images about his father:

> I understand now that each fact is nullified by the next fact, that each thought engenders an equal and opposite thought. Impossible to say anything without reservation: he was good, or he was bad; he was this, or he was that. All of them are true. (61)

But he concludes the passage on a note of acceptance for his father's being "set adrift" and for a world of incomplete and "anecdotal" knowledge:

> At times I have the feeling that I am writing about three or four different men, each one distinct, each one a contradiction of all the others. Fragments. Or the anecdote as a form of knowledge. (61)

The narrator is invariably and increasingly pleased with this revelatory form: anecdote depicting coincidences that rely on the narrator's observations and "exterior chance or precedent" (Austin 23). Glimmers, glimpses, and coincidences (e.g., A.'s son resembling Mallarmé's son; S. being born in the same year as A.'s father; A. being born in the same year as S.'s son) provide the needed epistemological "connections," authenticity. A. sees that there is something beyond the intellect, but "it is only at those rare moments when one happens to glimpse a rhyme in the world that the mind can leap out of itself and serve as a bridge for things across time and space" (161). "Our lives," Anna Blume tells us *In the Country of Last Things*, "are no more than the sum of manifold contingencies and no matter how diverse they might be in their details, they all share an essential randomness in their design: this then that, and because of that, this" (143–44).

Auster's postmodernist world grants only an unpredictable "brush[ing] up against the mysteries," a configuration of glimpses (*Art* 277). At the end of "Portrait of an Invisible Man," Auster again refers to the "blank photograph album" that he cannot hope to fill permanently. Having made his father momentarily "visible," Auster now sees that his father "has become invisible again" (68). In taking possession of his father's "objects" (his watch, sweater, car), Auster has appropriated the images; he has, in the words he cites from Kierkegaard, "give[n] birth to his own father"—but only momentarily. The images of his father will soon "break down, fall apart, and as a glimpsed achievement, "have to be thrown away" (68). Auster combines the tragic and the optimistic at the very end of "Portrait": the disappearance of his father with the "image" of his son Daniel asleep upstairs in a crib. He ends with this.

The second part of *Invention*, "The Book of Memory," sustains the view of tragic optimism while it simultaneously reverts to and subverts postmodernistic modes. Again, there is the motif of an invisibility or blankness—this time taking not the form of an empty photo album but simply a blank piece of paper, to be filled by the narrator A. A. begins his inward journey, his "hermetic season," by burrowing down to a place of "almost vanished memory" (78, 80). The second part of *Invention* is Auster's attempt to share the nostalgia for the unattainable, a nostalgia that at once evokes the pain of withdrawing from the world and the solitude made palpable by such a withdrawal.

But Auster also shares his versions of the postmodern typology. As Jacqueline Austin noted in her 1983 review of *Invention*, Auster "springs out" in "The Book of Memory" the full panoply of postmodern techniques: defamiliarization, self-reflectiveness, irony, metalinguistic play. Indeed, in "reconquer[ing] the emptiness," Auster increases his reliance on coincidence in his five-part commentary on the "nature of chance" and his thirteen "Books of Memory"; his ponderings on the "double" become more pronounced ("A world in which everything is double, in which the same thing always happens twice" [83]); his stress on rhymes and word play increases (159–60); and his emphasis on "the limits of the known world" (98) takes on an added urgency. Austin argues that in "The Book of Memory" such techniques are overused and that "huge amounts of material had been denied for over-fashionable reasons, perhaps despair at encompassing the subject, perhaps something more rarefied" (23).

But Auster's postmodern investigations provide the starting point for his own epistemology of sovereignty. Although at the beginning of the "Book of Memory," A. has a "nostalgia for the present," he discovers that he is no longer able to "dwell in the present" (76, 87). At certain points in A.'s commentaries, memory becomes "atemporal" and takes as its embodiments "a place ... a building ... a sequence of columns, cornices, porticoes" (82). From Pascal's advice, which becomes A.'s refrain ("All the unhappiness of man stems from one thing only: that his is incapable of staying quietly in his room"), A. begins to write the book of memory in his room on Varick Street. He then describes Anne Frank's room in Amsterdam and in a later section, the room of his friend S. that S. has turned into a miniature "cosmology":

> It was a shrine, hardly bigger than a body, in praise of all that exists beyond the body: the representation of one man's inner world, even to the slightest detail. S. had literally managed to surround himself with the things that were inside him. (89)

All of this is A.'s attempt to "encompass the subject," solitude—for the best way to begin understanding one's connection to others is to be alone. "And the more intensely you are alone," Auster argues, "the more deeply you plunge into a state of solitude, the more deeply you feel that connection" (*Art* 309).

Solitude therefore allows A. to become "inhabited by others" and to find the world outside, which is why Auster terms *Invention* "a collective work" (*Art* 309). Auster is not undertreating the material, as Austin believes, but instead, in "The Book of Memory," further expands on his epistemology based on momentary, ephemeral recognitions. That explains his use of so many authors, artists, references, quotations, and allusions, which is particularly pronounced in the second part of *Invention*.

I want to return for an instant to Racevskis's postmodernist cultural paradigm. It must be emphasized that Auster elaborately deconstructs the postmodernist aesthetic of expression, all the while operating from within it. Racevskis concludes his argument in "the modernity of moralistes" by stressing this postmodernist "revelation":

> The force of the postmodernist argument resides in the demonstration that the discourse of humanism, or rationalism, and of morality serves only to hide an irrational operation of interests that are bound to a will unfettered by any morality. (279)

But "The Book of Memory" uses the postmodern to join the will to an individual and collective morality. Auster constantly emphasizes moral choices in his relations with the surrogate father, S., feeding him, taking care of his physical needs; with his dying grandfather; and with his infant son who contracts pneumonia and nearly dies. A. judges the conditions that the United States had created in Cambodia and ironically evokes the visit of Rosalynn Carter and her entourage to a Cambodian refugee camp:

> The President's wife arrived, followed by a swarm of officials, reporters, and cameramen. There were too many of them, and as they trooped through the hospital, patients' hands were stepped on by heaving Western shoes, I.V. lines were disconnected by passing legs, bodies were inadvertently kicked. (156)

Most important, A., because "the world is monstrous," is morally committed to the image of his son. "And not just his son, but any son, any daughter, any child of any man or woman" (156). *Invention* is irrevocably fettered to self and pluralized forms of covering all spheres: cognitive, expressive, and moral.

Frederic Jameson in "Postmodernism, or The Cultural Logic of Late Capitalism" extends Racevskis's point on morality by arguing that postmodernism will presumably signal

> the end, for example, of style, in the sense of the unique and the personal, the end of the distinctive individual brushstroke (as symbolized by the emergent primacy of mechanical reproduction). As for expression and feelings or emotions, the liberation, in contemporary society, from the older *anomie* of the centered subject may also mean, not merely a liberation from anxiety, but a liberation from every other kind of feeling as well, since there is no longer a self present to do the feeling. (72)

Contravening Jameson's conception of the postmodernist self, "The Book of Memory" places a new value on the elusive and discloses a longing for a stable self. Auster's style, dipped in the postmodern condition, signals not the end of "the unique and the personal" but the beginning. *Invention* is foremost a story arising from the power of memory: "a way of living one's life so that nothing is ever lost" (138). "And even if the things to be seen are no longer there, it is a story of seeing" (154). Discursive, fragmented, the story is attached to Auster's singular epistemology of deferral, accretion, and *continuance*. After the things are seen, intuited, glimpsed, the imagination must then take over, for "like a child" man must be allowed to dream and to enter the imaginary (154).

Invention ends with a description of A. in a room looking at a "blank piece of paper," which he soon fills with contradictory images of the earth, the sky, and time. As in "Portrait of an Invisible Man," Auster returns to the images at the beginning of the narrative: more blankness or invisibility. A. must forever continue to reflect on the human condition, to make "visible" the ethical component of literary expression. Auster, it appears, feels an obligation to bring back selected values, but in a way that recognizes the ruptures caused by the postmodern. It can be said then, that *Invention* signals the emergence in contemporary epistemology of an aesthetic model opposed to the notion of not taking responsibility for the aesthetic self. Herein lies *Invention*'s "forward gropings ... [its] anticipation of an undefined future" (Habermas 98).

Any analysis of the postmodern must be necessarily unfinished and tentative. "[I]t is far from clear," Zygmunt Bauman reminds us, "which among the many topics of the [postmodernist] discourse signal lasting and irreversible tendencies, and which will soon find their place among the passing fads of a century notorious for its love of fashions" (139). What can be said with certainty is that the most "solid and indubitable accomplishment of the postmodern debate has been thus far the proclamation of the end of modernism" (139).

That end, and the dialectical oppositions of postmodernism to modernism can help us locate the genre (or anti-genre) of *Invention*. As a self-propelling, self-divisive, and self-perpetuated narrative, *Invention* derives its knowledge not from the traditional modes of writer as "legislator" but from writer as "interpretor," which is an irrevocable change. *Invention* is not weaker from this apparent diffusion of authority; rather the diffusion reinforces the power of individual perception. Values are thus best articulated by the state itself: Auster's reach through the glimmers to an authenticity.

All of this leads not to Lyotard's nostalgia for a sublime transcendent, but rather perhaps to the sighting of a shape against an unsatisfying relativism. The closing sentences of *Invention* present us with another deferral ("He wakes up. He walks back and forth between the table and the window. He sits down. He stands up."), another dislocation and reengagement ("He finds a fresh sheet of paper. He lays it out on the table before him and writes these words with his pen."), and then a tragic but affirmative continuance:

It was. It will never be again. Remember. (172)

NOTES

1. See Christopher Norris's comments on Lyotard, the "abyss of heterogeneity," and the futility of understanding "history in rational, purposive ... terms" in his study on postmodernism, *What's Wrong With Postmodernism: Critical Theory and the Ends of Philosophy?*, (Baltimore: Johns Hopkins UP, 1990) 6–16.

2. See for example Charles Jencks, "The Postmodern Agenda" and Ihab Hassan, "Pluralism in Postmodern Perspective" in *The Post-Modern Reader*, ed. Charles Jencks (New York: St. Martin's, 1992).

3. Although I use this conventional dialectic for the discussion that follows, the relationship between modernism and postmodernism, of course, is not so neatly bifurcated. See for example Linda Hutcheon, "Theorising the Postmodern"; John Barth, "The Literature of Replenishment" in *The Post-Modern Reader*; and Anthony J. Cascardi, "History, Theory, (Post)Modernity" in *After the Future: Postmodern Times and Places*, ed. Gary Shapiro (Albany: State U of New York P, 1990).

4. For a call to wage war on "totality," see Lyotard, "Answering" 149. For discussions of pluralism as a defining feature or motif of postmodernism, see, for example, Ihab Hassan, *The Postmodern Turn: Essays in Postmodern Theory and Culture* (Columbus: Ohio U State P, 1987); David Harvey, *The Condition of Postmodernity*, (Oxford: Blackwell, 1989); Jean-François Lyotard, *The Postmodern Condition: A Report on Knowledge* (Manchester: Manchester UP, 1984).

5. I am indebted here to Felicity A. Nussbaum's "Toward Conceptualizing Diary," *Studies in Autobiography*, ed. James Olney (New York: Oxford UP, 1988) 128–139. "Postmodern theory recognizes," Nussbaum writes, "that the self is less a reified thing than an ideological construct articulated in the language available to the individual at a particular historical moment" (131).

WORKS CITED

Auster, Paul. *The Art of Hunger*. New York: Penguin, 1992.

———. *In the Country of Last Things*. London: Faber and Faber, 1987.

———. *The Invention of Solitude*. Boston: Faber and Faber, 1982.

Austin, Jacqueline. "The Invention of Solitude," *American Book Review* 6.1, November–December 1983: 23.

Bauman, Zygmunt. "The Fall of the Legislator." *Postmodernism: A Reader*. Ed. Thomas Docherty. New York: Columbia UP 1993. 128–140.

Couser, Thomas G. *Altered Egos: Authority in American Autobiography*. New York: Oxford UP, 1989.

Eakin, Paul John. *Fictions in Autobiography: Studies in the Art of Self-Invention*. Princeton: Princeton UP, 1985.

Gergen, Kenneth J. "Theory of the Self: Impasse and Evolution'" *Advances in Experimental Social Psychology*. Ed. Leonard Berdowitz. New York: Academic, 1984.

Hassan, Ihab. "Pluralism in Postmodern Perspective." *The Post-Modern Reader*. Ed. Charles Jencks. New York: St. Martin's, 1991. 196–207.

Jameson, Frederic. "Postmodernism, or The Cultural Logic of Late Capitalism."
    Postmodernism: A Reader. Ed. Thomas Docherty. New York: Columbia UP,
    1993. 62–92.
Lyotard, Jean-François. "Answering the Question: What is Postmodernism."
    Postmodernism: A Reader. Ed. Thomas Docherty. New York: Columbia UP,
    1993. 38–50.
———. *The Differend: Phrases in Dispute.* Trans. Georges van den Abbeele.
    Minneapolis: U of Minnesota P, 1988.
Norris, Christopher. "How the Real World Became a Fable: The Gulf War,
    Postmodernism, and the Politics of Theory." *Works and Days: Essay in the Socio-
    Historical Dimensions of Literature and the Arts.* Indiana, PA (W&D). 9.2 (1991):
    7–38.
Racevskis, Karlis. "The Modernity of Moralistes and the (A)morality of
    Postmodernists. *The Antioch Review.* 45.3 (1987): 275–279.
Rowen, Norma. "The Detective in Search of the Lost Tongue of Adam: Paul Auster's
    City of Glass. Critique. 32.4 (1981): 224–234.

JOHN ZILCOSKY

The Revenge of the Author:
Paul Auster's Challenge to Theory

Edgar Allan Poe's legendary detective, Dupin, insisted that the good detective know how to *read* his criminal, how to decipher his "intellect" and "identify" with it ("The Purloined Letter" 118). Dupin's theory, a kind of intentional fallacy for detectives, is conceptualized in the 1928 "rule" of detective fiction advanced by influential detective novelist and critic S. S. Van Dine. In any good detective novel, Van Dine writes, the following "information" homology must be observed: "author:reader = criminal: detective" (Todorov 49). For Van Dine, the reader should be dependent on the author for information-clues just as the detective is dependent on the criminal. Postwar novelists such as Alain Robbe-Grillet and Michel Butor, however, found such a dependence downright criminal. They, like Poe, allegorized detectives as readers, but they deliberately overturned Van Dine's traditional hierarchy. In Robbe-Grillet's *The Erasers* (1953), the detective literally replaces the criminal. He shows up early at the scene of the crime and commits the murder himself, thus "erasing" the criminal from the plot and usurping his role as originator of clues and narratives.

This "new," "oedipal" detective symbolized, according to Frank Kermode, the larger political program of literature and literary theory in postwar left-intellectual France: the revolutionary detective becomes the "herald of the new [readerly] order" (Kermode 168). Robbe-Grillet's upstart

From *Critique: Studies in Contemporary Fiction* 39, no. 3 (Spring 1998). © 1998 by the Helen Dwight Reid Educational Foundation.

detective, indeed, exemplified the postwar reader. In the work of Roland Barthes, an admirer of Robbe-Grillet, that reader is "liberate[d]" from the tyranny of the author ("Death" 147). It is important to note that Robbe-Grillet's 1953 oedipal detective *preceded* Barthes's virtuosic reader of 1968. The "new" detective story, we could argue, anticipated, even preempted its theorization.

What has become of the "metaphysical" detective novel—the genre that intermixes fiction with literary theory—in the four decades since Robbe-Grillet? In this essay, I will investigate one example: Paul Auster's genre-crossing *The New York Trilogy* (1985–86), a work esteemed by mystery connoisseurs and professors of postmodernism alike.[1] In the light of *The New York Trilogy*, I will discuss the metaphysical detective novel's continued and often competitive engagement with literary theory.

PAUL AUSTER'S CHALLENGE TO THEORY

Auster, in a 1987 interview, claimed to be using the popular detective genre for much the same reason that a Beckett employed the standard vaudeville routine. He wanted to reinvigorate his writing, to bring it "to another place, another place altogether" (*Art of Hunger* 261). At the same time, Auster also was using the detective story to explore theories of reading à la Poe and Robbe-Grillet. Each of Auster's novels features a detective who literally reads the manuscripts of his criminal. Auster's detectives thus are vehemently readers, so much so that Auster considered inaugurating his trilogy with this epigraph from Wittgenstein: "And it also means something to talk of 'living in the pages of a book'" (*Art of Hunger* 263).

But Auster's reader-detectives are very different from those imagined by Robbe-Grillet and later theorized by Barthes. Auster's detectives are dependent, often desperately so, on their criminals. Each reads carefully his criminal's books and notebooks; Quinn, the hero of volume one, even turns his criminal's daily walks into a text: he traces the paths of his criminal's journeys onto a piece of paper and reads them as letters in the alphabet. Not until the last section of each novel does the criminal disappear from the narrative—finally leaving a space for a newly liberated detective to emerge. But the reader-detective (with the eventual exception of the hero of volume three) is, *pace* Barthes and Robbe-Grillet, not triumphantly "born"; rather, he devolves into a deranged vagabond (*City of Glass*), disappears into the narrator's vague fantasy of freedom by sailing to China (*Ghosts*), and dissipates (initially) in a phantasmagorical binge (*The Locked Room*). It is as though Auster's 1986 detectives had not yet discovered the literary theory of 1968. They must learn all over again, step by step, that the author is a construct, a false endpoint of reading.

But Auster's plot strategy is neither amnesiac nor regressive. Instead, it is an assertion—at the familiar crossroads of detective story and literary theory—that Barthes's readerly revolution was more theoretical than actual. Indeed, in American book-culture, the notion of the "author" as a single personality is probably more entrenched now than it was twenty-five years ago. Within a shrinking industry, publishers construct increasingly convincing and compelling personalities on book jackets, and present-day readers, like Auster's detectives, ardently pursue their authors at popular book signings and readings. Moreover, a professorial industry now flourishes around authors such as Barthes, Foucault, and Derrida.

According to Barthes, that fetishizing of the author should have ended long ago. In his famous 1968 essay, he sentenced the author to "death"—for criminally "limiting" interpretative thought. There, Barthes replaces the author with the "modern scriptor," whom he grants only a marginal existence: as a "being" that abides only in the process of writing ("Death" 145). The truly (post)modern author should, according to Barthesian politics, either efface his person, or, as in the contemporaneous schema of Foucault, accept dispersal into historical "functions" (107–120).

Within that hostile poststructuralist landscape, authors have tended to hide themselves, disguising authorial imprint beneath layers of artifice and quotation. But Paul Auster quite literally rejects theory's imperative to die or disperse: he appears, conspicuously, throughout his novels. Leaving behind disconnected, yet obvious fragments of autobiography and, once, even making a cameo appearance (as "Paul Auster" the writer, holding "an uncapped fountain pen.... poised in a writing position"), Auster blatantly exposes himself (*City of Glass* 143). He reveals his authorship, I would argue, the better to investigate the concept of authorship itself.[2] Instead of writing himself out of history in favor of either a "series of specific and complex operations" (Foucault 113) or a virtuosic reader (Barthes, "Death" 148), Auster experiments, in fictional practice, with the possibilities of life after authorial death. He authorizes his own (and several other criminal writers') disappearances to explore writing beyond authorship.

CITY OF GLASS

City of Glass, the first volume of *The New York Trilogy*, opens with a pseudonymous detective novelist, Daniel Quinn, being drawn into a real-life "tail-job." A stranger calls twice, asking for the Paul Auster Detective Agency, and Quinn, without knowing exactly why, agrees that he is Paul Auster and takes the case. Quinn, like the reader in Van Dine's homology, begins the case without significant information, either about himself or about the case (8, 14). He imagines his psyche splintered into three personalities: Daniel Quinn, the person who eats and sleeps and walks the streets; William Wilson, the Poe-inspired pseudonymous writer of detective novels; and Max Work, the self who, as the protagonist of the novels, is active in the world. Only when the case begins, when Quinn starts to pursue his real-life criminal, Stillman, does he gain a sense of himself as unified. He symbolically inaugurates his detectival quest by stripping naked and inscribing his own initials, not William Wilson's, onto the first page of his red case notebook (64).

Quinn achieves this sense of self, significantly, only as a reader, not as a writer. He gives up writing in order to pore over Stillman's cryptic book and follow him all over New York. A parody of the biographical literary critic, Quinn jots down Stillman's every move, assuming that each step, regardless of how insignificant, contains clues to Stillman's intentions. Quinn even reads Stillman's random paths as letters forming words. (Projecting an inherent logic onto random walks, he creates and completes an incomplete text, "OWEROFBAB" becomes "THE TOWER OF BABEL" [111].)

In this way, Quinn attempts to contain his criminal's haphazardness. He refuses, in the manner of Barthes's "classic" critic, to accept a disorderly narrative: "He ... disbelieve[d] the arbitrariness of Stillman's actions. He wanted there to be a sense to them" (109).

When Stillman finally disappears, Quinn is stupefied. Like Poe's Dupin (whose cases Quinn has read and admired), Quinn has trained himself to uncover the "intentions" of his criminal (141).[3] With Stillman gone, however, this traditional methodology is worthless: "Stillman was gone now.... Everything had been reduced to chance, a nightmare of numbers and probabilities. There were no more clues, no leads, no moves to be made" (141). Two-thirds of the way through the novel, then, the criminal author has disappeared, and the reader-detective is paralyzed by a surfeit of possibilities.

According to Foucault, the fear of such a surfeit is one of the major reasons that authors were constructed in the first place: "The author is ... the ... figure by which one marks the manner in which we fear the proliferation of meaning" (119). He states that we are afraid of plurality—personal, social, textual—and thus demand the circumscribing convention of the author: "[T]he great peril, the great danger with which fiction threatens our world" can only be reduced and encircled by recourse to the author (118). The "author-function," then, neutralizes contradiction and potentiality and leads to the consolidation of existing power relations. Only through the destruction of the author, Foucault surmises, can human possibility begin to unleash itself. Reading and writing will unfold and expand, and criticism will take up its vital task: to "locate the space left empty by the author's disappearance ... and watch for the openings that this disappearance uncovers." That new, author-free space is characterized by fragments—by "gaps and breaches"—not by unities (105). It is an area where, in Barthes's words, "everything is to be *disentangled*, nothing *deciphered*" ("Death" 147).

Quinn imagines that his new, criminal-free world is governed only by "fate." Fate, for Quinn, implies the acceptance of uncertainty, the slackening of his fierce, detectival desire for order: "Fate in the sense of what was, of what happened to be" (169). But Quinn cannot accept the vagaries of this new order. He remains the prototypical detective, ardently desiring a solution to his case. He regards the incessant busy signal at Virginia Stillman's as "fate," and he interprets it narcissistically: as a "sign" to continue with his case (169). Stillman is already gone, however, and Quinn— the detective in denial—stakes out a building that has no criminal inside.

Questioning Author-ity

In the penultimate section of *City of Glass*, after Quinn's failed stake-out, he becomes a writer again. He turns, like Paul Auster himself,[4] from writing detective fiction to autobiographical reflections—in Quinn's case, Baudelairean portraits of the city's downtrodden. Finally, in the novel's last section, Quinn disappears from the narrative completely. He is replaced by two writers: "Paul Auster," the writer whom Quinn visits earlier (whom I shall refer to as Auster, and to the real author as simply Auster),[5] and an unnamed first-person Narrator (for whom I will use a capital N) who claims to be the editor of Quinn's ever-present red notebook. The Narrator vehemently denies authorship of *City of Glass*, claiming that he did no more than edit Quinn's notebook. But this is clearly a lie: Quinn does not even buy the notebook until page 63 (which explains the Narrator's enigmatic comment in the final paragraph: "The red notebook, of course, is only half the story, as any sensitive reader will understand" [202]). Thus we can assume—in terms of Auster's conceit—that the self-effacing Narrator is responsible for most, if not all, of the story. He has created the characters (from Quinn to Paul Auster,) as well as the plot, which leads Quinn to solitude and madness. The Narrator, however, refuses responsibility for his

imaginative violence, laying the blame on Auster, instead: "[Auster] behaved badly throughout," he claims, and because of that, "our friendship has ended" (202–203). His hands now clean, the Narrator can carry on as the implied author of the entire trilogy.

Although this game of blame-shifting could be read as just that, a game, it also has important ethical ramifications. Paul Auster, we could argue, is trying to distance himself from his "bad behavior": his mistreatment of Quinn (his alter ego) as well as his writing a fiction too narcissistically tied to his own life. In the light of Auster's earlier work, it is indeed likely that here he is attempting to work through his ethical position as author. Referring to his memoir about his dead father, the first section of *The Invention of Solitude* (1982), Auster formulates his profound distrust of his own authority: "['Portrait of an Invisible Man'] still seems to me not so much an attempt at biography but an exploration of how one might begin to speak about another person, and whether or not it is even possible" (*Art of Hunger* 258). *The Invention of Solitude* immediately precedes *City of Glass*. In *City of Glass*, I would argue, Auster discovers how to speak about another person, himself, without wielding the authority he so distrusts.[6] By transferring authority from himself to the Narrator, he "kills" himself and reinvents himself as an implied author. Auster thus adds to Barthes: the author is dead, but his implied self, his "ghost," is alive and well.

GHOSTS

The second novel of the trilogy, *Ghosts*, by far the shortest of the three, begins on February 3, 1947 (the birth date of Paul Auster and thirty-five years before the start of the other two volumes, *City of Glass* and *The Locked Room*). Narrated in a shallow present tense that precludes any sense of past and featuring two-dimensional protagonists designated as Blue, Black, and Brown, *Ghosts* functions as a kind of scaffolding, a bare-bones framework for the other two novels. It brings out skeletally, like the middle section of a triptych, the structural elements shared by all three texts.[7] The detective protagonist, Blue, for example, is, like Quinn, a reader of his suspect's manuscript; Black, the criminal, is, like Stillman, an author. Blue reads what Black writes and also what Black reads (*Walden*), hoping, in the manner of a "classic" critic, to "solve" Black by going back to his literary sources. Blue believes, as do the protagonists of *City of Glass* and *The Locked Room*, that if he reads the criminal-author correctly, he will bring order both to the case and to his life. In the end, Blue kills Black, thus establishing the figure of the dead or dying author-criminal, common to all three novels. The Narrator, unseen throughout the novel, reverts to the first person in the final paragraph to announce, as in *City of Glass*, that the reader-detective has mysteriously disappeared.

THE LOCKED ROOM

In *The Locked Room*, similarly, a reader-detective (this time the Narrator himself) tracks and "reads" a fugitive author, Fanshawe. The Narrator, like Quinn, places all hope for resolution, personal and textual, in the figure of the author. The Narrator reads Fanshawe's letters and early poems, interviews Fanshawe's friends and relatives, and even plagiarizes Fanshawe's life: marrying his wife, adopting his son, sleeping with his mother. By getting closer to Fanshawe, by getting inside his skin, the Narrator hopes to come "into focus" for himself (57).

But Fanshawe proves to be untraceable, an imaginary fantasy. The Narrator sifts through Fanshawe's biography (reading letters and interviewing surviving friends and relatives) and is left with an inconclusive residue of rumors, stories, and possible lies (131–32). The Narrator despairs; he sets off on a hallucinatory binge on the rue Saint-Denis. He "los[es] track of [him]self," seeing the world in "fragments" and "bits and pieces that refuse to add up" (148). His new, authorless landscape exceeds the logic of his detective's search. Like Quinn following the death of Stillman, the Narrator has a crisis of purpose and identity: "[I felt] like a down-and-out private eye, a buffoon clutching at straws" (145).[8] For Quinn, the chaos of his criminal-less world is "fate"; for the Narrator, it is "randomness" (155). But the Narrator's reaction is diametrically opposed to Quinn's. The Narrator does not try to contain fate; rather, he accepts and welcomes it: "[T]hat … thrilled me—the randomness of it, the vertigo of pure chance" (155).

The Narrator's acceptance of author-less contingency is, I would argue, a metaphor for Auster's welcoming of a new type of "author-less" writing. Auster's earlier, less contingent mode of writing is represented by the writings of Quinn and Fanshawe.[9] Like the young Paul Auster, Quinn and Fanshawe begin their careers as intensely self-reflexive poets. Quinn writes an obscure poetry collection (*Unfinished Business*) and Fanshawe authors a collection (*Ground Work*) bearing the same title as Auster's self-probing collection (written between 1970–1979).[10] Both Quinn and Fanshawe, like Auster, eventually turn from poetry to prose, but their goals remain that of self-examination, or as Fanshawe puts it, "explanation" (175).

WRITING SOLITUDE

Tied to that motto of self-examination is the enduring image of solitude. As the Narrator writes, this image of the author is stamped indelibly in his mind: "Fanshawe alone in that [locked] room, condemned to a mythical solitude" (147). Two years before beginning *City of Glass*, indeed, Paul Auster was working out his own myth of solitude. Living alone in New York (his marriage and family having just broken up and his father having died), Auster writes in *The Invention of Solitude*: "[A.] is in New York, alone in his little room at 6 Varick Street" (76–77). This book features Pascal's famous quote on the importance of isolation: "As in Pascal: 'All the unhappiness of man stems from one thing only: that he is incapable of staying quietly in his room'" (76). It also is replete with references to solitary artists: Hölderlin (98–100), Emily Dickinson (122–23), Van Gogh (142–143), and others. Fanshawe claims, in the spirit of his artistic predecessors, to find in solitude "a passageway into the self, an instrument of discovery" (*Locked Room* 125).

Each of these "solitude" narratives, real and fictional, ends in some sort of madness. Auster's assessment of solitude thus seems to waver from a celebration of the mythical site of production to a fear of a cruel and un-representable loneliness:

> [T]he room is not a representation of solitude, it is the substance of solitude itself. And it is a thing so heavy, so unbreatheable, that it cannot be shown in any terms other than what it is. (*Invention of Solitude* 143)

It is precisely this unrepresentability, this dangerous emptiness, that Auster—as well as his later fictional stunt men, Quinn and Fanshawe—strived to represent in his early writings. Auster writes autobiographically about A.: "By staying in this room for long stretches at a time, [A.] can usually manage to fill it with his thoughts, and this in turn seems to dispel the dreariness ..." (77). Quinn later echoes A.'s sentiment in *City of Glass*, when, alone in his empty room, he dreams of "filling the darkness with his voice, speaking the words into the air, into the walls, into the city ..." (200). The lyricism of this passage notwithstanding, Auster is critical of Quinn's and his own artistic *modus operandi*. Like Fanshawe after him, Quinn is sentenced to madness—forced to live through a 1980s repetition of Hölderlin, Dickinson, and others. Hidden in Auster's critique is a condemnation of the literary tradition in which he is so well schooled. The intensely isolated self, Auster seems to be saying, can no longer "fill" a "darkness" with his voice nor presume to endow a world with meaning.

WRITING BEYOND SOLITUDE

The Narrator, Auster's final detective and final authorial stand-in, transcends that image of artistic isolation. Auster's Narrator begins the narrative trapped, like A. in *The Invention of Solitude*, within an image of his past self: he sees himself only as the inferior boyhood rival of Fanshawe: "[W]ithout [Fanshawe] I would hardly know who I am" (7). This crippling imaginary fantasy drives the Narrator to thoughts of murder or, better, of schizophrenic suicide. After physically attacking "Fanshawe," the Narrator remarks that he can suddenly see "[him]self dead" (161).[11] The specter of his own corpse, as ubiquitous and undeniable as an "odor," now replaces his image of himself as Fanshawe (156). The new sensation—of death—remains with the Narrator for the rest of the novel. It leads him, like Auster after the death of his father, to reinvent himself. (According to Auster, "[M]y father's death saved my life [*Art of Hunger* 288].) The Narrator abandons his manhunt for himself and evolves instead into what he calls a "self ... in the world" (143), a father among a family ("the bodies I belonged to" [162])—a being awash through death in human life and living.[12]

Following that confrontation with death, the Narrator "officially" gives up writing (160). New modes of storytelling, such as his stepson's improvised fable about elephants and emperors, enter the Narrator's life, and he is no longer driven to acquire significance through a Fanshawean mode of authorship. When Fanshawe, intimating his residual authorial power over the Narrator, says, "I'm just reminding you of what I wrote," the Narrator responds confidently, "Don't push me too far, Fanshawe. There's nothing to stop me from walking out" (167). When the Narrator does leave, he reads Fanshawe's red notebook, which, even more than the red notebook in *City of Glass*, functions as an *Urtext*.[13] But the Narrator immediately tears it up, even though it seems "unfinished" and begs "to be started again" (179).

WRITING AND DEATH

Quinn, Auster's first authorial stand-in, has an antithetical reaction to the "end" of the red notebook: he equates it with the end of his life. Premonitions of death do not free him for new modes of storytelling. Rather, they entrench him deeper into his existing method. Like Scheherezade in Auster's account of *The Thousand and One Nights*, Quinn believes in the dictum, "as long as you go on speaking, you will not die" (*Invention of Solitude* 149). Quinn tries to ward off death through writing, longing to postpone what Foucault calls "the day of reckoning that [will] silence the narrator" (102). Sequestered in his room, Quinn does not experience death as immanent in storytelling and living; on the contrary, writing remains his hope of transcendence. He writes instead of eating, writes smaller and smaller to conserve pages, and hopes that he will be able to "face the end of the red notebook with courage" (200).

In the end, however, Quinn does not die; his red notebook is read and related to us by the Narrator, allowing Quinn to live on through fiction. At the end of the trilogy, we discover that he has survived as a character behind the scenes of *The Locked Room*—relentlessly tracking Fanshawe across the country, attempting to solve yet another case. That second case, like the first, is one Quinn seems afraid to solve. He shudders at the prospect of a resolution, perhaps because it would signify the closure he both desires and fears. As Fanshawe remarks, Quinn never apprehends him, not because he was unable to but rather because "I scared him to death" (169).

It is important to remember that the Narrator—despite the fact that he "officially" gives up writing—does, like Quinn, create a text. The vital difference is that Quinn's writing expresses only narcissism and fear: he desires to "fill" a world and to ward off death. For the Narrator, such fantasies of omnipotence are distant memories. "[T]he truth," he claims, is "no longer important" (160). The Narrator's writing is now rooted in supersubjective contingency: the "anything-ness," of the world. "It is the power of this anything, I believe," he writes, "that has made the story so difficult to tell. For when anything can happen—that is the precise moment when words begin to fail" (161). The Narrator realizes that self-expression— storytelling—is difficult, if not impossible, in a world where subjective will is muddled in a pool of infinite possibilities. However, if every contingency, even death, is accepted as given, the story will begin to tell itself. As the Narrator explains, his courage in accepting the state of things allowed language itself to divulge the tale:

> [A] moment came when it no longer frightened me to look at
> what had happened. If words followed, it was only because I had
> no choice but to accept them, to take them upon myself and go
> where they wanted me to go. (149)

The Narrator's writing, steered by chance, is more than a surrender of self to language. It is a "struggle" to "say goodbye to something" (149)—an effort continuously to self-transcend, to speak while dying. His writing is born of an oedipal destruction that will repeat itself for as long as he lives.

He will never fill the void left by the dead author-criminal. His writing, beginning and ending in absence, is not, like Quinn's, an attempt to saturate the darkness. Rather, it happens in the gray spaces of his living, in the hollows of the bodies he belongs to. Perhaps it is this kind of writing—produced within contingency, beyond solutions and the usual suspects—that enacts a birth.

We could argue that Auster, in the guise of his final and most accomplished stand-in, emerges from the rubble of dead author-criminals to become a virtuosic Barthesian "producer"—a reader who rewrites while reading (S/Z 4).[14] But Auster, it is important to remember, vehemently emphasizes his "authorship." He appears repeatedly among (and inside of) his characters to announce, "I'm the writer!" (*City of Glass* 190). Such a brash assertion of authorship traditionally brings with it, in the paradigms of Barthes and Foucault, claims to authority. Not so for Auster. By appearing and disappearing randomly throughout his three-volume text (in the guise of Quinn, Paul Auster, Fanshawe, and the Narrator), Auster disrupts the notion that an author "controls" his fiction. His "biography" floats from one character to the next, and, in the end, Auster inheres only as another two-dimensional character in his refracting city. We, like the reader-detectives of *The New York Trilogy*, discover that our "author" exists—but only as shards, as pieces of his fictionalized personal history.

EPILOGUE: WRITING FOR THE BOOK INDUSTRY

For Auster, as for most successful authors, including Barthes and Foucault, there is an ironic epilogue. Auster's creation of the virtuosic anti-author, followed by the publication of the last installment of *The New York Trilogy*, led to the birth of another "author"—Paul Auster himself. *The New York Trilogy*, Auster's first work of fiction, was published in three volumes by a small press (Sun and Moon), then quickly rereleased (just past Auster's fortieth birthday) by Penguin. In 1990, Penguin published a one-volume edition. That edition includes an impressive literary biography ("Paul Auster's work has been translated into fifteen languages," "*The New York Trilogy* won the Prix France-Culture de Littérature Étrangère for the best work by a foreign author.") and, for the first time, the dates corresponding to Auster's work on each volume ("1981–1982," "1983," "1984"), were written on each final page. These temporal markers uphold, however ironically, the singularity of the act of creation—by one "author" at a certain moment in history (Lavender 236). Is Paul Auster—now firmly entrenched in the complicated nexus of public readings, promotional "bios," and book signings—destined to repeat the errors of Quinn? Will he, despite his revision of author-ity, necessarily become an "author," a subjectivity stable and expansive enough to "fill" a world?

Auster, I would argue, continues to undermine his own "author-function" through the alliance with contingency developed at the end of *The New York Trilogy*. In a 1990 interview, Auster claims that his goal is to remain "open" to the "anything-ness" of the world: "The unknown is rushing in on top of us at every moment. As I see it, my job is to keep myself open to these collisions ..." (*Art of Hunger* 273). Auster's estimation of chance collisions is evidenced by the plots of his more recent novels, which often develop out of accidents not unlike the wrong number that "started it" all in *City of Glass*.[15] Moreover, Auster allows his day-to-day writerly practice to be affected by what he calls "the powers of contingency" (*Art of Hunger* 271).[16] In a recent work, "The Red Notebook" (1993), Auster describes a chance collision that led directly to more writing and, at the same time, reminded him "that it is possible for stories to go on writing themselves without an author" (253). Ten years after completing *City of Glass*, "Auster" remembers sitting at his desk, "trying to work," when the phone rings. It is a stranger, asking three times for a "Mr. Quinn." Another wrong number, "Auster" claims, and again his writing begins (253).

ACKNOWLEDGMENT

The author thanks Rita Barnard and Kerry Sherin for their careful readings of this essay.

NOTES

1. *City of Glass*, the first installment, was nominated for the Edgar Award for the best mystery novel of the year (1985).

2. I agree with the point of William Lavender (in his article on *City of Glass*) that Auster's work engages contemporary literary theory. But Auster's encounter with theory does not stop with the formal concerns—point-of-view, character, plot—that Lavender highlights. As I argue below, Auster inquires into the nature of authorship and its claims to authority.

3. Earlier in *City of Glass*, Quinn quotes Dupin's theory of reading, and identifying with, his opponent's intellect (65).

4. Auster, like Quinn, began his career as a little-known poet and later wrote a pseudonymous detective novel. Like Quinn at the end of *City of Glass*, Auster turned to autobiographical prose in 1982, with *The Invention of Solitude*.

5. Notice the intentional blurring of the two figures: Both Austers have a wife named Siri and a son named Daniel; moreover, Auster$_1$, during his brief appearance in *City of Glass*, is vehemently an "author," holding a "fountain pen ... poised in a writing position" (143).

6. That process of discovering how to write about the Other, who is oneself, begins in the second section of *The Invention of Solitude*: "As in Rimbaud's phrase: 'Je est un autre'" (124). Auster comments on this section of *The Invention of Solitude* in *The Art of Hunger* (259).

7. The triptych tends to have a static middle section, which, like *Ghosts*, serves as a still model for the wings, where the action occurs. I thank Thomas Dertwinkel for bringing this to my attention.

8. Although the Narrator is not actually a detective (neither is Quinn), he refers to himself as such at least one other time: "I was a detective, after all, and my job was to hunt for clues" (131).

9. Fanshawe's biography is very similar to Auster's: They are exactly the same age (*Locked Room* 45); both began their careers as poets and published collections called *Ground Work*; and both house-sat and wrote in a cottage in the South of France. For the biographical similarities between Auster and Quinn, see note 4.

10. *Ground Work: Selected Poems and Essays 1970–1979*. The collection contains titles such as "In Memory of Myself," "Searching for a Definition," and "Autobiography of the Eye."

11. This man is probably not really Fanshawe, only the Narrator's fantasy of him.

12. See Auster's remarks on family and fatherhood in a 1990 interview: "Becoming a parent connects you to a world beyond yourself, to the continuum of generations, to the inevitability of your own death.... You begin to let go, and in that letting go—at least in my case—you find yourself wanting to tell stories.
When my son was born twelve years ago, Charlie Simic ... wrote me a letter of congratulations in which he said, 'Children are wonderful. If I didn't have kids, I'd walk around thinking I was Rimbaud all the time'" (*Art of Hunger* 290).

13. Fanshawe filled his red notebook in a "brick" house on "Columbus" Square in "Boston" under the pseudonym "Henry Dark"—all details that are strongly reminiscent of Stillman's linguistic paradise, "New Babel" (in *City of Glass*), where language promises to regain its lost unity in the New World.

14. The Narrator does not "create" *The New York Trilogy*; rather, he, like Barthes's "producer," reads texts (Quinn's and Fanshawe's) more or less creatively and re-assembles them.

15. *The Music of Chance* (1990) begins with a man haphazardly meeting a stranger—who changes the man's life and kick-starts the plot of the book—on the side of the road. *Leviathan* (1992) begins with a young writer meeting another writer at a joint reading that both almost canceled out of; the latter eventually becomes the subject of the former's book, *Leviathan*.

16. According to Auster, a chance tele-miscommunication led to his writing of *City of Glass*: "One day, ... the telephone rang, and the person on the other end asked if he had reached the Pinkerton Agency. I said no, you've got the wrong number, and hung up.... [T]he very next day another person called and asked the same question. "Is this the Pinkerton Agency?" Again I said no, told him he'd dialed the wrong number, and hung up. But the instant after I hung up, I began to wonder what would

have happened if I had said yes. Would it have been possible for me to pose as a Pinkerton agent? And if so, how far could I have taken it? The book grew out of those telephone calls.... The wrong numbers were the starting point" (*Art of Hunger* 294).

WORKS CITED

Auster, Paul. *The Art of Hunger: Essays, Prefaces, Interviews*. Los Angeles: Sun & Moon, 1992.

———. *City of Glass*. Los Angeles: Sun & Moon, 1985.

———. *Ghosts*. Los Angeles: Sun & Moon, 1986.

———. *Ground Work: Selected Poems and Essays* 1970–1979. London: Faber and Faber, 1990.

———. *The Invention of Solitude*. 1982. New York: Penguin, 1988.

———. *The Locked Room*. Los Angeles: Sun & Moon, 1986.

———. *The New York Trilogy*. New York: Penguin, 1990.

———. "The Red Notebook." *Granta* 44 (1993): 236–53.

Barthes, Roland. "The Death of the Author." *Image-Music-Text*. Trans. Stephen Heath. New York: Hill and Wang, 1977. 142–48.

———. *S/Z*. Trans. Richard Miller. New York: Hill and Wang, 1974.

Foucault, Michel. "What is an Author?" Trans. Josué V. Harari. *The Foucault Reader*. Ed. Paul Rabinow. New York: Pantheon, 1984. 101–20.

Kermode, Frank. "Novel and Narrative." *The Theory of the Novel: New Essays*. Ed. John Halperin. New York: Oxford, 1974. 155–74.

Lavender, William. "The Novel of Critical Engagement: Paul Auster's *City of Glass*." *Contemporary Literature* 34 (1993): 219–39.

Poe, Edgar Allan. "The Purloined Letter." *The Tell-Tale Heart and Other Writings*. New York: Bantam, 1982. 108–26.

Todorov, Tzvetan. "The Typology of Detective Fiction." *The Poetics of Prose*. Trans. Richard Howard. Ithaca: Cornell UP, 1977. 42–52.

WILLIAM LAVENDER

The Novel of Critical Engagement: Paul Auster's City of Glass

*C*ity *of Glass*, the first of three short novels included in Paul Auster's *New York Trilogy*, is, like its two companions, a detective novel. Its protagonist plays the role of a detective, takes a case, and embarks upon a program of surveillance and decipherment to solve a mystery. In this it partakes of a tradition of the popular form of the twentieth-century detective novel. Peter Brooks, in *Reading for the Plot*, uses a Sherlock Holmes story ("The Musgrave Ritual") to illustrate how the process of mystery solving can be seen as a model of the narrative act, citing Tzvetan Todorov and other critics who have noted the exemplary character of detective fiction (23–27). *City of Glass*, we might say, takes up where Brooks leaves off (in this instance), posits the detective novel as an allegory for novels in general and then uses it to examine the possibilities of the form. In this it partakes of a somewhat more rarefied, metafictional tradition, of which Michel Butor's *Passing Time* is a notable example.

Butor's focus is the fictional representation of temporality. *City of Glass* also considers this question, but it differs from *Passing Time* in the central position it assigns to theory in general. In broad strokes, we can say that Auster poses the question, How many of the normally assigned qualities of the novel, especially those qualities that have become attached to it through critical exegesis, formulation and application of theory, and scientific or semiotic analysis, can be abandoned, mutilated, ruined in and by a narrative

From *Contemporary Literature* 34, no. 2 (Summer, 1993). © 1993 by the Board of Regents of the University of Wisconsin System.

that remains identifiable as a novel? Auster's handling of literary theory resembles, in many ways, the treatment of philosophical concepts we find in the novels of Samuel Beckett, *Watt* for example. There is also a resemblance to the critical self-reflexivity of John Barth's *Lost in the Funhouse*. In these two writers literary representation is undermined by their respective theoretical concerns (for Beckett existential philosophy, for Barth postmodern self-consciousness), but, simultaneously, the works are restabilized along these new, theoretical axes. In Auster no such realignment occurs; both the form and the theory shift beneath our feet.

City of Glass, then, is a deconstruction. Or a sabotage. It deconstructs the form of the novel, the canons of criticism, theory, and tradition, and it deconstructs itself, as it literally falls apart in its progression. Characters appear, they are sketched full of potentials which we logically expect to be fulfilled, and then they walk off the page never to return. One character, Stillman (senior), returns again and again but is a completely different person each time, having no memory of what has happened to him previously in the story. A mystery is presented, investigated, drawn out to what we feel is its midpoint, that place where it is most profligate of potential solutions, and then abandoned never to be solved. A figural third-person point of view is scrupulously maintained until the last two pages, when an enigmatic "I" suddenly reveals itself. These are just a few of the glaring literary violations that Auster commits upon the form and substance of the novel. Without making any claim of exhaustive analysis, I will proceed by examining some of the more subtle, or subterranean, or subversive attacks upon literature and upon theory, returning at the end to more general considerations of genre and the place of this work in literary history.

Let us turn first to a consideration of the novel's point of view. The protagonist, Quinn, as I have mentioned, pretends to be a detective. He must pretend because in "real life" he is not a detective but a writer of detective novels, under the pseudonym William Wilson. Quinn's, or William Wilson's, principal character is named Max Work. Quinn, we learn, "had, of course, long ago stopped thinking of himself as real. If he lived now in the world at all, it was only at one remove, through the imaginary person of Max Work. His detective necessarily had to be real. The nature of the books demanded it" (9–10). We have, then, for Quinn, at the outset, a layering:

Quinn → Wilson → Work

The situation becomes somewhat more complex when Quinn, through the chance occurrence of a telephone call, a wrong number, decides to play the role given to him by the call, that of a detective named, coincidentally, Paul Auster. Of course the reason Quinn is interested in playing this role is his identification with his character, Work. Therefore we can posit Auster as posterior to Work, so:

Quinn → Wilson → Work → Auster

There is, alas, another complication in that Paul Auster also happens to be the name of the author of this novel, so Quinn, Wilson, Work, Auster, and all the rest are, properly speaking, his creations. This necessitates a further modification of our model as follows:

$Auster_1$ → Quinn → Wilson → Work → $Auster_2$

Now, Seymour Chatman, in "Discourse: Nonnarrated Stories," gives us a general model of narrative structure that can further enlighten our understanding of this text, as follows ("narrator" and "narratee" are given in parentheses because of their optional nature):

Real Author → Implied Author → (Narrator) →
(Narratee) → Implied Reader → Real Reader
(374)

If we consider, for the time being, only the "author" side of this model (the first line, as shown above), we see first of all that our $Auster_1$ should be placed either as a real or implied author. In considering this placement, we can look to the text for guidance, for this novel gives rather more explicit guidelines in this regard than we are used to seeing. Of Quinn we are told:

> it did not occur to him that he was going to show up for his appointment. Even that locution, his *appointment*, seemed odd to him. It wasn't his appointment, it was Paul Auster's. And who that person was he had no idea....
> It was not until he had his hand on the doorknob that he began to suspect what he was doing. "I seem to be going out," he said to himself. "But if I am going out, where exactly am I going?"
> (14)

Here we, along with Quinn, see, or sense, the presence of an author (someone who makes and keeps *appointments*). This author is *implied* as the motivation that places Quinn's hand upon the doorknob. This motivation cannot be seen as implying the presence of the real author, for the real author is required to embed the connotation, the paradoxical self-apprehension of a character realizing himself as a puppet, which leads us to the logical discernment of a cause, a puppeteer. The implied author's function, on the other hand, is strictly limited to manipulating Quinn's control strings. This implied author must be the construction that we have labeled $Auster_1$, since it is logically impossible for it to be $Auster_2$, who appears in the novel as a normal character. Therefore we must posit yet another Auster, an $Auster_0$, as the real author, giving:

$$Auster_0 \rightarrow Auster_1 \rightarrow Quinn \rightarrow Wilson \rightarrow Work \rightarrow Auster_2$$

We must still account, however, for the third transformation in Chatman's diagram, the "narrator" function. The novel is written, for the most part, in what is usually called figural narration, that is, third person, but more or less strictly from Quinn's point of vantage; Quinn is the only character whose thoughts and private moments are revealed to us, until the end. In the last two pages an "I" suddenly appears, and an unnamed narrator reveals himself. This narrator is a friend of "Auster," and is, in fact, made aware of Quinn's mystery by "Auster," in another case of rather blatant implied authorship. Together they discover Quinn's notebook which, the narrator alleges, was the entire basis of the story he has told: "There were moments when it was difficult to decipher, but I have done my best with it, and have refrained from any interpretation" (158). Therefore we must position the narrator, whom we shall designate as "I," posterior to, or perhaps simultaneous with, Quinn, giving:

$$Auster_0 \rightarrow Auster_1 \rightarrow Quinn/I \rightarrow Wilson \rightarrow Work \rightarrow Auster_2$$

It is $Auster_2$, the character in the novel, who gives this notebook to the narrator, suggesting that he keep it: "The whole business had upset him so much that he was afraid to keep it himself" (158). This suggests the possibility that $Auster_2$ might need to be located anterior to the narrator, which would give:

$$Auster_0 \rightarrow Auster_1 \rightarrow Quinn \rightarrow Wilson \rightarrow Work \rightarrow Auster_2 \rightarrow I$$

But then it is the narrator who tells the story of Quinn and the others. It is even, in this strange case, the narrator who, apparently, embeds the signs of the implied author. Thus it appears that we might need to position "I" between $Auster_0$ and $Auster_1$. The situation is further complicated by the fact that the novel itself seems to have an opinion on the matter, rendered allegorically in the scene where Quinn meets the Auster character ($Auster_2$). Their conversation turns to Don Quixote, about whom Auster is writing an essay. In his essay, he tells Quinn (and the reader), he is presenting a theory that the real author of the book is Sancho Panza, with the stenographic aid of the barber and the priest:

> It seems perfectly possible to me that [Sancho Panza] dictated the story to someone else—namely, to the barber and the priest, Don Quixote's good friends. They put the story into proper literary form—in Spanish—and then turned the manuscript over to Samson Carrasco, the bachelor from Salamanca, who proceeded to translate it into Arabic. Cervantes found the translation, had it rendered back into Spanish, and then published the book *The Adventures of Don Quixote*.
>
> (118)

It is, then, possible in this strange world for a character in a novel to be its author. Thus we can give our final diagram of the author side of Chatman's construction as:

$$Auster_0 \rightarrow Auster_1 \rightarrow Quinn \rightarrow Wilson \rightarrow Work \rightarrow Auster_2 \rightarrow I$$

The construction is circular and seamless. It is final, however, only by our own critical whim, since, as will be seen below, Quinn adopts still more pseudonyms, one of which, while he is posing as Detective Auster, is Daniel Quinn ($Quinn_2$). We have not even attempted to diagram the reader side of the Chatman model, but the mention of Quinn's notebook, which the narrator professes to be the source of the text, which is written, technically, by Detective Auster and then labored over, "read," first by Quinn, then by $Auster_2$ and "I," gives us a hint that simplicity is not what such a diagram would reveal. We wonder, even, if discreteness between the two sides of the transaction could be maintained, if the layers of readers would not simply distribute themselves among the strata of authors. The illusion, then, is one of infinity.

The point is that *City of Glass* suggests, allegorically, a hopelessly complex, paradoxical, self-referential system of geneses that parodies not only Chatman's model but the very idea of models of narrative structure by making itself into a model of itself. We could say that it naively takes the critics at their word, writes itself according to the plan, the critical blueprint, even takes it a step further (if three layers are good, shouldn't six, or ten, be better?), and erects the lopsided monument of its structure as the most eloquent comment on the theory. The extent to which this engagement is "conscious" or "intentional" is endlessly arguable and finally moot; whether or not Auster had Seymour Chatman specifically in mind when he constructed his point of view is irrelevant. What matters is that the discursive milieu in which the novel (and the trilogy) positions itself is critical as well as novelistic. The characterization of the author's namesake as an essayist makes this conclusion unavoidable.[1]

Alison Russell, in "Deconstructing *The New York Trilogy*: Paul Auster's Anti-Detective Fiction," has noted that the three works "employ and deconstruct the conventional elements of the detective story, ... the Romance, 'realistic' fiction, and autobiography" (71), but this approach leaves several of the most prominent devices in *City of Glass* unexplained, including the indeterminate reflexivity of point of view described above. As will be seen below, the parodic forms employed in character and plot also refuse definitive positioning in relation to popular genres, but refer in every instance to critical models.

We turn now to a consideration of character. In the first half of the twentieth century, character was considered by many novelists and critics to be the very fundament of the novel. Virginia Woolf, in "Mr. Bennett and Mrs. Brown," gives the most explicit formulation of this trend, saying, "I believe that all novels ... deal with character, and that it is to express character ... that the form of the novel ... has been evolved" (31). E. M. Forster, in "Flat and Round Characters," also espouses the primacy of character. And, perhaps most important, Henry James, in "The Art of Fiction," says: "What is either a picture or a novel that is not of character? What else do we seek in it and find in it?" (19). In later, structural or poststructural critics, we find a very different view. William H. Gass, for example, in "The Concept of Character in Fiction," argues against the analysis of characters as if they were people. "A character, first of all, is the noise of his name, and all the sounds and rhythms that proceed from him," he writes (49). He then explains how characters need not be persons, but can in fact be anything that serves as a fixed point, a structural reference in the narrative.

We pass most things in novels as we pass things on a train. The words flow by like the scenery. All is change. But there are some points in a narrative which remain relatively fixed; we may depart from them, but soon we return, as music returns to its theme. Characters are those primary substances to which everything else is attached.

(49)

This is a notion of character that is very different from Woolf's and Forster's, yet we can see an agreement across the decades in the positioning of character as primary in the novel. We find concurrence with this view across a wide range of critics and theorists. Fernando Ferrara, for example, in a rigorously austere analysis based on communication theory, defines fiction as "communication through characters" (250).

In *City of Glass* we find a rather enigmatic assortment of these humanoid narrative functions. As we have seen, Quinn himself is problematic, with his layers of assumed identities, one of which is the author's. The character of Auster and that of the narrator, especially in their circular relation to Quinn, also present a structural aspect that, it appears, would be difficult to define as a "fixed point." And yet these three can be seen to be drawn in sharp relief when compared to the Peter Stillmans. The first of this strange father–son pair that we meet is the son. It is the son who has called Quinn, looking for Auster, the detective. When Quinn goes to meet him, we get this report of his entering the room:

The body acted almost exactly as the voice had: machine-like, fitful, alternating between slow and rapid gestures, rigid and yet expressive, as if the operation were out of control, not quite corresponding to the will that lay behind it. It seemed to Quinn that Stillman's body had not been used for a long time and that all its functions had been relearned, so that motion had become a conscious process, each movement broken down into its component submovements, with the result that all flow and spontaneity had been lost. It was like watching a marionette trying to walk without strings.

(17)

Peter, then, is a character somehow cut loose from his author. This is, in fact, the case, for Quinn is, in this scene, impersonating "Auster." Peter Stillman called for Paul Auster, but Quinn came instead, and Quinn has come to listen, not to empower. The author sent a mere character in his place, and so "poor Peter Stillman" must muck his way through his narrative on his own, unauthored.

Peter describes to Quinn his horrible childhood, how he was locked away in the dark until he was twelve, the victim of his father's linguistic experiment, the search for "God's language." His father was put in prison for his treatment of his son, but now he has served his time and is returning, Peter thinks, to kill him. "Wimble click crumblechaw beloo," says Peter, and "I am the only one who understands these words" (20), alternating outbursts of strange gibberish with moments of relative lucidity, during which he manages to get his story across to "Mr. Auster." Peter's narrative occupies some nine pages of uninterrupted direct quotation, but at the end of it Quinn realizes that an entire day has elapsed and that they are now sitting "in the dark." Thus it must be that the unauthored character is rather a slow speaker. His speaking, in fact, seems to resemble his walking:

> "There are many more words to speak. But I do not think I will speak them. No. Not today. My mouth is tired now, and I think the time has come for me to go. Of course, I know nothing of time. But that makes no difference. To me. Thank you very much. I know you will save my life, Mr. Auster. I am counting on you. Life can last just so long, you understand. Everything else is in the room, with darkness, with God's language, with screams. Here I am of the air, a beautiful thing for the light to shine on. Perhaps you will remember that. I am Peter Stillman. That is not my real name. Thank you very much."
>
> (26)

Peter has sent for Auster his author to save his life. Without his author, he must remain in darkness, unknown, off the page; his name cannot be "real." But Quinn is only a character; he cannot save him. Peter Stillman walks off page 28 and never returns. Peter Stillman the elder suffers a rather different malady from his son's. If Stillman junior may be said to suffer from a narrative anemia, a rarefaction of authority, so to speak, Stillman senior is afflicted by a prolixity, a chronic proliferation which causes him to vibrate with activity. His potential is so enormous, so meaningful, so authoritative that he literally cannot contain himself, as we see in this scene at the train station, where Quinn begins his surveillance.

> As Stillman reached the threshold of the station, he put his bag down ... and paused.... What happened then defied explanation. Directly behind Stillman, heaving into view just inches behind his right shoulder, another man stopped, took a lighter out of his

pocket, and lit a cigarette. His face was the exact twin of Stillman's. For a second Quinn thought it was an illusion, a kind of aura thrown off by the electromagnetic currents in Stillman's body. But no, this other Stillman moved, breathed, blinked his eyes; his actions were clearly independent of the first Stillman.

(67–68)

This character is so vital, so full of possibilities, that he undergoes mitosis before our eyes. When the two of him walk away in separate directions, Quinn first follows the second one, then runs back and takes up the trail of the first. We never see this second Stillman again; we can only wonder, with Quinn (154), what story we might have ended up in if we had followed the second instead of the first. As he disappears into the corpuscular New York traffic stream, we can imagine an infinite number of future divisions, infecting God-knows-how-many novels along the way.

After some thirteen days of meticulous surveillance, during which Quinn observes only the most banal, if enigmatic, behavior, and certainly nothing that hints of Stillman being a threat to his son, Quinn is finally overcome by sheer boredom and decides that he must speak to Stillman. At the first meeting, Quinn, deciding that he must conceal his identity as Detective Paul Auster, introduces himself as:

> "... Quinn. Q-U-I-N-N."
> "I see [says Stillman]. Yes, yes I see. Quinn. Hmmm. Yes. Very interesting. Quinn. A most resonant word. Rhymes with twin, does it not?"
> "That's right. Twin."
> "And sin, too, if I'm not mistaken."
> "You're not."
> "And also in—one n—or inn—two. Isn't that so?"
> "Exactly."
> "Hmmm. Very interesting. I see many possibilities for this word, this Quinn, this ... quintessence ... of quiddity. Quick, for example. And quill. And quack. And quirk. Hmmm. Rhymes with grin. Not to speak of kin. Hmmm. Very interesting. And win. And fin. And din. And gin. And pin. And tin. And bin. Hmmm. Even rhymes with djinn. Hmmm. And if you say it right, with been. Hmmm. Yes, very interesting. I like your name enormously, Mr. Quinn. It flies off in so many little directions at once."

(89–90)

If a character is, as Gass tells us, the sound of his name, it would seem that Stillman has Quinn, so to speak, pegged. Noticeably absent from the exchange is any hint whatsoever that the dialogue represents an interaction of two humans. That is, there is no "hello," "pleased to meet you," "lovely day for a walk," or any of the banal expressions two strangers might exchange upon first meeting. Stillman reacts to Quinn *as if* he were a character as defined by Gass.

The next day Quinn confronts Stillman again. Since Stillman appears to have no memory of their previous meeting, Quinn introduces himself this time as Henry Dark, which is the name of a prophetic character, introduced to us earlier in the novel, upon whom Stillman wrote his dissertation. Stillman replies:

> "Unfortunately, that's not possible, sir."
> "Why not?"
> "Because there is no Henry Dark.... You see, there never was any such person as Henry Dark. I made him up. He's an invention.... a character in a book I once wrote. A figment."
>
> (96)

Thus there is given to us an inequality: a character is not a person; a person is not a character. This is, in summary, Gass's formulation. But what are we to make of the fact that this axiom is itself given by a character? Since speech is a faculty limited to persons, a character denying characters their personhood suggests a paradox along the order of *I cannot speak*, which is simply another form of the paradox of Epimenides, *I am lying*. The loop is actually a double one, for Stillman is addressing Quinn, a character, assuming, necessarily, in order to continue speaking, that he is a person. Thus he tells a character that he cannot be a character because he is a person. The effect of this dialogue is to point out the contradiction inherent in Gass's seemingly straightforward rule.

At the third meeting, Quinn has grown accustomed to Stillman's lack of memory and introduces himself as Peter Stillman.

> "That's my name," answered Stillman. "I'm Peter Stillman."
> "I'm the other Peter Stillman," said Quinn.
> "Oh. You mean my son. Yes, that's possible. You look just like him. Of course, Peter is blond and you are dark. Not Henry Dark, but dark of hair. But people change, don't they? One minute we're one thing, and then another another."
>
> (101)

Stillman, it seems, is wise to the ways of the Auster novel. Why shouldn't his son, blond yesterday, be dark today?

There follows then a parody of the novelistic treatment of family, with Stillman passing on some of his Austerly wisdom to his son Quinn in the form of such timeless verities as "you shouldn't put all your eggs in one basket. Conversely, don't count your chickens before they hatch" (102). Ever conscious, though, of his paper flesh, of the ink in his veins, Papa Stillman adds:

> "Lying is a bad thing. It makes you sorry you were ever born. And not to have been born is a curse. You are condemned to live outside time. And when you live outside time, there is no day and night. You don't even get a chance to die."
>
> (102)

and:

> "A father must always teach his son the lessons he has learned. In that way knowledge is passed down from generation to generation, and we grow wise."
>
> "I won't forget what you've told me" [Quinn replies].
>
> "I'll be able to die happily now, Peter."
>
> "I'm glad."
>
> "But you mustn't forget anything."
>
> "I won't, father. I promise."
>
> (103–4)

At this point Stillman senior, following in the tradition of his son, disappears from the page forever. Stillman, we know by now, is a "lie," a fiction. So we see by his own wistful statement that he is "sorry [he was] ever born." But the logical move to the next sentence is a strange one: "And not to have been born is a curse." In the world of fiction, of lying, to wish for something is to cause it to happen. To be "sorry" he was ever born is enough to cause, in his very next breath, a whole new history to be written, one where he was not "born." A similar move takes place in relation to his death: "I'll be able to die happily now" follows, in this fictional logic, "you don't even get a chance to die."

Thus not only is the concept of character that we saw in Woolf and Forster undermined but that of Gass and Ferrara also. For to Gass's fixed point is opposed a protean changeling, to Ferrara's communicative mode a babble of empty cliches and immediate self-contradiction. Both modern and postmodern notions of character are exploded. This is revealed most succinctly in the pun on Stillman's name, since he is "a still man," lifeless, mere paper, but he is also "still a man," because a paper character can exist only as a comparison to a "real person."

Having seen how Auster has sabotaged point of view and character, we now turn to search for remnants of that third bulwark of the narrative art, plot. There is a critical trend that identifies in the detective novel a special relationship to plot and to story. Todorov, for example, posits the crime and the work of its detection as the *fabula* and *sjuzet*, thus making the detective novel an allegory for narratives in general (Brooks 24–25). For Brooks, the detective's uncovering of the crime is analogous to the reader's deciphering of the plot (23–29). Plot, then, in contemporary critical theory, tends toward its meaning of "subterfuge," an enigma to be uncovered, as much as the Aristotelian "sequence of actions." These two lexical possibilities can be said to form subdivisions of the term "plot." They find expression in Roland Barthes's hermeneutic and proairetic codes (*S/Z* 19), which may be defined, briefly, as follows: the hermeneutic code is the code of enigmas and their solutions, of questions and answers, mysteries and solutions; the proairetic code is the code of actions, of events in temporal or narrative sequence.

We will examine two instances of plot in *City of Glass*, one of them a subplot, or rather a plot allegory, contained within the novel, the other the story of the novel in summary. The subplot occurs during Quinn's surveillance of Stillman. Quinn begins his surveillance by reading Stillman's dissertation, which concerns, among other things, the Tower of Babel. The details need not concern us here. He then follows Stillman every day for thirteen days, noting everything that he does in his notebook. Here we have, literally, "a condition of all classic detective fiction, that the detective repeat, go over again, the ground that has been covered by his predecessor, the criminal" (Brooks 24). After these thirteen days, frustrated by a seeming lack of clues, Quinn sits down with his notebook and, from his notes, "sketched a little map of the area Stillman had wandered in" (80). We should note that "to plot" can also mean "to map." Thus Quinn "plots" Stillman's course for each of the days he has observed him, excluding the first four, for which his notes are not precise enough. He finds that the graphics he has produced, in sequence, resemble (in the vaguest sense of the word) the letters OWER OF BAB. Assuming that the first four days would have yielded THE T, and that the two to come will yield EL, "the answer seemed inescapable: THE TOWER OF BABEL" (85). Was Stillman, then, sending a message?

on second thought this did not seem apt. For Stillman had not left his message anywhere. True, he had created the letters by the movement of his steps, but they had not been written down....

And yet, the pictures did exist—not in the streets where they had been drawn, but in Quinn's red notebook. He wondered if Stillman had sat down each night in his room and plotted his course for the following day or whether he had improvised as he had gone along. It was impossible to know.

(85–86)

First of all we might compare this to Brooks's description of plotting in "The Musgrave Ritual": "The central part of the tale displays a problem in trigonometry in action, as Holmes interprets the indications of the ritual as directions for laying out a path on the ground, following the shadow of the elm when the sun is over the oak, pacing off measurements, and so forth: he literally plots out on the lawn the points to which the ritual, read as directions for plotting points, refers him" (24). Quinn's plotting seems to resemble that of both Holmes and Brooks, except that Quinn is somewhat less sure of himself than either of these competent detectives. Quinn's wondering whether Stillman "plotted or improvised" is obviously a parody of literary interpretation, the mapping itself a parody of Holmes-style "trigonometry in action." And the fact that the letters only exist in "Quinn's red notebook" (and, of course, in our paperback copy of *City of Glass*) leads us to wonder, with Quinn, if it is a delusion or if it is "real," if Auster is improvising or plotting. There is thus an enigma, a question, identical for Quinn and for ourselves: Is there a plot? Is there a subterfuge? Is there, in fact, an enigma?

In *S/Z*, Barthes, speaking of Balzac's *Sarrasine*, defines for us the

morphemes (or the "hermeneutemes") of this hermeneutic sentence.... They are: (1) *thematization*, or an emphasizing of the subject which will be the object of the enigma; (2) *proposal*, a metalinguistic index which ... designates the hermeneutic ... genus; (3) *formulation* of the enigma; (4) *promise of an answer*; (5) *snare* ...; (6) *equivocation* ...; (7) *jamming*, acknowledgment of the insolubility of the enigma; (8) *suspended answer* ..., (9) *partial answer* ...; (10) *disclosure, decipherment*....

(209–10)

In our text, we find the "thematization" and "proposal" in this segment, in which Quinn has paused after mapping the third day to meditate upon his enterprise:

Quinn paused for a moment to ponder what he was doing. Was he scribbling nonsense? Was he feeble-mindedly frittering away the evening, or was he trying to find something? Either response, he realized, was unacceptable. If he was simply killing time, why had he chosen such a painstaking way to do it? Was he so muddled that he no longer had the courage to think? On the other hand, if he was not merely diverting himself, what was he actually up to? It seemed to him that he was looking for a sign.

(83)

The "thematization" is contained in the questions, since they all point toward the ultimate, metaquestion: Is there an enigma? The "proposal" is contained in the final sentence, since it tells us that a semiotic enterprise, a hermeneutic, is about to begin. The "formulation" comes after Quinn maps the next letter, the R:

As with the others, it was complicated by numerous irregularities, approximations, and ornate embellishments.... Still clinging to a semblance of objectivity, Quinn tried to look at it as if he had not been anticipating a letter of the alphabet. He had to admit that nothing was sure: it could well have been meaningless.

(84)

For brevity, we will skip the "promise," "snare," "equivocation," "jamming," and "suspended and partial answer." We leave it to faith that, with appropriately Barthesian hermeneutic rigor, there could be found examples of each. We turn, expectantly, to the "disclosure" or "decipherment," the object, the complement of the sentence. But it never comes. The last two days are never plotted. The enigmatic Tower of Babel, a motif for forty pages, is never mentioned again, and both the plot and the plot theory, the subterfuge and the sequence, the hermeneutic and the hermeneutemes drift into insignificance. But perhaps, we conjecture, this is the answer. For to answer "Is there an enigma?" with "Yes" leaves the question unanswered, and to answer with "No" denies the question's predicate. So this hermeneutic sentence is closed, not with the "*period* of truth" (Barthes 209) but the ellipsis of silence.

The movement of the novel as a whole can be plotted as a series of these ellipses. First Stillman Jr. simply erases himself without explanation. (Stillman's "plot" to kill his son might be said to have been realized, as the elder character simply replaces the younger in the print.) Then Stillman Sr.

disappears. Quinn, having discovered that Stillman Sr. has checked out of his hotel, and having tried to telephone his employer every twenty minutes for two days, hearing nothing but busy signals, suddenly finds himself, on page 132, alone in his novel:

> he realized that he had come to a decision about things. Without his even knowing it, the answer was already there for him, sitting fully formed in his head. The busy signal, he saw now, had not been arbitrary. It had been a sign, and it was telling him that he could not yet break his connection with the case, even if he wanted to. He had tried to contact Virginia Stillman to tell her he was through, but the fates had not allowed it. Quinn paused to consider this. Was "fate" really the word he wanted to use?
>
> (132)

I want to answer this question, for Quinn. To bring his (self–)critical lexicon up to date, I suggest that the word he is looking for is *overdetermination*. Christine Brooke-Rose gives the definition of this term as follows: "A code is over-determined when its information (narrative, ironic, hermeneutic, symbolic, etc.) is too clear, over-encoded, recurring beyond purely informational need" (106). We can see an example of overcoding of the hermeneutic code in the sheer abundance of question marks in the quotation from page 83, above. But this sequence ends, as we have noted, in ellipsis. In Stillman Sr. we see something resembling an overdetermination of character (semic code), but of a very strange sort, since he appears as three different characters, each overcoded. But in Quinn we find semic overcoding of a more straightforward variety, realized in moments when he suddenly apprehends himself as being out of his own control, as being manipulated by an other (which he can never quite identify as an author), as being, in other words, semically overcoded.

One example of this self-apprehension is the scene in which Quinn finds his hand being placed for him on the doorknob (14, quoted above). Another is the section just quoted, where he finds a thought, a decision, implanted in his mind, a manipulation which he names "fate." This overcoding is made abundantly clear to the reader by the simple inclusion of "Auster" in the cast of characters, the simple repetition of the name in the narrative being sufficient to keep the author's hand always in view. This knowledge that is continually imparted to the reader and continually kept from Quinn has a curious correlative: it becomes the overcoded hermeneutic sentence of the text. The hand of the author takes the place, in this mystery, of the crime. The enigma becomes not who committed the crime, not how Stillman plans to kill his son, but rather *what will the author do next*? And thus the paradox of the semes: although Quinn is decidedly overdetermined, anything can happen to him.

This situation reaches its climax when Quinn, after having spent a period of months staking out Stillman Jr.'s apartment, during which time he sees no one and squanders all his money, calls Auster. Auster tells him that he has tried to call him "a thousand times." He is surprised to hear that Quinn is still working on the case:

> "I don't believe you don't know. Where the hell have you been? Don't you read the newspapers?"
>
> "Newspapers? Goddamit, say what you mean. I don't have time to read newspapers."
>
> There was silence on the other end, and for a moment Quinn felt that the conversation was over, that he had somehow fallen asleep and had just now woken up to find the telephone in his hand.
>
> "Stillman jumped off the Brooklyn Bridge," Auster said. "He committed suicide two and a half months ago."
>
> (145–46)

Now in a "normal" narrative, this revelation would close a hermeneutic sentence. But in this narrative it cannot. In this respect the hermeneutic code resembles the semic, for even though it is overdetermined, the enigma of what the author will do remains open until the last word, the last punctuation mark of the novel. Quinn, receding now into denouement, goes to Stillman's apartment, which he finds open and empty. There he remains for six pages, writing in his red notebook, approaching his end as the pages run out. "The last sentence of the red notebook reads: 'What will happen when there are no more pages in the red notebook?'" This unanswered question ends the proairetic (what happened/happens to Quinn) and semic (Quinn is a writer contemplating his self-creation/destruction) sequences; Quinn fades to ellipsis. But it opens another mini-hermeneutic. At this point the narrator appears. Never evident before, ellipsis, as it were, in front of him rather than behind, on the next-to-last page he suddenly commandeers the text:

> At this point the story grows obscure. The information has run out, and the events that follow this last sentence will never be known. It would be foolish to even hazard a guess.

> I returned home from my trip to Africa in February, just hours before a snowstorm began to fall on New York. I called my friend Auster that evening, and he urged me to come over to see him as soon as I could. There was something so insistent in his voice that I dared not refuse, even though I was exhausted.
>
> (157)

In this short sequence we are veritably showered with codes. The narrator closes the mini-hermeneutic of the sentence before, once again with ellipsis ("will never be known"); he opens two more hermeneutics (who am I? why is Auster upset?); he closes a proairetic sequence that has never been opened ("returned home") and opens one that will never be closed ("snowstorm began"); he introduces, also, a new set of cultural codes (Africa, snowstorm in New York) and semes (I travel, Auster is my friend, Auster is upset). Overcoded, to say the least, but at the same time undercoded, for what is transmitted? Nothing but the irony that something so full could at the same time be so empty.

All the codes, then, decipher to ellipsis, including the grand hermeneutic of what the author will do next, since it leads us out of *City of Glass* and on to other texts. The work is, after all, the first segment of a trilogy; another novel begins on the next page. And it is, in fact, after the end, not (to paraphrase Kafka) on the last word, but on the very last, that the novel's most ironic turn occurs, for at the bottom of the page, in the tradition of Joyce and the modernist artificers, we find the date (1981–1982), so that the work, with all its indeterminate self-reflection, all its postmodern "floating signifiers," is positioned at a concrete point of time, place, and authorship, signed, as it were, and affirmed as a crafted artifact.

Nor is this arguably negligible textual feature the only evidence of this affirmation. Russell has noted parallels between Quinn's and Paul Auster's (Auster$_0$'s) careers (73). Quinn, before he started writing detective novels, "had published several books of poetry, had written plays, critical essays, and had worked on a number of long translations" (4), just like Paul Auster. Norma Rowen, in "The Detective in Search of the Lost Tongue of Adam: Paul Auster's *City of Glass*," mentions the similarities between Stillman's interest in prelapsarian language and the focus of one of Auster's essays. These biographical projections, which are highlighted by Auster's inclusion of himself as a character, are also anchors in the concrete. They are not, as Barthes notes of Balzac's insertion of historical characters in his fiction, details included to enhance an effect of reality; they are too esoteric to function at the level of effect. They are, rather, kernels of reality buried in a text that everywhere seeks an effect of unreality. The parody is not of realism, but of irrealism. To the postmodern statement that fiction is not truth, it opposes a new paradox: fiction cannot lie.

In "'From Work to Text': The Modernist and Postmodernist *Künstlerroman*," Carl D. Malmgren notes the debilitating effect of literary tradition on the postmodern novelist. Pertinent to John Barth in *Lost in the Funhouse*, he says, "From the point of view of the hag-ridden postmodernist writer, the inescapability of the inter-text is an hysterical/historical burden. The inter-text lays waste to his powers of description, contaminates his discourse, and ultimately renders impotent his imagination. Inter-textuality is a form of castration" (23). This captures the postmodern dilemma which Barth perhaps best exemplifies, that the form is exhausted, that everything has already been said. There is an atmosphere of suffocation, a stricture, a narrowing of the field of the possible and a simultaneous demand for originality. *City of Glass*, like *Lost in the Funhouse*, wrestles with the inter-text, but rather than admit (tragic) defeat, it asserts its potency: it chokes the inter-text with text.

The work of this novel is, for Paul Auster, a necessary engagement. To poststructuralism, the author is a "function .... not defined by the spontaneous attribution of a discourse to its producer, but rather by a series of specific and complex operations" (Foucault 113). *City of Glass*, with its confused abundance of authors, writers, narrators, pseudonyms, and impersonations, is the *künstlerroman* of these "complex operations." It is Auster's portrait of the author as a developing function, a search through the labyrinth of theory and tradition for a new authorial identity, one that can survive in an age when authority is not necessarily bound to text by "spontaneous attribution." In this way, to be sure, the scope of the project is limited. Perhaps it is only in Auster's later work, such as *The Music of Chance*, that its success or failure can be gauged.

In the last paragraph of *City of Glass*, the narrator tells us, "As for Auster, I am convinced that he behaved badly throughout" (158). The narrator, then, is also a critic, reminding us that this character that has authored his novel has allowed his other characters to disappear, his point of view to become hopelessly refracted, his plots to end unresolved, his overdetermination to lead to indeterminacy, and his codes to dead-end in indecipherability. But what critic, now, would use the word "badly"? Doesn't the postmodern critic merely *describe*? Isn't the task of structuralism taxonomy, of semiotics theory? In short, isn't evaluation as a critical enterprise a profoundly modernist (that is, dead) concern? Perhaps merely to list the truisms reveals them as such, and it is not necessary to mention that simply to select an example is to evaluate; one way or another, examples are always "exemplary."

"The novel," says M. M. Bakhtin, "gets on poorly with other genres. There can be no talk of a harmony.... The novel parodies other genres ...; it exposes the conventionality of their forms and their language," and the "ability of the novel to criticize itself is a remarkable feature of this ever-developing genre" (51, 52). Bakhtin's comments have special significance when we consider that critical theory is itself a genre—and when we realize that the relation of writer to critic, of the novel to theory, of literature to semiotics, of art to science, is one of an essential, if subterranean, hostility. "The experts have not managed to isolate a single definite, stable characteristic of the novel—without adding a reservation, which immediately disqualifies it altogether as a generic classification.... The novel, after all, has no canon of its own.... It is plasticity itself" (Bakhtin 54, 66). We see in metafiction a shape-shifting, a protean refusal to let itself be pinned down, classified, dissected, conquered. Metafiction deserves its prefix not because it is "above" (an etymological anomaly), but because it is changing, fiction in a state of metamorphosis.

Art and science are two very different social functions; the engagement of each by the other is a phenomenon peculiar to our age, one whose implications we have barely begun to explore. Metafiction is the novel's defense, and its counteroffensive. The fact that it engages through parody rather than polemic, through laughter rather than rigor, through metamorphosis rather than taxonomy is its vital distinction.

It could be argued that Auster's seemingly obsessive engagement of theory reduces the novel to an academic enterprise, robbing the form of social and political relevance. It could be argued that there is no place in the novel for theory to be tested, that art should ignore criticism and proceed with its treatments of life. If, however, literature does have value beyond the codification of dominant ideologies, if it is, in other words, relevant, why would it shrink from this very affirmation? In the engagement of theory by representation, both are exposed, and exercised, in all their capabilities and limitations. The value of the novel of critical engagement is that it clears a space where representation can once again close with politics and society and, at least for the moment, be equal to the task.

Note

1. It should be noted, relative to intentionality, that other of Auster's fictional works cannot be positioned in this same discursive constellation. *The Music of Chance* (1990), for example, engages the Rousseauist social allegory, and in *Moon Palace* (1989) the discourse is purely novelistic.

Works Cited

Auster, Paul. *City of Glass*. 1985. *The New York Trilogy*. New York: Penguin, 1990.

Bakhtin, M. M. "Epic and Novel: Toward a Methodology for the Study of the Novel." *The Dialogic Imagination: Four Essays*. Ed. Michael Holquist. Trans. Caryl Emerson and Michael Holquist. Rpt. in Hoffman and Murphy 49–69.

Barthes, Roland. *S/Z*. Trans. Richard Miller. New York: Hill, 1974.

Brooke-Rose, Christine. *A Rhetoric of the Unreal: Studies in Narrative and Structure, Especially of the Fantastic*. Cambridge: Cambridge UP, 1981.

Brooks, Peter. *Reading for the Plot: Design and Intention in Narrative*. New York: Knopf, 1984.

Chatman, Seymour. "Discourse: Nonnarrated Stories." *Story and Discourse: Narrative Structure in Fiction and Film*. Ithaca: Cornell UP, 1978. Rpt. in Hoffman and Murphy 367–79.

Ferrara, Fernando. "Theory and Model for the Structural Analysis of Fiction." *New Literary History* 5 (1974): 245–68.

Forster, E. M. "Flat and Round Characters." *Aspects of the Novel*. Harcourt, 1954. Rpt. in Hoffman and Murphy 41–47.

Foucault, Michel. "What Is an Author?" Trans. Josué V. Harari. *The Foucault Reader*. Ed. Paul Rabinow. New York: Pantheon, 1984. 101–20.

Gass, William H. "The Concept of Character in Fiction." *Fiction and the Figures of Life*. 1970. Boston: Godine, 1989.

Hoffman, Michael J., and Patrick D. Murphy, eds. *Essentials of the Theory of Fiction*. Durham: Duke UP, 1988.

James, Henry. "The Art of Fiction." *The Future of the Novel*. Ed. Leon Edel. New York: Vintage, 1956. Rpt. in Hoffman and Murphy 15–23.

Malmgren, Carl D. "'From Work to Text': The Modernist and Postmodernist *Künstlerroman*." *Novel* 21.1 (1987): 5–28.

Rowen, Norma. "The Detective in Search of the Lost Tongue of Adam: Paul Auster's *City of Glass*." *Critique* 32 (1991): 224–34.

Russell, Alison. "Deconstructing *The New York Trilogy*: Paul Auster's Anti-Detective Fiction." *Critique* 31 (1990): 71–83.

Todorov, Tzvetan. *The Poetics of Prose*. Trans. Richard Howard. New York: Cornell UP, 1977.

Woolf, Virginia. "Mr. Bennett and Mrs. Brown." *The Captain's Death Bed and Other Essays*. New York: Harcourt, 1950. Rpt. in Hoffman and Murphy 25–39.

ALISON RUSSELL

Deconstructing The New York Trilogy: Paul Auster's Anti-Detective Fiction

Detective fiction comprises a genre seemingly at odds with American experimental writing. The detective story's highly stylized patterns are derivative of the Romance, an extremely conventional literary genre. Recent experimental novelists, however, are taking advantage of these conventions to create what Stefano Tani has called "anti-detective fiction."[1] Pynchon's *The Crying of Lot 49* and Nabokov's *Pale Fire* illustrate this postmodern mutation in their parodic forms and subversions of the end-dominated detective story. A more recent example of anti-detective fiction is Paul Auster's *The New York Trilogy*, a highly entertaining yet sophisticated work, amenable to the deconstructive principles of Jacques Derrida. Auster's novels have attracted the attention of a wide range of readers: *City of Glass*, the first volume of the trilogy, was nominated for an Edgar Award for best mystery of the year, but this recognition by a non-academic community may account for the lack of critical attention given to *The New York Trilogy*. The fact that Auster is known primarily as a poet and translator may also account for his exclusion from recent studies of American experimental fiction. This essay offers a Derridean analysis of Auster's trilogy, which will hopefully attract further academic attention to *The New York Trilogy*.

The three novels comprising the trilogy—*City of Glass*, *Ghosts*, and *The Locked Room*—are essentially retellings of the same story. All three employ

From *Critique: Studies in Contemporary Fiction* 31, no. 2 (Winter 1990). © 1990 by the Helen Dwight Reid Educational Foundation.

and deconstruct the conventional elements of the detective story, resulting in a recursive linguistic investigation of the nature, function, and meaning of language. The trilogy also parodies and subverts the Romance, "realistic" fiction, and autobiography, thereby exploding the narrative traditions associated with these genres. By denying conventional expectations of fiction—linear movement, realistic representation, and closure—Auster's novels also deconstruct logocentrism, a primary subject of Derrida's subversions. Logocentrism, the term applied to uses and theories of language grounded in the metaphysics of presence, is the "crime" that Auster investigates in *The New York Trilogy*. In each volume, the detective searches for "presence": an ultimate referent or foundation outside the play of language itself. This quest for correspondence between signifier and signified is inextricably related to each protagonist's quest for origin and identity, for the self only exists insofar as language grants existence to it.

In *Writing and Difference*, Derrida states that "the absence of [a presence or] a transcendental signified extends the domain and play of signification infinitely."[2] As a retelling of the same story, each volume of Auster's trilogy illustrates this Derridean dissemination; each text denies any one meaning or "solution." Like language itself, the three texts are an incessant play of "différance," which Derrida defines in *Positions* as "the systematic play of differences, of the traces of differences, of the spacing by means of which elements are related to each other."[3] Meaning is deferred in an endless movement from one linguistic interpretation to the next. Auster reinforces this deconstructive effect through the use of other language games, such as intertextual references, mirror images, and puns, thereby exploding the centering and unifying conventions of detective stories. The distinction among author, narrator, and character is increasingly blurred. Similarly, the textual boundary of each volume of the trilogy disintegrates: characters in one book dream of characters in another or reappear in different disguises. For obvious reasons, it may be inappropriate to discuss these books separately, just as it may be equally inappropriate to use the terms "author," "narrator," and "protagonist"; for the sake of convention, however, this approach and these terms will be used to analyze Auster's trilogy.

The title of the first volume, *City of Glass*, is a play on Augustine's *The City of God*, a neoplatonic treatise that suggests that an eternal order exists outside the realm of sense: Augustine's work posits transcendence or, in Derrida's terms, presence. The title *City of Glass* also connotes transparency; thus Daniel Quinn, the novel's detective and protagonist, becomes a pilgrim searching for correspondence between signifiers and signifieds. The search for transparent language is predominantly visual, a characteristic alluded to in the narrator's discussion of the phrase "private eye" in the novel's first chapter.

> The term held a triple meaning for Quinn. Not only was it the letter "i," standing for "investigator," it was "I" in the upper case, the tiny life-bud buried in the body of the breathing self. At the same time, it was also the physical eye of the writer, the eye of the man who looks out from himself into the world and demands that the world reveal itself to him.[4]

Quinn, as a writer of mystery novels, exists in a world dominated by signifiers and assumed solutions. The first chapter of *City of Glass* describes the function of the writer-detective and reveals the metaphor that will be employed—and deconstructed—in all three volumes of *The New York Trilogy*: "The detective is one who looks, who listens, who moves through this morass of objects and events in search of the thought, the idea that will pull all these things together and make sense of them. In effect, the writer and the detective are interchangeable" (15). This passage offers a multiplicity of orientations, as the detective metaphor applies to Quinn, to Auster, and to the relationship between the two. It is also a "clue" to the mystery of *The New York Trilogy* because Auster is always both inside and outside his three texts. The narrator of the first volume continually denies any one locus of meaning, yet teases the reader with the possibility of one: "The center, then, is everywhere, and no circumference can be drawn until the book has come to its end" (15). By directing our attention to the end of the book and to a possible solution, the narrator forces us to participate in the detective's game.

As a genre, the detective story is end-dominated, and its popularity attests to Western culture's obsession with closure. By denying closure, and by sprinkling his trilogy with references to other end-dominated texts, Auster continually disseminates the meaning of this detective story. The detective story also necessitates a movement backward in time, from the corpse to the crime, so to speak. In *City of Glass*, Quinn's quest for an ultimate referent leads him into an investigation of the origin of logos; his quest becomes a pursuit of paternal authority associated with creation and also a quest for his own identity. In the beginning of the novel, Quinn is described as a mystery novelist who writes stories about the detective Max Work under the pseudonym William Wilson (an allusion to Poe's story about doubles and, later in the novel, to the baseball player Mookie Wilson). The narrator alludes to Quinn's identity crisis by withholding information: "Who he was, where he came from, and what he did are of no great importance" (7). Essentially, Quinn is a paper-Auster, a mere linguistic construct of the author himself: "As a young man he had published several books of poetry, had written plays, critical essays, and had worked on a number of long translations" (9). Although Quinn suspects that he is not real, he is not aware that he is Auster's creation. The novel becomes increasingly comic when Quinn receives middle-of-the-night telephone calls for the Paul Auster Detective Agency. Quinn tells the mysterious caller, "[T]here is no Paul Auster here" (13).

Logocentrism in *The New York Trilogy* is closely associated with paternal authority. Quinn's unconscious denial of his creator's presence suggests the loss of the Father, the ultimate authority and founder of logos—the word. Quinn usurps the role of the Father when he assumes the identity of Paul Auster (of the detective agency)—when he meets his client, Peter Stillman, he thinks of "his own dead son," but "just as suddenly as the thought had appeared, it vanished" (25). Quinn is unable to posit the determinacy characteristic of paternal authority. The interview with Stillman strikes Quinn as strange and unreal, and "as a consequence, he could never be sure of any of it" (23). Significantly, Quinn is hired to find and tail the father of his client, also named Peter Stillman. The elder Stillman had attempted to find God's language thirteen years earlier by keeping his young son in a locked dark room for nine years. As a product of this experiment, the son babbles incoherently to Quinn, unable to affirm his own identity: "For now, I am Peter Stillman. That is not my real name. I cannot say who I will be tomorrow.... But that makes no difference. To me. Thank you very much. I know you will save my life, Mr. Auster. I am counting on you" (36–37). Like his language, Stillman himself lacks solidity—he moves like a marionette "trying to walk without strings" and dresses completely in white (25). At one point in their meeting, "Quinn suddenly felt that Stillman had become invisible" (26). Everything about Stillman and the Stillman case lacks substance, for they are fictions within the larger fiction of *City of Glass*.

Quinn's pursuit of the Father is a search for authority and "authority." In looking for the creator of logos, he is looking for his own creator as well, but his investigation is subverted by Auster's authorial duplicity. In many ways, *City of Glass* is a reworking of *Don Quixote*, a book that also denies its own authority while claiming to be a true story. When Virginia Stillman tells Quinn that she was referred to the Paul Auster Detective Agency by Michael Saavedra (Cervantes's family name), Quinn becomes the quixotic hero, the unknowing victim of a strange conspiracy. This possible "solution" to *City of Glass* is exfoliated in chapter ten, when Quinn decides to contact the "real"

Paul Auster for help with his case. This Auster claims to know nothing about a detective agency. He is a writer, he explains to Quinn, working on an essay about the hoax of *Don Quixote*. Don Quixote "orchestrated the whole thing himself," Auster tells Quinn, duping Cervantes into "hiring Don Quixote to decipher the story of Don Quixote himself" (153–54). This analysis, when applied to *City of Glass*, raises a number of questions about the book's authorship, and results in endless doublings and mirror images. When Quinn meets Auster's young son, also named Daniel, he tells the boy, "I'm you, and you're me." The boy replies, "and around and around it goes" (157).

Quinn's investigation becomes an obsessive search for an ultimate authority, for his research on the elder Stillman leads him to believe that this "father" holds the key to finding a way back to pure logos. He reads Stillman's book, *The Garden and the Tower. Early Visions of the New World*, in which Stillman analyzes *Paradise Lost*, identifying words that embodied two equal and opposite meanings—"one before the fall and one after the fall" (70). This ironic deconstructive reading of Milton's text results in Stillman's own quest for prelapserian language: he prophecies a new paradise based upon his reading of Henry Dark's pamphlet, *The New Babel* (75). According to Derridean philosophy, Dark's (and Stillman's) return to pure logos is impossible because of the nature of language. As a play of differences, language offers no basis for attributing a determinate meaning to any word or utterance.

The quixotic Quinn, deluded by Stillman's book, stalks the old man throughout the labyrinth of New York City, recording Stillman's every move in a red notebook (possibly a parodic allusion to Wittgenstein's *The Blue and Brown Books*). By keeping Stillman in his sight, Quinn is attempting to retain "presence," but in rereading his notebook, he "often discovered that he had written two or even three lines on top of each other, producing a jumbled, illegible palimpsest" (100). Words continually fail to produce an absolute meaning for Quinn, for Stillman's movements always remain divorced from the words in the red notebook. Repeatedly frustrated in his attempts to decipher the meaning of Stillman's patterned walks through the city, Quinn decides to confront physically the logocentric father. Presenting himself alternately as Paul Auster, Henry Dark, and Peter Stillman, Quinn discusses language, lies, and history with the old man. Stillman tells Quinn, "A lie can never be undone.... I am a father, and I know about these things. Remember what happened to the father of our country" (133). By referring to one of the most popular fictions of American history, Stillman unwittingly subverts his own authority. His attempt to rename the world is doomed to failure.

By the end of the novel, fiction is piled upon fiction, negating any one meaning or solution to the mystery of *City of Glass*. The narrator interrupts his own narrative in Cervantes's fashion, claiming both ownership and authorship of the text: "Since this story is based entirely on facts, the author feels it his duty not to overstep the bounds of the verifiable, to resist at all costs the perils of invention. Even the red notebook, which until now has provided a detailed account of Quinn's experiences, is suspect" (173). The narrator is a self-undermining linguistic agent, offering truth and then subverting the possibility of truth, continually denying his readers any one locus of meaning.

As the novel "ends," *City of Glass* illustrates Derridean dissemination. Quinn literally vanishes from the text when he runs out of space in his red notebook, seemingly imploding into the text of *City of Glass*: "It was as though he had melted into the walls of the city" (178). Similarly, Peter Stillman and his wife have disappeared, while the elder Stillman has supposedly committed suicide. In *City of Glass*, characters "die" when their signifiers are omitted from the printed page. All that remains is the cryptic conclusion of the narrator, who claims to have received Quinn's notebook from his friend, the writer Paul Auster.

> As for Quinn, it is impossible for me to say where he is now. I have followed the red notebook as closely as I could, and any inaccuracies in the story should be blamed on me. There were moments when the text was difficult to decipher, but I have done my best with it and have refrained from any interpretation. The red notebook, of course, is only half the story, as any sensitive reader will understand. As for Auster, I am convinced that he behaved badly throughout. If our friendship has ended, he has only himself to blame. As for me, my thoughts remain with Quinn. He will be with me always. And wherever he may have disappeared to, I wish him luck. (202–03)

The narrator's conclusion shows this fiction to be a game against itself. His assertion deconstructs itself through references to the indeterminacy of the red notebook. *City of Glass* is a paranoid text in its uncertainty and contradictory frames of reference.

In *Ghosts*, the second volume of the trilogy, Auster presents another version of this detective story. This text, as a repetitive but also differing collection of signifiers, continues to illustrate Derridean différance, both within the text itself and in its differences from *City of Glass*. Like its predecessor, *Ghosts* defers the possibility of a solution or meaning. Again, Auster explores and deconstructs the logocentric quest for origin—the origin of language, but also the origin of "self." The story begins on February 3, 1947 (the author's birthdate), a movement backward in time appropriate to the text's illustration of différance. In *Speech and Phenomena*, Derrida explains that

> différance is what makes the movement of signification possible only if each element that is said to be "present," appearing on the stage of presence, is related to something other than itself but retains the mark of a past element and already lets itself be hollowed out by the mark of its relation to a future element. This trace relates no less to what is called the future than to what is called the past, and it constitutes what is called the present by this very relation to what it is not, to what it absolutely is not; that is, not even to a past or future considered as a modified present.[5]

Thus, in *Ghosts*, we read the narrator's statement, "the time is the present," followed two pages later by a contradicting statement: "It is February 3, 1947.... But the present is no less dark than the past, and its mystery is equal to anything the future might hold."[6] *Ghosts* is a "trace" of a past element that was never fully present; therefore, the novel's detective protagonist, Blue, is shown to be increasingly obsessed with "presence." Like Daniel Quinn, Blue's identity is inextricably related to language. Since différance destroys the notion of a simple presence, identity and the origin of self are equally destroyed, for origin is always other than itself.

The title of *Ghosts*, like *City of Glass*, suggests transparency, the ideal logocentric relationship between signifier and signified, but it also connotes a lack of substance. *Ghosts* contains fewer pages, characters, and plot complications than the other two volumes of the trilogy. The book is a "ghost" of *City of Glass* and of the detective story genre: the "meat" of the text is stripped down to a generic level, reinforced by Auster's rejection of nomenclature and his use of Film Noir signifiers. Auster's reductionist technique in *Ghosts* is in itself a form of deception—it suggests that the details of the story will be presented in black-and-white, transparent facts that will lead to the solution of the trilogy. The opening lines of the book are equally deceptive in their sparing use of language and their structural similarity to Biblical syntax: "First of all there is Blue. Later there is White, and then there is Black, and before the beginning there is Brown" (7). These bare "facts," with their connotations of creation, begin the deconstructive process of the text by illustrating the movement of signification as a distortion of the linear regression to origin.

Ghosts, as an investigation of origin, also suggests the parallel search for truth—truth as measured by visual presence. Blue, the protagonist-detective, is hired by White "to follow a man named Black and to keep an eye on him for as long as necessary" (7). Truth, for Blue, is always limited to that which he can see: "Words are transparent for him, great windows that stand between him and the world" (23–24). Blue dutifully writes his reports on Black for the never present or visible White, but he becomes frustrated with the ineffectiveness of language: "He discovers that words do not necessarily work, that it is possible for them to obscure the things they are trying to say" (25–26).

Blue's obsession with transparency is rooted in the primacy he gives to visual perception. He attends a baseball game, "struck by the sharp clarity of the colors around him," and is fond of movies because "the pictures on the screen are somehow like the thoughts inside his head" (42, 44). When Blue's vision is obscured, language (and therefore truth or meaning) becomes opaque to him: "Without being able to read what Black has written, everything is a blank so far" (11). Significantly, when Blue experiences this failure of language, he begins to think about his dead father and other dead or rejecting father figures. Blue's memories of lost fathers result in the loss of his own identity. He feels as if he is becoming one with Black, "so completely in harmony ... that to anticipate what Black is going to do, to know when he will stay in his room and when he will go out, he needs merely to look into himself" (38).

Although Blue occasionally ventures out of his room, he exists essentially in a hermetic space. *Ghosts* is a self-enclosed structure of self-mirrorings, but it is also a mirror image, in some ways, of the first and third volumes of *The New York Trilogy*. Much of the book consists of Blue looking out of his window to observe and write about Black, who sits by a window in a building across the street writing and looking back at Blue. Blue reads *Walden* because he sees Black reading *Walden*, but he feels trapped in the process: "He feels like a man who has been condemned to sit in a room and go on reading a book for the rest of his life ... seeing the world only through words, living only through the lives of others" (57). Blue's description of *Walden* is self-reflexive: "There is no story, no plot, no action—nothing but a man sitting alone in a room and writing a book" (58). Blue becomes trapped in the hermetic world of the text: "How to get out of the room that is the book that will go on being written for as long as he stays in the room?" (58). Blue verges on insanity when Black claims that he, too, is a private detective hired "to watch someone ... and send in a report about him every week" (73). Experiencing complete ontological instability, Blue tries to recover language by verbally cataloguing objects according to their color, but he realizes that "there is no end to it" (77). The colors blue, black, and white are meaningless distinctions, he realizes, for each can be applied to any number of people, places, and things.

Ghosts is not merely a reductive version of City of Glass, despite its stripped-down quality and bared concepts. In many ways, the second volume of the trilogy offers itself as a collection of the signs that make up American culture, taken from baseball, popular movies, and the canonical texts and authors of nineteenth-century literature. These artifacts of our collective identity haunt the pages of Ghosts, raising the issue of whether or not original discourse is possible. Just as language is divorced from the things it signifies, texts themselves become divorced from their creators. When Black recounts anecdotes about the "ghosts" of New York City, he provides Blue with a lesson about the flesh and spirit of the writer. Whitman's brain, Black recalls, was removed from his body to be measured and weighed, but it was dropped on the floor: "The brains of America's greatest poet got swept up and thrown out with the garbage" (63). Black is equally amused by Thoreau's visit to Whitman, a meeting that took place next to Whitman's full chamber pot.

> That chamber pot, you see, somehow reminds me of the brains on the floor.... There's a definite connection. Brains and guts, the insides of a man. We always talk about trying to get inside a writer to understand his work better. But when you get right down to it, there's not much to find in there—at least not much that's different from what you'd find in anyone else. (65)

Black's anecdotes reveal his concern with the solipsistic existence of the writer's life. He tells Blue how Hawthorne sat in a room for twelve years to write, a situation similar to his own: "Writing is a solitary business. It takes over your life. In some sense, a writer has no life of his own. Even when he's there, he's not really there" (66). The writer is a ghost, a trace. In Of Grammatology, Derrida explains that there is nothing outside of textuality, outside of "the temporalization of a lived experience which is neither in the world nor in 'another world.'"[7]

This "problem" is the crux of the mystery in Ghosts. Black and Blue are both inside and outside one another, oppositions of what Derrida calls a "violent hierarchy": "one of the two terms governs the other (axiologically, logically, etc.) or has the upper hand. To deconstruct the opposition, first of all, is to overturn the hierarchy at a given moment."[8] Throughout Ghosts, Black has the upper hand, as it is he who hired Blue. When Blue decides that he must deny Black's existence in order to prove his own, he sets out "to erase the whole story" (89). In the novel's final scenes, Blue and Black are intent upon killing one another, and their physical struggle illustrates Derrida's "violent hierarchy." Although Blue appears to be the victor, he is not sure whether the sound of Black's breath is coming from Black or from himself (94).

The final volume of *The New York Trilogy*, *The Locked Room*, takes its title from a popular motif of detective novels: a murdered body is discovered in a sealed room, the exits of which have been locked from the inside. Auster complicates the conventional puzzle by omitting the corpse in *The Locked Room* (another denial of presence). The third version of this repeating story continues to keep différance in play by rejecting the binary opposites inherent in Western traditions and philosophies. In *The Locked Room*, each side of the dualism is inextricably related to the other; thus, like Black and Blue in *Ghosts*, the narrator (the protagonist of this volume) and his counterpart Fanshawe experience a mutually parasitic relationship.

Binary opposition is deconstructed on a larger scale throughout *The New York Trilogy*, not only because the work is in three parts, but because the texts are linked parasitically: references to Quinn, Stillman, and Henry Dark reappear in *The Locked Room*, just as subtle allusions in the first and second volumes foreshadow events in the third. The oscillation of the dominating term of any hierarchy is also illustrated by the changing hierarchy of the terms "writer" and "detective": Daniel Quinn is a writer turned detective, Blue a detective turned writer, and the narrator of *The Locked Room* a writer turned detective. Since deconstruction rejects the notion of a single self, these three novels, as linguistic constructs, also serve as the selves of Auster.

The logocentric quest in *The Locked Room* differs from that of the preceding volumes in several ways. Quinn and Blue are able to confront Stillman and Black physically, but the narrator of *The Locked Room* is frustrated in his attempts to find evidence of the physical presence of his childhood friend, Fanshawe, who has mysteriously disappeared. He has only the words of Fanshawe, the unpublished novels he inherits as Fanshawe's literary executor. As soon as he gains possession of Fanshawe's manuscripts, he usurps the role—the life—of his friend. He marries Fanshawe's wife, adopts his son, and considers the idea of publishing Fanshawe's books as his own. Unlike Quinn and Blue, the narrator of *The Locked Room* has access only to the language, the signifiers, of his counterpart, never to his physical presence. When he learns that Fanshawe is not dead, he sets out to recover and re-create presence in a search that takes him to Fanshawe's mother and childhood home, to his haunts in Paris, and, finally, to a locked room. His quest for Fanshawe turns out to be a quest for himself, for his own identity, since like Black and Blue, the narrator and Fanshawe are inseparable.

If these novels are linguistic constructs of the author, Paul Auster, their protagonists' quests for an ultimate authority and identity serve as ironic frames for the author's own logocentric quest for origin, a quest he himself continually deconstructs. Early in *The Locked Room*, the narrator wonders "what it means when a writer puts his name on a book, why some writers choose to hide behind a pseudonym, whether or not a writer has a real life anyway."[9] This echo of Black's reference to Hawthorne (*Fanshawe*, ironically, is the title of an early novel by Hawthorne) raises again the question of the writer's nonlife. In *The Locked Room*, Auster suggests that language can destroy identity as well as create it. The narrator, in attempting to write a biography of Fanshawe, realizes that life, the "essential thing," resists telling.

> We imagine the real story inside the words, and to do this we substitute ourselves for the person in the story, pretending that we can understand him because we understand ourselves. This is a deception. We exist for ourselves, perhaps, and at times we even have a glimmer of who we are, but in the end we can never be sure, and as our lives go on, we become more and more opaque to ourselves, more and more aware of our own incoherence. No one can cross the boundary into another—for the simple reason that no one can gain access to himself. (80–81)

This is the problem of the writer, as well as of the reader. *The Locked Room* is a "locked room" for Auster himself: it contains the life of Auster, not only in the sense that it contains his words, but also in its biographical elements. Auster is inside and outside his text, fighting for the upper hand of Derrida's "violent hierarchy." Since the self in the text must die when the story ends, the rewriting of the detective story in *The New York Trilogy* is also a deferment of death for the author. The narrator says, however, that "stories without endings can do nothing but go on forever, and to be caught in one means that you must die before your part in it is played out" (63). The solution for Auster, then, is to posit no one self but many selves.

The narrator's logocentric quest for origin (for his search for Fanshawe is undertaken ostensibly to collect data for a biography of his friend) involves a deterministic single-minded approach to what he sees as a self-contained entity. Instead, he accumulates information and learns that Fanshawe has many lives.

> A life touches one life, which in turn touches another life, and
> very quickly the links are innumerable, beyond calculation....
> Faced with a million bits of random information, led down a
> million paths of false inquiry, I had to find the one path that
> would take me where I wanted to go. (131)

In Paris, where words become a "collection of sounds" without meaning, the narrator loses the ability to distinguish between signifiers and signifieds: "Thoughts stop where the world begins.... But the self is also in the world" (143). In place of stable meaning, he finds what Derrida calls "free-play." He becomes exhilarated by this freedom of language and his ability to name things at random. He usurps the role of the creator of logos and becomes mad with this power: he "names" a girl in a bar Fayaway and himself Herman Melville, recalling the naming of the narrator in *Moby-Dick* (a book the narrator's wife had given him). When the narrator meets a vaguely familiar young man, he decides that this person will be Fanshawe: "This man was Fanshawe because I said he was Fanshawe" (152). The narrator is unable to retain his naming power, however, for the "Fanshawe" claims that his name is Peter Stillman (153). When the two men fight, they reenact the battle for identity between Black and Blue in *Ghosts*. This time the battle also suggests two texts, or versions of the story, grappling for supremacy. In accordance with the oscillating dominance of the "violent hierarchy," the narrator loses the battle, getting pummeled by Stillman before blacking out.

In this same chapter, the narrator claims authorship of *The New York Trilogy* and reveals his own interpretation of the books: "These three stories are finally the same story, but each one represents a different stage in my awareness of what it is about. I don't claim to have solved any problems.... The story is not in the words; it's in the struggle" (149). This "author," who intrudes into his narrative to assert his intentions and conclusions, is also a self-undermining linguistic agent within the text. He offers a kind of closure to the puzzle of *The New York Trilogy* but undermines this solution by continuing the story in the following chapter.

The relationship between the narrator and Fanshawe is extremely complicated throughout *The Locked Room*. An examination of the "clues" invites us to infer that the narrator and Fanshawe are one and the same; if so, this person is the victim of the sort of quixotic conspiracy promoted by the writer Paul Auster in *City of Glass*. This solution is subverted in the last chapter of the story, in which the textual boundaries of the trilogy disintegrate: Fanshawe may also be Daniel Quinn, Peter Stillman, and Henry Dark, in accordance with the deconstructive denial of a single self.

When the narrator is summoned by Fanshawe, he goes to the locked room in Boston expecting to find a presence outside of himself, a correspondence between his thoughts and external reality. (Significantly, Fanshawe summons the narrator in a letter, implying the possibility of correspondence.) The locked room in which Fanshawe "exists" is located on Columbus Street in Boston—place names associated with the discovery of a new Eden and with the founding fathers of this country. Fanshawe is thus associated with paternal authority, but he denies both his name and his presence to the narrator: they communicate through the door of the locked room.

In an ironic subversion of theistic authority and logocentrism, Fanshawe reveals that he is going to kill himself: "I've proved the point to myself. There's no need to go on with it. I'm tired. I've had enough" (174). The narrator blacks out and wakes up to darkness—the fallen world— holding the red notebook left behind by Fanshawe. The authority of logos is completely deconstructed in this paternal message to the narrator:

> All the words were familiar to me, and yet they seemed to have been put together strangely, as though their final purpose was to cancel each other out.... Each sentence erased the sentence before it, each paragraph made the next paragraph impossible. It is odd, then, that the feeling that survives from this notebook is one of great lucidity. It is as if Fanshawe knew his final work had to subvert every expectation I had for it.... He had answered the question by asking another question, and therefore everything remained open, unfinished, to be started again. I lost my way after the first word, and from then on I could only grope ahead, faltering in the darkness, blinded by the book that had been written for me. (178–79)

The red notebook illustrates Derrida's writing "sous rature"—writing under erasure, a ceaseless undoing and preserving of meaning. Even these words are suspect, however, the narrator tells us, leading him to destroy the paternal message: "One by one, I tore the pages from the notebook, crumpled them in my hand, and dropped them into a trash bin on the platform. I came to the last page just as the train was pulling out" (179).

Throughout *The New York Trilogy*, Auster parodies elements and motifs of the Romance in order to bare the formulaic expectations associated with this genre. According to Northrop Frye, in *The Secular Scripture*, "most romances exhibit a cyclical movement of descent into a night world and a return to the idyllic world."[10] Ostensibly, the failure to ascend or return characterizes a failed quest. Ironically, Auster's protagonists, by continually descending into darker and darker worlds, are freed from the tyranny of their logos-motivated quests. In Frye's mythological universe, based upon Judeo-Christian polarities of Heaven and Hell, "themes of descent are connected with the establishing of order, authority, and hierarchy."[11] In *The New York Trilogy*, these concepts of power and control are repeatedly denied to each of the protagonists because they are logocentric ideals, the subjects of Auster's subversions. Quinn, Blue, and the narrator of *The Locked Room* are parodic romantic heroes. Like Don Quixote, they are all bewitched by books, especially books of a romantic nature: "Quinn had been a devoted reader of mystery novels. He knew that most of them were poorly written, that most could not stand up to even the vaguest sort of examination, but still, it was the form that appealed to him" (14); Blue is "a devoted reader of *True Detective* and tries never to miss a month" (16); the narrator of *The Locked Room* reads *Moby-Dick*, *Robinson Crusoe*, and other travel-oriented books (24, 54, 85, 91).

Similarly, the themes and conventions associated with descent in Romance—confused identities, twins, doubles, and mirror images—appear repeatedly in the trilogy: in *City of Glass*, Quinn starts to follow Stillman but sees another man whose face is "the exact twin of Stillman's" (90); Blue, in spying on Black, feels as though he were "looking into a mirror" (20); the narrator of *The Locked Room* reads one of Fanshawe's stories, which hinges on "the confused identities of two sets of twins" (30). According to Frye, "[A]t the lower levels the Narcissus or twin image darkens into a sinister doppelganger figure, the hero's shadow and portent of his own death or isolation."[12] Auster subverts this binary opposition characteristic of Romance by insisting upon a "both/and" oscillating movement: he denies romantic hierarchization by refusing to privilege permanently one term of an opposition over another. Blue is Black, for example, and also not Black.

The detective story is closely affiliated with the Romance (despite its "gritty" realism) through its solitary quest and in its emphasis on "reintegrating the existing order."[13] The detective in conventional fiction discovers "the truth," but in the deconstructive anti-detective novel, "the inanity of the discovery is brought to its climax in the nonsolution, which unmasks a tendency toward disorder and irrationality that has always been implicit within detective fiction."[14] The lack of any one single solution leaves the narrator, and implied author, of the trilogy free to choose any or none of the potential solutions available to him; he is free to begin another quest in a new world full of possibilities.

The New York Trilogy is in many respects a travel narrative—a semantic journey through fictional space and an ontological voyage for a paradise of pure presence. The implied author of the trilogy, and perhaps Auster himself, crosses the boundaries of fictional zones to rediscover himself through self-exploration. In romantic literature, the hero often returns to his native land; in *The New York Trilogy*, the return to origin is impossible. Each volume serves as a trace or recording of the travel, and each concludes with a reference to other travels: at the end of *City of Glass*, the narrator claims to have just returned from Africa (201); at the end of *Ghosts*, the narrator says he likes to think of "Blue booking passage on some ship and sailing to China" (96); at the end of *The Locked Room*, the narrator stands on the platform waiting for a train (179).

The travel theme of the trilogy is reinforced through references to fictional, nonfictional, and imaginary travel narratives: *Moby-Dick, A. Gordon Pym, Robinson Crusoe, Don Quixote*, Raleigh's *History of the World, The Journeys of Cabeza de Vaca*, Peter Freuchen's *Arctic Adventure*, Marco Polo's *Travels*, Fanshawe's *Neverland*, and many others. The protagonists of these books, like those of *The New York Trilogy*, are exiles, pilgrims, and explorers who claim unknown regions through language. The traveler's attempt to name things and to decipher "signs" is also the function of the ontological voyager, for adventures only "exist" in language—when they are told or written down. Since language is unstable and its meaning indeterminate, no place can be completely claimed or owned by its discoverer. The uncertainty of language also denies the self-exploring traveler access to an absolute origin, or self. As a travel narrative, *The New York Trilogy* is nomadic in nature: the semantic journey never ends but consists of a never-ending loop of arrivals and departures. The Chinese box structure of the trilogy offers vertical, as well as horizontal, travel. The references to historical texts allow travel through time as well as space, as does the trilogy's movement from present to past to present. This plurality of orientations results in endless shifting frames of references that continually deny any one locus, or "place," of meaning for the infinite traveler.

NOTES

1. Stefano Tani, *The Doomed Detective* (Carbondale: Southern Illinois UP, 1984).

2. Jacques Derrida, *Writing and Difference*, trans. Alan Bass (Chicago: U of Chicago P, 1978) 280.

3. Jacques Derrida, *Positions*, trans. Alan Bass (Chicago: U of Chicago P, 1981) 27.

4. Paul Auster, *City of Glass* (1985; New York: Penguin, 1987) 15–16. Subsequent references are to this edition.

5. Jacques Derrida, "Différance," *Speech and Phenomena and Other Essays on Husserl's Theory of Signs*, trans. David B. Allison (Evanston: Northwestern UP, 1973) 142–43.

6. Paul Auster, *Ghosts* (1986; New York: Penguin, 1987) 7, 9. Subsequent references are to this edition.

7. Jacques Derrida, *Of Grammatology*, trans. Gayatri Chakravorty Spivak (Baltimore: Johns Hopkins UP, 1976) 65.

8. Derrida, *Positions* 41.

9. Paul Auster, *The Locked Room* (1986; New York: Penguin, 1988) 64. Subsequent references are to this edition.

10. Northrop Frye, *The Secular Scripture: A Study of the Structure of Romance* (Cambridge: Harvard UP, 1976) 54.

11. Frye 182.

12. Frye 117.

13. Frye 138.

14. Tani 46.

STEVEN E. ALFORD

Chance in Contemporary Narrative: The Example of Paul Auster

> "If the world is not made up of texts, none can talk about it and, if it is made up of stories, one can only discuss it through them."
>
> —Mark Chénetier

INTRODUCTION

The concept of chance is a culturally pervasive phenomenon. In popular culture, singer/songwriters from Leonard Cohen to Sting compare love to a game of cards. During the Vietnam war, the American government determined the fates of 19-year-olds through a conscription lottery, and today states "solve" their financial problems by legislating a "stupid tax"— the lottery. Heisenberg demonstrated the role of chance in physics, undermining the assumed causal and deductive determinism of that discipline.[1] In the controversial arena of recovered memory, victims supposedly come to understand how their lives have been determined from a repressed traumatic memory of sexual abuse, but the return of this memory is caused by a chance encounter with a childhood friend, or the Proustian intersection of the individual with a smell, taste, or other sensory experience.

From *LIT: Literature Interpretation Theory* 11, no. 1 (July 2000). © 2000 by OPA (Overseas Publishers Association).

Hence, when one comes to the phenomenon of chance in narrative, the concept carries with it its own cultural charge. Authors, their narrators and characters reveal their assumptions about the universe through how they understand the operation of chance. To consider chance in narrative, then, is to uncover larger metaphysical and/or epistemological assumptions that can be examined and tested through argument.

In interviews, memoirs, and fiction, Paul Auster exhibits an ongoing concern with the phenomenon of chance. Yet Auster's texts offer examples of the operation of chance that seem to contradict one another. I will show that significant metaphysical and epistemological assumptions about the world are implicit in one's understanding of chance. Further, the seeming contradictions that Auster's texts exhibit result from overlooking the temporal structures of narratives (both autobiographical and fictional) and from assuming that there is a meaningful sense to the term "world" independent of our constitutive ascription of meaning to it.

In studying chance in Auster's work, I will record the instances of chance in Auster's narratives, distinguish between those in which Auster speaks in his own voice (in his nonfiction works) and those in his novels, in which narrators or characters make claims about chance. Among the nonfiction works are his memoir, *The Invention of Solitude* and the lengthy essay, "Hand to Mouth" as well as interviews, collected in *The Art of Hunger*. The fictional works examined include *The New York Trilogy*, *Moon Palace*, and *The Music of Chance*.

PAUL AUSTER ON CHANCE

Paul Auster is fascinated with chance. As he says in his interview with Larry McCaffery and Sinda Gregory, "Chance is a part of reality: we are continually shaped by the forces of coincidence, the unexpected occurs with almost numbing regularity in all our lives" (*Art* 269). Indeed, in many instances, what Auster means by chance is a surprising coincidence such as "Meeting three people named George on the same day. Or checking into a hotel and being given a room with the same number as your address at home" (270). Parts of Auster's Memoir, *The Invention of Solitude*, are introduced as "commentaries" on the nature of chance. Each of the four commentaries is presented as a set of two coincidental events.[2] He defines coincidence as "to fall on with; to occupy the same place in time or space" (*Invention* 162).[3] Here is an exemplary passage, from the first commentary:

During the war, M.'s father had hidden out from the Nazis for several months in a Paris *chambre de bonne*. Eventually, he managed to escape, made his way to America, and began a new life. Years passed, more than twenty years. M. had been born, had grown up, and was now going off to study in Paris. Once there, he spent several difficult weeks looking for a place to live. Just when he was about to give up in despair, he found a small *chambre de bonne*. Immediately upon moving in, he wrote a letter to his father to tell him the good news. A week or so later he received a reply. Your address, wrote M.'s father, that is the same building I hid out in during the war. He then went on to describe the details of the room. It turned out to be the same room his son had rented. (80)

As for his own life, Auster says, "Things like that happen to me all the time" (*Art* 270).

What does Auster make of the recurrence of coincidences in his life? He has given two different answers. In one interview he says, "Chance? Destiny? Or simple mathematics, an example of probability theory at work? It doesn't matter what you call it. Life is full of such events" (Art 270).[4] However, from his other writings, one can see that it matters very much to Auster what one calls it, because in understanding it one comes to a greater self-understanding.

At the core of Auster's cosmology is the contention that life is literally meaningless. His memoir records this personal reflection (couched in the third person):

At his bravest moments, he embraces meaninglessness as the first principle, and then he understands that his obligation is to see what is in front of him (even though it is also inside him) and to say what he sees. He is in his room on Varick Street. His life has no meaning. The book he is writing has no meaning. There is the world, and the things one encounters in the world, and to speak of them is to be in the world. (*Invention* 148–149)

In this passage, Auster embraces the world of Newton and Hobbes, of blind causal forces compelling atoms to ricochet about, creating the universe and ourselves as part of it. Our own impulse as humans is "to give it a meaning, to look beyond the bare fact of its existence, [...] to build an imaginary world inside the real world," but "he knows it would not stand" (*Invention* 148).

Not only are our fictional creations untrue, the very act of attempting to understand the world and ourselves is itself a fictional construct, one born of our timorous epistemological cowardice. The world and the lives we live in it are literally "meaningless"; meaningfulness, the act of signification, is for Auster a supplementary act on our part, lighting the fire of signification to keep away the frightening beast of chance.

The "brave" Auster sees the world as it is, meaningless. The "weak" Auster gives in to the impulse to paper over the world and its randomness with acts of understanding that obscure the world's fundamental meaninglessness. However, Auster does not maintain this view (that the world is "meaningless" and that our acts of understanding are supplemental) with any consistency. He sees another way of looking at the world as something that carries within it a "mystery." A coincidence is a brief flash of the mystery showing its ordinarily hidden face: "Reality [is] a Chinese box, an infinite series of containers within containers" (*Invention* 117). In his interview with Joseph Mallia, Auster says "the world is filled with strange events. Reality is a great deal more mysterious than we ever give it credit for" (*Art* 260).

What is the mystery? For Auster, the mystery lies in the conflict between our understanding of lived experience[5] as an unfolding temporal sequence and the ultimately "psychological" character of time: time is not a property of the "real" world, a world that, while it contains us, exists independently of both our intentions and attempts to understand it. In the real world there is no time; all events that apparently occur sequentially in fact coexist simultaneously. As he says in the Mallia interview, "The central question in the second part [of *The Invention of Solitude*] was memory. So in some sense everything that happens in it is simultaneous. But writing is sequential, it unfolds over time" (*Art* 259).

To sense that two events are coincidental depends on the ability to remember. Memory is important because it allows us to hold up two seemingly non-simultaneous, yet eerily linked events and see them in their atemporal connectedness. To remember is not to go back in time, but to bring the seemingly past event into its proper place in the "present."[6]

> Memory, then, is not so much as the past contained within us, but as proof of our life in the present. If a man is to be truly present among his surroundings, he must be thinking not of himself, but of what he sees. He must forget himself in order to be there. And from that forgetfulness arises the power of memory. It is a way of living one's life so that nothing is ever lost. (*Invention* 138)

Temporally, the only "time" that is truly real is the simultaneity of the "present," the knowledge of which is given to us through the agency of memory.

For Auster, the "chanceness" embedded in a coincidence is not a fantastic event, but a Borgesian Aleph that gives one a glimpse into the mysterious structure of the universe.[7] The key quality of a coincidence, any coincidence, is that in it two seemingly divergent events are in fact the same event, changing only the actors who engage unconsciously in the seeming repetition. Indeed, the repetition inherent in coincidence could be "read" either way, depending on one's point of view. To support this claim he quotes Leibniz:

> [...] every body experiences everything that goes on in the universe, so much so that he who sees everything might read in any body what is happening anywhere, and even what has happened or will happen. He would be able to observe in the present what is remote in both time and space [...]. A soul, however, can read in itself only what is directly represented in it; it is unable to unfold all at once all its folds; for these go on into infinity. (*Invention* 160–161)

Thinking, like walking, necessarily occurs in a sequence:

> if we were to try to make an image of this process in our minds, a network of paths begins to be drawn, as in the image of the human bloodstream (heart, arteries, veins, capillaries), or as in the image of a map (of city streets, for example, preferably a large city, or even of roads, as in the gas station maps of roads that stretch, bisect, and meander across a continent), so that what we are really doing when we walk through the city is thinking, and thinking in such a way that our thoughts compose a journey, and this journey is no more or less than the steps we have taken [...]. (*Invention* 122)

Hence, we need to think, to walk, and to trace a path, so that by reflecting on the path we have taken we might see inscribed in it its "meaning," that is, our place in the simultaneity of the universe.

Another example of Auster's insight into the deceptive temporality of the world occurs when he visits the elderly Madame Follain, daughter of the painter Maurice Denis, and sees her standing in front a portrait of her as a youth:

> For that one instant, he felt he had cut through the illusion of
> human time and had experienced it for what it was: no more than
> a blink of the eyes. He had seen an entire life standing before
> him, and it had been collapsed into that one instant. [...] Time
> makes us grow old, but we do not change. (*Invention* 145)

One might describe Auster's position as a Parmenidean vision that has been "psychologized" by introducing memory as the central cognitive capacity that awakens us to the illusion of time.[8]

 As even this casual contact with his ideas shows, philosophically, this position is vague and deeply problematic. Among the problems is, for example, the point that if the world's operation is a mystery and beyond our understanding, then how can we "understand" that time is an illusion? The only answer consistent with Auster's position would be that he possesses a type of gnosis or mystical insight that permits him to know something that he claims is outside knowledge, or that, since the world is essentially meaningless, the claim to have knowledge about the nature of the world is to claim that the false constructs of the imagination are true. Yet, given the tenor of his other comments, one could not responsibly make such an inference. If we live in the "world," how can we speak knowingly of this place where we live as the site of our situatedness to ourselves?

For Auster's notion of the essential "meaninglessness" of the world to work, we would have to first assume the truth of the naturalistic, scientific account of nature and equate that with the "real." In so doing, as noted, we would be reverting to a Hobbesian understanding of the world in which passions (Hobbes) or essentially fictive interpretations (Auster) are "added to" the world and taken as real by the unreflective. However, this account assumes a theory-neutral status of the scientific account of nature which few would accept.

Auster sees chance, as coincidence, manifesting itself in one of two ways: one, as an aspect of the meaningless randomness of our existence, and two, as an entrée into the mystery of the atemporal status of the world. What responsibility do these views impose on the author of fiction? Auster feels a moral responsibility to reflect this insight into the nature and function of coincidence in the plot structure of his novels.

> As a writer of novels, I feel morally obligated to incorporate such
> events into my books, to write about the world as I experience
> it—not as someone else tells me it's supposed to be. The
> unknown is rushing in on top of us at every moment. As I see it,

my job is to keep myself open to these collisions, to watch out for all these mysterious goings-on in the world. (*Art* 273)

Earlier in this interview, he speaks more specifically about the nature of a novelistic coincidence and how it should be represented:

> When I talk about coincidence, I'm not referring to a desire to manipulate. There's a good deal of that in bad eighteenth- and nineteenth-century fiction: mechanical plot devices, the urge to tie everything up, the happy endings in which everyone turns out to be related to everyone else. No, what I'm talking about is the presence of the unpredictable, the utterly bewildering nature of human experience. From one moment to the next, anything can happen. Our life-long certainties about the world can be demolished in a single second. In philosophical terms, I'm talking about the powers of contingency. Our lives don't really belong to us, you see—they belong to the world, and in spite of our efforts to make sense of it, the world is a place beyond our understanding. We brush up against these mysteries all the time. The result can be truly terrifying-but it can also be comical. (269)

Auster's claim that time is a psychological illusion and his seemingly gnostic insight into the world's timelessness involve a paradox. The deployment of chance in fictional narratives involves another paradox, one granted to us as part of the temporal structure of literary narration (which I will discuss below). Let us now seek to understand how these ideas about chance, coincidence, mystery and the world occur in his novels.

CHANCE IN AUSTER'S FICTION

In the fictional works we can assume that ideas about chance will manifest themselves in two ways. First, the author will insert "chance" events to accurately reflect the world of lived experience. Second, the narrator can take an intentional stance with respect to chance in his interpretation of the characters whose lives he purports to tell, or characters can make claims about chance which reveal their views of how chance operates. While they are obvious fictions, narrators' and characters' claims can be understood as arguments about the "real" world, the world of lived experience where we, as readers, assume them to "live" as part of our contract with the author.[9]

CHANCE AS COINCIDENCE REFLECTING LIVED EXPERIENCE

Most of Auster's fiction is structured around coincidental events, and is reflective of his claim that, in the interest of mirroring the operation of the world of lived experience in the world of fiction, the author's obligation is to structure the plot so that coincidental events move the action forward.[10] Auster's justly celebrated *The New York Trilogy* abounds in plot coincidences. In *City of Glass*, Peter Stillman's first name is that of Quinn's son (42). Henry Dark predicts that in 1960 the "new Babel would begin to grow up," the same year that Stillman locked up his son (59). Quinn sits down on the subway, only to find the woman next to him reading a work he had written under the name William Wilson (which, coincidentally, is also baseball player Mookie Wilson's real name) (64). When Quinn, as "Auster," tracks the people disembarking from a train, he discovers that, coincidentally, two people on the train look exactly like Stillman. The Pope decanonizes Christopher, the patron saint of travel, in the same year that people land on the moon (154). In *Ghosts*, Blue relates the story of the young man hiking in the Alps who discovers his dead, frozen father who had perished there years before. *Moon Palace* continues this interest in coincidence. Marco Stanley Fogg meets a man named Neil Armstrong in Boise, Idaho, and then watches astronaut Armstrong on television (32). Fogg ducks into a movie theater in New York (53), only to find it showing *Around the World in Eighty Days*, and recalls the first time he saw it eleven years ago with his Uncle Victor, who claimed that, in seeing it, Marco "confronted himself" on the screen (via the protagonist Phileas Fogg).[11] A series of chances propels Jim Nashe, the protagonist of *The Music of Chance*. Inheriting money,[12] meeting with "Jackpot" Pozzi, "one of those random, accidental encounters that seem to materialize out of thin air" (1), engaging in an affair with Fiona Wells, "like most of the things that happened to him that year, it came about purely by chance" (14)—these seemingly random events almost destroy him, as he and Pozzi are consigned to building an enormous wall in a meadow, an utterly senseless assignment whose origins lie in the impenetrable concatenation of a series of chance events.

CHANCE AS METAPHYSICAL SYNCHRONICITY

These examples of chance as coincidence function to reflect mimetically Auster's experience in the lived world. However, *Moon Palace* also features characters making claims about the metaphysical status of chance connections between two events. While the first type of chance event examined in *The New York Trilogy* and *Moon Palace* functions mimetically for the purposes of narrative verisimilitude, other instances of chance-as-coincidence involve characters making claims about the nature of the universe (the one the characters purportedly share with us, as noted above). In these instances, coincidence serves to reinforce Auster's claim that coincidence is an entrée into the mystery of the temporal simultaneity of the world of lived experience.

In the course of narrating his life story, Thomas Effing remarks repeatedly that there is no such thing as mere coincidence (104, 197). Fogg, finding an eerie connection between Tesla, Effing, and the message in a fortune cookie, remarks, "The synchronicity of these events seemed fraught with significance, but it was difficult for me to grasp precisely how. It was as though I could hear my destiny calling out to me, but each time I tried to listen to it, it turned out to be talking in a language I didn't understand" (233). Unfortunately, the sensation reminds him of another character, the paranoid lunatic Charlie Bacon, who sees in baseball scores hints about America's nuclear readiness. Fogg claims that coincidence "was too difficult a subject for me to handle, and in the end I put it to the side, telling myself that I would return to it at some later date. As chance would have it, I never did" (234).

COINCIDENCE AS METAPHYSICAL CORRESPONDENCE

For Fogg, more telling than the synchronicity he observes in the universe are what he calls correspondences, which belie the seeming randomness of the universe and our lives' pathways.

> Everything works out in the end, you see, everything connects. The nine circles. The nine planets. The nine innings. Our nine lives. Just think of it. The correspondences are infinite. (14)

Correspondences among seemingly unrelated events seem to reveal, if only obliquely, an order to the universe ordinarily hidden from us.[13] Following the sale of his Uncle Victor's books, Fogg is plunged into economic and material oblivion. At the same time, he feels he is on the verge of an important insight into the nature of things, thoughts that originally seemed to be "clusters of wild associations, a rambling circuit of reveries," but which he now understands as "significant" (32). Running through a series of seemingly unrelated coincidences, he says that

The more I opened myself up to these secret correspondences, the closer I felt to understanding some fundamental truth about the world. I was going mad perhaps, but I nevertheless felt a tremendous power surging through me, a gnostic joy that penetrated deep into the heart of things. (32)[14]

Although he later loses this sense of mystic insight, the feeling remains that correspondences—coincidences, chance connections among disparate elements of the world—are an entry point to revealing the world ordinarily shielded from us by our intrusive consciousness. The lesson to be learned is that "causality was no longer the hidden demiurge that ruled the universe. [...] Heraclitus had been rescued from his dung heap, and what he had to show us was the simplest of truths: reality was a yo-yo, change was the only constant" (62).

Both Fogg and Auster claim that coincidence, properly understood, gives one an insight into the nature of the world. Yet, an interesting divergence obtains here between the narrator Fogg's claim that change is the only constant, and author Auster's claim that correspondences established through an act of memory reveal that change is an illusion. I will forego discussion of this intriguing connection until later.

Chance as an Affirmation of the Universe's Meaninglessness

Claims that change is the only constant or that change is an illusion support the idea that the universe is in principle knowable. This epistemological optimism can reveal verities about the world independent of our participation in it, with the implication that we can order our lives properly in light of this knowledge. However, the narrators of *The New York Trilogy* doubt that this is the case.[15] In *The Locked Room* we are told that "In the end, each life is no more than the sum of contingent facts, a chronicle of chance intersections, of flukes, of random events that divulge nothing but their own lack of purpose" (256). Indeed, for this narrator,

In general, lives seem to veer abruptly from one thing to another, to jostle and bump, to squirm. A person heads in one direction, turns sharply in mid-course, stalls, drifts, starts up again. Nothing is ever known, and inevitably we come to a place quite different from the one we set out for. (297)

Hence, chance events are just that and nothing more; they reveal nothing to us except the meaninglessness of our existence. This is much like the "brave" Paul Auster, the one who wants to assert that life is indeed meaningless (see above, p. 3). The "weak" Auster would, given the understanding that the world is indeed meaningless, construct stories about it that would assuage his fear.

GAMES OF CHANCE AS REFLECTIONS OF THE UNIVERSE'S STRUCTURE

Perhaps the most well known of Auster's reflections on chance is found in his novel, *The Music of Chance*, which was made into a feature film. A recondite allegory, the novel features two central events, a poker game and the building of a wall. While the novel comments on chance as a random event in life,[16] as well as the idea of a "curious correspondence" (49), the central locus of chance is the individual wager. After receiving his inheritance, but before meeting Pozzi, Nashe goes on a "gambling jag" in Las Vegas (13) and later bets on horses in Saratoga (19). Following the assault on Pozzi and his subsequent (and suspect) trip to the hospital, Nashe plays pool with Floyd for money (212).

These bets are thematically secondary to the central poker game between Pozzi and Flower and Stone. Pozzi's loss in this game results in his assault and possible death, and Nashe's unexplained, but surely injurious fate following his nighttime car trip back from the bar with which the book ends. Had Pozzi won, he and Nashe would have left Flower and Stone's estate wealthy; having lost, they subjected themselves to months of backbreaking work, physical injury, and possible death.

Auster claims that he includes chance events in his narratives to better reflect the operation of the world of lived experience. Couldn't we reverse the direction and say that the world of lived experience can best be represented as the seemingly random events one experiences in a game of chance? Don't we all "take a chance" daily, invariably with insufficient information to properly predict the outcome of our action? Aren't getting married, moving to a new town, taking a job, and so forth all gambles, just like a card game?

Nicholas Rescher's book, *Luck*, argues succinctly against this analogy:

It makes no sense to assimilate personal fate to games of chance, because with games there is always antecedently a player to enter into participation, while with people there is no antecedent, identity-bereft individual who draws the lot at issue with a particular endowment. (31)

To put it another way, gambling involves adopting an intentional stance toward a state of affairs; a wager involves putting your own future condition (marital, financial, professional) "on the line." If "life" itself were a wager, it would require an individual who runs the universe adopting an intentional stance with respect to the possible future events in it that would in turn affect the individual's status. Even religious people would reject this claim, on one of two grounds: either the deity knows the future, in which case wagers lose their meaning, or the deity is understood to be all-powerful and thus unaffected by the events transpiring in the universe.

To repeat, while individuals adopt intentional stances as a consequence of interacting with the world, the world itself is not the consequence of anyone's intentional stance. Hence, from a cosmic point of view, "life" cannot be a "game."[17] Thus, we need to separate the two claims. On the one hand, we could say that our lives are ruled by chance, that chance is a name for cosmic randomness. On the other hand, we could say that taking chances is part of life. The first is a claim about the nature of the cosmos (made by the "brave" Auster); the latter is a truism. To link them through the metaphor of gambling is logically unsound.

CHANCE AND FATE

The evidence in *Moon Palace* presents an inconsistent view of fate and its relation to chance. In Fogg's discussion of the death of Cyrano de Bergerac, he asks, "Had one of his enemies murdered him, or was it simply a matter of chance, of blind fate pouring destruction down from the sky?" (38). Clearly, chance and fate are opposed terms, and to equate the two isn't conceptually appropriate. As Leland Monk says,

> Chance (from the Latin *cadere*, to fall) can mean a totally haphazard event (the fall of the dice) or an opportunity (your turn to throw the dice) or a lucky break (the fall of the dice that wins the game). Fate, on the other hand, refers to events that fall out in a manner predetermined by a higher power (the loaded dice of the gods). What seems like chance to us, throwing the dice, becomes a way of divining our fate (from the Latin *fatum*, the gods' sentence). (2)

For Fogg to say that chance and blind fate can be equated fails to acknowledge the very real difference between the two terms.

In another instance, Fogg ascribes Effing's paralyzing injury to cosmic retribution:

> [...] the purest kind of justice had been meted out; a harsh and anonymous blow had descended from the sky, and he had been crushed, arbitrarily and without mercy. There had been no time to defend himself or plead his case. Before he knew it had begun, the trial was over, the sentence had been handed down, and the judge had disappeared from the courtroom. (188)

Clearly, the cases of Cyrano and Effing are comparable (Cyrano's death, Effing's injury); yet Fogg makes two contradictory claims about the nature of the cosmos: fate is "blind" to Cyrano, while it functions as karmic retribution toward Effing. One can't have it both ways.

Auster's most celebrated work, *The New York Trilogy*, also concerns itself with fate. In the *Trilogy* we discover two different claims about fate that dovetail, in that one of them suggests the conditions of our epistemological orientation toward others while the other is a cosmological claim.

In *Ghosts*, Blue had "thought of himself as essentially free. [...] Now, after the incident with the masked man and the further obstacles that have ensued, Blue no longer knows what to think. It seems perfectly plausible to him that he is also being watched, observed by another in the same way that he has been observing Black. If that is the case, then he has never been free" (200). Later, during a Thoreauvian reverie, Blue imagines himself free of the tyranny of his job, "walking through the woods and swinging an axe over his shoulder." But, he realizes that, wherever he goes, Black will be there, too, shadowing him, and "there will never be any end to it. This is what the ancients call fate, and every hero must submit to it. There is no choice, and if there is anything to be done, it is only the one thing that leaves no choice" (222). Here we can note one of the principal thematic claims of *The New York Trilogy*, that we can have no knowledge of ourselves without the participation of an Other. (In Blue's case this inspires a Sartrean round of despair, followed by aggressive anger). Our desire for self-knowledge requires involvement with others. In Blue's case, he interprets this condition as a type of psychic tyranny over his dream of freedom. He calls that tyranny "fate."

Quinn, in *City of Glass*, ponders the telephone busy signal he received when calling Virginia Stillman, and wonders what to think of it. "It had been a sign," he decides, that "the fates" were preventing him from contacting her.

"Was 'fate' really the word he wanted to use," he wonders, "It was such a ponderous and old-fashioned choice. And yet, as he probed more deeply into it, he discovered that was precisely what he meant to say" (132).

However, still not pleased with the term, he reflects further.

> Fate in the sense of what was, of what happened to be. It was something like the word "it" in the phrase "it is raining" or "it is night." What that "it" referred to Quinn has never known. A generalized condition of things as they were, perhaps; the state of is-ness that was the ground on which the happenings of the world took place. He could not be any more definite than that. But perhaps he was not really searching for anything definite. (133)[18]

We might be able to link these various meanings of fate and the attendant concept of chance, if we understood the term "fate" as a word for the causal chain of significance that is inevitable in any act of understanding. The problem with the presentation of fate in these accounts is that they fail to understand the temporal character of what they call fate and displace the actions of fate into something they call the "world," instead of understanding fate as another word for causal linking in language. These two problems, temporality and assuming there is a "world" independent of our constitutive acts of signification, are features both of Auster's nonfiction and his fiction. To better understand what is at issue, let us now consider more generally time and the "world," and their relation to chance.

TIME AND ITS CONNECTION TO THE FATED, THE CAUSED, AND CHANCE

Speaking broadly, we can say that a chance event is an uncaused event, one that is a consequence neither of the whimsical act of a Greek god, the moralistic intervention of a Hebrew one, nor the play of a cosmologically omnipresent or divine fate. Fate might work impersonally, as do the Greek fates; cyclically, as does *Fortuna*; or morally, as does the variously understood force of karma. In turn, chance can be understood as just "what happens," the outcome of a series of probabilistically understood possibilities, or the (in principle) unpredictable outcome of an algorithm (as illustrated in information theory by Conway's game of Life).

Looking more closely at the relation between fate and chance, we could say that, in the modern world, understood retrospectively, the cause of an event is often called "fate." That is, retrospectively, fate is understood as a force that dovetails with our intentional acts. Kismet, for example, the romantic inevitability of two lovers being joined, can only be understood through an act of remembering the various seemingly (at the time) chance events that brought the two lovers together. Prospectively, fate can act when someone "takes a chance," whether that chance be taking a job, choosing a lover, or betting money on a horse. In that sense, "taking a chance" in many ways is simply making a choice in the ignorance of the possible consequences, and the consequence of the choice is better understood not as a "fated" event, but as a caused one. Making a bet in poker is taking a chance from the point of view of the bettor, but if one knew the order of cards in the deck, the bet would be not taking a chance at all; instead the bettor would understand the unfolding of the game as caused by the necessary relationship of the cards relative to the series of choices the players make, both in taking a card or holding, and betting. In more modern terms, we understand the consequences of our actions to be what information theorists call "sensitive dependence on initial conditions." Taking a chance in that sense once again means being ignorant of the combined elements that converge to cause a state of affairs. Fate in either of these senses doesn't mean the actions of a cosmological force, but the result of ignorance regarding the states of affairs that cause, and are consequences of, an intentional act. Fate, classically understood—in Greek tragedy or Hebrew theology or the actions of karma—functions as a moral force in the world. Causes—whether of the scientific or probabilistic form—merely describe or circumscribe an amoral property or relation between material objects.

Taking potential future and actual antecedent events relative to an intentional act into account implicitly assumes that chance and time are in some way related. An event is "chancy" relative to one's temporal and epistemological position with respect to it. One avenue into exploring the differences between chance in lived experience and chance in literature would be to examine the difference in temporal status between experiencing the sensory world and concretizing a text hermeneutically (understanding, of course, that in a sense reading is itself a sensory experience).

Both people and fictional characters respond to their respective sensory worlds within the temporal realms of past, present and future. However, readers are placed in a different position with respect to the act of understanding a fictional narrative. In the act of reading the reader is placed in two separate temporal worlds. First, sitting in the chair, following the narrative, the reader experiences a series of unfolding events which occur in the readerly present. The narrator tells us that the character disembarks from the train, picks up her suitcase, and moves into the railway terminal. However, there is a second temporal level to the event of reading, given that the story that is unfolding before us has already happened, *from the standpoint of the narrator*. What seems to be happening in a narrative time analogous to our own lived time has in fact been arranged by the narrator to happen in a particular sequence for particular narrative purposes. The unfolding events in fact occurred in the (narrator's) past, and are linked owing to their significance with respect to an event that the narrator finds important. After the character leaves the railway station, she will get into a taxi that will, ten minutes later, plunge over a precipice. The reader was ignorant of the accident, but the narrator wasn't—the temporal structuring of the tale is based on something that has already occurred and structured owing to its significance with respect to another event.[19]

Hence, narratives don't transpire in a single temporal sequence, but occur simultaneously in two temporal ways, the readerly present, and the narrative (i.e., remembered) past unfolding in the present as the narrator putatively "tells" the story. Unlike lived experience, which moves only forward, the seemingly prospective "moving forward" of the readerly present is, from the standpoint of the narrator, a retrospective examination of events, usually to understand their cause. (Other terms for these two elements in narrative are "story"—the events in their temporal sequence and "plot"—the events in their causal sequence). The reader makes concrete what *seems* to her to be a story, which is in fact a plot.

These remarks should help us understand how chance works in narrative. From the point of view of the story (the reader, or the narrator as he "lived" the experience prior to setting it down on paper), chance events do indeed "just happen"; they exist as unrelated and uncaused from the standpoint of the person who experiences them (life, as we are told, does not narrate). However, when chance events are understood retrospectively, a divide occurs between reader and narrator, based on the narrator's attaching significance to the events in the past and on what they brought to fruition in the narrator's experience. The death of the woman in the taxi (who we learn was the narrator's hated wife) enabled the narrator to marry his one true love. Hence, the "accident" of the plunge over the precipice is an accident as it *happens*, but becomes, through the narrator's attempt to understand his life, an element in the ordered chain of caused events which brought the narrator together with his one true love. The accident is *both* a chance event *and* a significant element in a causal chain responsible for bringing the two lovers together. The narrator (now) knows that the chance event is significant; the reader doesn't. Within the story, the narrator arranges the accident so it seems to the reader to have been accidental, but from the standpoint of the narrator's individual interests, it isn't an accident at all.

While this describes the condition of a fictional narrative, isn't this also the same condition we experience when we try to make sense of our lives through telling ourselves our individual stories? We exist in the (seemingly "random") present, yet our lived present only becomes *significant* as it is linked to past events through the agency of memory. Lived experience is indeed meaningless; it gains its meaning only through retrospection. The events of lived experience are "chancy"; what moves them from the realm of chance to becoming part of a causal chain is one's attaching the chance event, through an act of telling oneself one's story, to another, significant event. From the intentional perspective of the fictional narrator, *or the actual person*, chance events are simply those that fall outside the chain of significance established through the act of telling oneself one's story. The world may be random and "meaningless" as it is lived, but claiming to have access to such a world, outside of blind sensation, is an abstraction, since one of the criteria of "having an experience" is that it is meaningful; it occurs within the context of signification.

Hence, except insofar as they are placed there as such by the author for the purposes of verisimilitude, there are no chance events in fictional narrative. As narrator Jack Gladney said in Don DeLillo's *White Noise*, all plots move deathward—narratives, as narratives, free isolated events from their aleatory contingency in the narrative act of making sense of them. This freeing from contingency, seen from the standpoint of lived experience, is a loss of freedom. In our own nonfictional acts of autobiography, telling ourselves a story helps us understand ourselves, but in understanding it seems as if we are unfree, since actions we deem significant derive their significance from their connection within a determined causal chain. If we are unfree, then, seemingly there must be a "cause" for our actions, other than our own voluntary act of narrating the events in our lives. What agency could that possibly be? Fate, *Fortuna*, karma—forces we introduce into the stories we tell ourselves, which are in fact reifications of the conditions of narrativity itself.

This seems to be the paradox of our condition: in seeking to make sense of our life, to make our life a life, we engage in the free act of signification that seems to erase our freedom. Both chance events and acts of free will are reduced, in their own way, to a caused element in our respective stories. The paradox of chance in lived experience derives from our lack of ongoing awareness of our dual temporal orientation—the "forwardness" of lived sensory experience, the arena of random, chance events—and the atemporality of memory's act of joining past events with present events we deem significant. The paradox of chance in literature derives from its "as-if" character. With respect to the reader, strictly speaking there are no chance events. But as the reader "lives" the story forward, seeming chance events occur. Hence, chance events in literature are not "chancy" from the standpoint of the narrator, but are such from the standpoint of the reader, so long as the reader understands the narrative as a story and not a plot.

CONCLUSION

Throughout the course of this discussion, we have come across a series of seeming contradictions, both in Auster's view of the role of chance in lived experience, and his narrators' and characters' accounts of the operation of chance and its relation to what they call fate. To best understand these various claims, we should now see them not as contradictions, but rather as poles of a series of paradoxes that arise owing to the dual temporal structure of narrative.

Let's restate some of the claims we have examined in our discussion. Auster claims variously that life is meaningless (i.e., its events as experienced are random), and that insight into life's meaning (and time's illusory character) can be understood through analyzing the operation of memory (the "mystery" of life). Auster claims that time is an illusion (and therefore change doesn't occur), while Fogg, one of his characters—siding with Heraclitus—claims that change is constant (suggesting that temporal succession is all there is, with the attendant problems with respect to identity). Both Auster and his characters variously claim that life is in principle unknowable, and that it is knowable in that it is ruled by "fate." We can express some of these oppositions more clearly, if also more inelegantly, through a chart:

Change is an illusion.	Change is ongoing.
Life is meaningless.	Life is meaningful, though such meaning is "supplementary."
The events in life are random.	Life is a "mystery" whose operation can be revealed to us.
Life is ruled by chance.	Life is ruled by fate/causes outside ourselves.
The universe is unknowable.	The universe is knowable.

Given our discussion thus far, we can see that these views are not opposed, but rather result from privileging one of two differing temporal stances with respect to both lived experience and, respectively, the hermeneutical act of concretizing a text and telling ourselves the story of our lives (i.e., understanding our experience). Auster's random world is that of a life (or text) lived forward; it's one damn thing after another, with no seeming meaning. Meaning arises owing to an act of signification that ascribes acts as meaningful insofar as they are part of a causal chain linked to an event deemed significant. Chance events in life are events outside the narrative; in literature, there are no chance events, except insofar as they appear that way to the reader.

The origin of the seeming problem, both for Auster and his narrators and characters, is their collective assumption that the random, meaningless world is somehow available to us outside narrativity. As Mark Chenitier's epigraph to this essay suggests (echoing Wittgenstein), if there is something outside our capacity to talk about it, it's unavailable to us. Our error, and conceivably heartaches, begin when we constitute such a putative world outside language and then claim that it has certain qualities that create for us metaphysical problems. Whether this is Kant's noumenal world, science's world of blind causal forces, or Auster's random world, these are all posited abstractions that in fact exist as second order reifications beyond our originary constitution of the world through language. Chance, then, would be a word to describe elements of this, or another world outside of signification. Chance, in other words, signifies nothing.

NOTES

1. As Rescher says, "Step-by-step, modern science has been moving away from determinism and toward a doctrine of chance limited by law" (45).

2. See 80, 88, 134–35, 143–44. See also Auster, *Hand* 106.

3. Auster's definition seems to connect with the classical understanding of the term "chance": "*Tuchē* does not imply randomness or absence of causal connections. Its basic meaning is 'what just happens'; it is the element of human existence that humans do not control" (Nussbaum 89). "Although chance (*tyche*) is initially mentioned by the Greek philosopher Empedocles, it is first consistently thematized by the atomists Leucippus and Democritus in the fifth century B.C. But they considered chance only to deny its existence [owing to the deterministic quality of atoms' movement]. [...] According to the early atomists, when we designate or experience something as chance, we do so simply because we are ignorant of its determinant cause. [...] For Aristotle, the two forms of chance (*automaton* and *tychē*) both exist in our everyday experience, and are as real as other forms of causation.

They are alike in that they are both causes of effects that happen *incidentally*; they are different in that chance as *automaton* operates in the realm of *nature* ('both in the lower animals and in many inanimate objects') while the chance called *tyche* operates in the realm of *mind*. *Tyche* is experienced by agents capable of moral action and is predicated on deliberate inattention" (Monk 16–17). Compare as well with Kavanagh's etymology: "The English 'chance,' like the German *Zufall*, the Spanish *casualidad*, and the Italian *caso*, all, in terms of their roots either in the Germanic *Fall* or the Latin *cadere*, evoke the idea of 'what falls out,' 'what is coming down.' They leave undecided the question of whether the event in question is causally motivated or fortuitous" (6). Rescher offers this: "Throughout the Western philosophical tradition, chance (*tuch?*, *casus*, *Zufall*) has been defined as an accidental concurrence of independent eventuations, which, as such, are inherently unpredictable and exempt from any mode of lawful regularity" (225, n. 24). See also Monk's discussion (5).

4. The role of chance in culture, from ideas of destiny to those of probability, have been examined by, for example, Nussbaum, Daston, Kavanagh, Mitchell, Banerjee, Rescher, and Oriard. See also Monk 16–31, 79–82.

5. I will employ the infelicitous "lived experience" or "lived world" to denote our immediate sensory experience of the world, to avoid using the more problematic terms "real world" or "reality." Of course, after Derrida, even the assumption of the immediate presence of the sensory to consciousness is itself problematic.

6. Given Auster's metaphysical stance with respect to temporality, the "present" is a misnomer, since its meaning derives from the sequential elements of past, present and future, a relationship Auster denies.

7. See Borges, "The Aleph": "What my eyes beheld was simultaneous, but what I shall now write down will be successive, because language is successive" (26). For commentary, see Bell-Villada 219–229. Relevant here also is Borges' "Funes the Memorious," in which ironically (for us), the capacity to remember everything renders elements of memory not comparable, but unique "it bothered him that the dog at three fourteen (seen from the side) should have the same name as the dog at three fifteen (seen from the front)" (*Labyrinths* 65). For another connection between Borges and Auster, see Bray (85).

8. In this connection, see Borges, "A New Refutation of Time": "The denial of time involves two negations: the negation of the succession of the terms of a series, negation of the synchronism of the terms in the two different series. In fact, if each term is absolute, its relations are reduced to the consciousness that those relations exist" (*Labyrinths* 232).

9. For studies of chance in literature, as, for example, paired with the idea of *moera* in Greek tragedy, or the surrealist experiments with chance, see Bell, Biard, Madoff, Monk, Paulson, Porter, and Wilson. A related and fecund approach involves looking at how narratives handle causation, and the role of chance as the counterpoint to cause, as evidenced in Brian Richardson's fine book. See also the citations listed in his book (187, n. 3).

10. Referring to the "paradox" of chance in fictional narrative, Richardson notes, "its absence indicates a specious causalism that posits a seamless and unreal chain of cause and effect; its presence, however, invariably reveals authorial intervention, since chance in fiction is never a chance occurrence" (166).

11. For further examples in *Moon Palace* see 35, 104, 184, and 196. For the French view of *Moon Palace*, see the special issue of *Q/W/E/R/T/Y*, published in October 1996.

12. Instances of good and bad fortune figure as well in Auster's life and works. Auster himself inherited money following his father's sudden death. In *Moon Palace*, Fogg's mother gets hit by a bus, which results in a substantial financial settlement for the young Fogg. And what propels Nashe on his journey in *The Music of Chance* is a familial inheritance. The idea of one's "fortunes" being down one day and up the next has, of course, a long history in the west. "For Fortuna accordingly became a goddess with her own cult and numerous temples (one on the Tiber just outside the city). Early in the third century B.C., a colossal bronze statue of the goddess *Tychē* (Fortuna) as civic deity was erected in Antioch by Eutychides, a pupil of Lysippus. [...] Fortuna was deemed to be the firstborn daughter of Jupiter and a prime personage among the gods. [...] Yet another sector of the Roman iconography of luck relates to the wheel of fortune (*rota fortunae*), which became one of the most popular and widely diffused secular icons of the Middle Ages. It was commonly depicted as a great wheel on the order of a mill wheel, ridden by people, some on the way up, others on the way down, some 'on top of the world,' others 'hitting bottom'" (Rescher 9–11). See also Daston.

13. Compare to the comment of Tim Woods: "In the final analysis, chance or accident is regarded as an unknowable and impenetrable possibility of pattern, although always obscurely evading specific definition and tangible isolation" ("Music" 145). I don't think that chance evades *specific* definition, but in Auster's novels we are offered a series of definitions.

14. Compare this character's claim with Auster's comments on the "mystery," p. [x] above.

15. For an analysis of the narrators of *The New York Trilogy*, see Alford.

16. See 1, 14, and 20.

17. In his discussion of the transformation of the concept of fortune to that of chance in literary narrative, Richardson notes, "In medieval, Renaissance, and Restoration texts, fortune had generally been viewed in relation to individual desires and ambitions, and it invariably implies a larger, governing (though often obscure) supernatural design. Chance, on the contrary, is impersonal, arbitrary, and subject to statistical quantification, while its effects on human aspirations are random and incidental. Major metaphors of fortune are the wheel, the moon, the tides, and a fickle woman; the dominant trope of chance, whether couched in terms of dice, cards, or lotteries, typically comes from gambling. (It is perhaps no coincidence that speculation on joint-stock companies, an extremely proper and profitable form of gambling, emerges around the same time.)" (23–24).

18. See Sorapure's discussion, in which she claims that "Quinn here reconceives of fate in a way that displaces the belief in a controlling or omniscient authority and instead sees it as descriptive of a ground-level perspective, characterized in this instance by the detective's immersion in the world of the text rather than the author's position above or beyond it" (170). Compare as well with Heidegger's discussion of the "es gibt" in *Being and Time*, and the translator's commentary (255 n. 1).

19. Champigny has made a similar argument regarding probability in the detective genre.

Works Cited

Alford, Steven E. "Mirrors of Madness: Paul Auster's The New York Trilogy." *Critique* 37 (Fall 1995): 16–32.

Auster, Paul. *The Art of Hunger: Essays, Prefaces, Interviews.* Los Angeles: Sun & Moon P, 1992.

———. *Hand to Mouth.* New York: Henry Holt, 1997.

———. "Interview with Joseph Mallia." *The Art of Hunger: Essays, Prefaces, Interviews.* Los Angeles: Sun and Moon P, 1992. 256–68.

———. "Interview with Larry McCaffery and Sinda Gregory." *The Art of Hunger: Essays, Prefaces, Interviews.* Los Angeles: Sun and Moon P, 1992. 269–312.

———. *The Invention of Solitude.* 1982. New York: Penguin, 1988.

———. *Moon Palace.* New York: Viking, 1989.

———. *The Music of Chance.* New York: Viking, 1990.

———. *The New York Trilogy: City of Glass, Ghosts, The Locked Room.* 1985. New York: Penguin, 1986.

Banerjee, Amal. "The Triumph of Chance Over Necessity." *Journal of European Studies* 23 (September 1993): 315–24.

Bawer, Bruce. "Doubles and More Doubles." *The New Criterion* 7 (1989): 67–74.

Bell, David F. "'Ce Soir Àsamarcande': Baudrillard and Russet on Chance." *Chance Culture and the Literary Text.* Ed. Thomas M. Kavanagh. Ann Arbor: U Michigan P, 1994. 87–103.

Bell-Villada, Gene H. *Borges and His Fiction: A Guide to his Mind and Art.* Chapel Hill: U North Carolina P, 1981.

Bernstein, Stephen. "Auster's Sublime Closure: *The Locked Room.*" *Beyond the Red Notebook: Essays on Paul Auster.* Ed. Dennis Barone. Philadelphia: U Pennsylvania P, 1995. 88–106.

Biard, J. D. "Chance Encounters as a Novelistic Device." *Journal of European Studies* 18 (March 1988): 21–35.

Borges, Jorge Luis. "The Aleph." *The Aleph and Other Stories: 1933–1969.* New York: E. P. Dutton, 1970. 15–30.

———. *Labyrinths: Selected Stories and Other Writings.* New York: New Directions, 1964.

Bray, Paul. "The Currents of Fate and The Music of Chance." *Review of Contemporary Fiction* 14 (Spring 1994): 83–86.

Champigny, Robert. *What Will Have Happened: A Philosophical and Technical Essay on Mystery Stories.* 1977. Bloomington: Indiana UP, 1995.

Daston, Lorraine. "Fortuna and the Passions." *Chance Culture and the Literary Text.* Ed. Thomas M. Kavanagh. Ann Arbor: U Michigan P, 1994. 25–47.

De Los Santos, Oscar. "Auster vs. Chandler or: Cracking the Case of the Postmodern Mystery." *Connecticut Review* 16 (Spring 1994): 75–80.

Handler, Nina. *Drawn into the Circle of its Repetitions: Paul Auster's New York Trilogy.* Ed. Dal Salwak. San Bernardino, Calif.: Borgo P, 1996.

Heidegger, Martin. *Being and Time.* Trans. John Macquarrie & Edward Robinson. London: SCM Press, 1962.

Kavanagh, Thomas M. "Chance and Probability in the Enlightenment." *French Forum* 15 (January 1990): 5–24.

Kirkegaard, Peter. "Cities, Signs and Meaning in Walter Benjamin and Paul Auster, or: Never Sure of Any of it." *Orbis Litterarum* 48 (1993): 161–79.

Madoff, Mark. "Inside, Outside, and the Gothic Locked-Room Mystery." *Gothic Fictions: Prohibition/Transgression.* Ed. Kenneth W. Graham. Vol. No. 5. AMS Ars Poetica. New York: AMC P, 1989.

Mitchell, Giles, and L. Robert Stevens. "Darwin and the Heroic Conception of Chance." *The Midwest Quarterly* 23 (Spring 1982): 304–16.

Monk, Leland. *Standard Deviations: Chance and the Modern British Novel.* Stanford: Stanford UP, 1993.

Moss, Maria. "Demons at Play in Paul Auster's *The Music of Chance.*" *Amerikastudien.* Vol. 40.4. Munich: Wilhelm Fink Verlag, 1995. 695–708.

The Music of Chance. Dir. Philip Haas. MP Studio, 1993.

Nussbaum, Martha. *The Fragility of Goodness: Luck and Ethics in Greek Tragedy and Philosophy.* New York: Cambridge UP, 1986.

Oriard, Michael. *Sporting With the Gods: The Rhetoric of Play and Game in American Culture.* Cambridge: Cambridge UP, 1991.

Paulson, William. "Chance, Complexity, and Narrative Explanation." *Sub-Stance* 74 (1994): 5–21.

Porter, Theodore M. "Statistical Subjects." *Chance Culture and the Literary Text.* Ed. Thomas M. Kavanagh. Ann Arbor: U Michigan P 1994. 49–63.

Q/W/E/R/T/Y: Arts, Littératures & Civilisations du Monde Anglophone. Special Issue on *Moon Palace.* 6 (October 1996).

Rescher, Nicholas. *Luck: The Brilliant Randomness of Everyday Life.* New York: Farrar, Straus, Giroux, 1995.

Richardson, Brian. *Unlikely Stories: Causality and the Nature of Modern Narrative.* Newark: U of Delaware P, 1997.

Rosello, Mireille. "The Screener's Maps: Michel de Certeau's 'Wandersmaenner' and Paul Auster's Hypertextual Detective." *Hyper/Text/Theory.* Ed. George P. Landow. Baltimore: The Johns Hopkins UP, 1994. 121–58.

Sorapure, Madeleine. "The Detective and the Author: *City of Glass.*" *Beyond the Red Notebook: Essays on Paul Auster.* Ed. Dennis Barone. Philadelphia: U Pennsylvania P, 1995. 71–87.

Weisenburger, Steven. "Inside *Moon Palace.*" *Beyond the Red Notebook: Essays on Paul Auster.* Ed. Dennis Barone. Philadelphia: U Pennsylvania P, 1995. 128–42.

Wilson, R. Rawdon. *In Palamedes' Shadow: Explorations in Game, Play, and Narrative Theory.* Boston: Northeastern UP, 1990.

Woods, Tim. "'Looking for Signs in the Air': In the Country of Last Things." *Beyond the Red Notebook: Essays on Paul Auster.* Ed. Dennis Barone. Philadelphia: U Pennsylvania P, 1995. 107–128.

———. "*The Music of Chance*: Aleatorical (Dis)harmonies Within 'The City of the World.'" *Beyond the Red Notebook: Essays on Paul Auster.* Ed. Dennis Barone. Philadelphia: U Pennsylvania P, 1995. 143–61.

Wordsworth, Ann. "Chance in Other Words." *Sub-Stance* 12 (1990): 227–32.

TIM WOODS

"Looking for Signs in the Air": Urban Space and the Postmodern in In the Country of Last Things

"Space is for us an existential and cultural dominant." So concludes Fredric Jameson, having described postmodernism's dependence on a "supplement of spatiality" that results from its depletion of history and consequent exaggeration of the present (365). Indeed, recent years have seen an increasing interest in the politics of place, the cultural function of geography, and the reassertion of the importance of space in any cultural study. The territory of these arguments is marked out in diverse areas in the work of people like Michel Foucault, Gaston Bachelard, David Harvey, Edward Soja, Doreen Massey, Fredric Jameson, Pierre Bourdieu, and Michel de Certeau. However, the most significant development of this "spatial turn" in recent theory is Henri Lefebvre's *The Production of Space* (1991), in which he rigorously argues that space is the key component in the analysis of economic production. As a consequence, one can no longer practice a historical analysis without taking account of the politics of spatialization embedded within the production process. Geography, place, space, locale, location—such terms form one of the lexicons gaining ascendancy within cultural analysis.

Lefebvre explores the "production of space," maintaining that space is produced and reproduced, thus representing the site and outcome of social, political, and economic struggles. Arguing that new modes of production

From *Beyond the Red Notebook: Essays on Paul Auster*, edited by Dennis Barone. © 1995 by the University of Pennsylvania Press.

137

exist in concomitant relation to new conditions of space, Lefebvre deconstructs the illusions of the naturalness and transparency of space and erects a typology of spatialities. The postmodern novel's deliberate foregrounding of the discourses of the sensual and the analytic, of private memory and public representation, of personal "lived" experience and "official" public constructions, parallels this "new geography" by showing how spatial constructions are created and used as markers of human memory and of social values in a world of rapid flux and change.

Lefebvre's conception of space as something that is "felt" as much as "known" or analyzed, leads to the emergence of two sorts of space. One is the empirical rational space or place perceived as a void to be filled up. The other is what might be termed "affective space," a space that is charged with emotional and mythical meanings, community symbolism, and historical significances. Space does not have an autonomous, objectively separate existence from subjects. Rather, as Henri Lefebvre has argued in *The Production of Space*, space is *produced* by the material forms of production. Consequently, Lefebvre conceives of the city as "a space of differences." His crucial distinction lies between a social space constituted by the activity of everyday life and an abstract space laid down by the actions of the state and the economic institutions of capital. The reproduction of social relations of capitalism is therefore accomplished as a constant struggle between these different modes of reproducing space.

It is increasingly being noted that Paul Auster's fiction frequently touches upon the postmodern preoccupations of subjectivity, sexuality, sublimity, and silence. However, *In the Country of Last Things* foregrounds Auster's engagement with an additional postmodernist "S" word—spatiality. As the novel gradually overlays discourses about spatial control and control by space, the complex complicity of these apparently different concerns emerges. Much of Auster's fiction pivots on spatial loci, on the actions of individuals within locked rooms, isolated garrets, enclosed spaces, circumscribed areas, and the effects of closure and openness on human consciousness: how a change in society's modes of production changes social conceptions of space and how, in turn, space constructs, and is constructed by, individual consciousness. A good deal of Auster's "Book of Memory" in *The Invention of Solitude*, for example, meditates upon the effects of being cut off and isolated from the world by one's spatial circumstances, like the recurrent image of Jonah being trapped within the belly of a whale (for example, see *The Invention of Solitude*, 89, 99–100, 124–126, 131, 157–159, 162–164). *In the Country of Last Things* explores, in particular, the urban space in a putative apocalyptic future, and the manner in which it is occupied, inhabited, and experienced both phenomenologically and emotionally, by individuals and communities. Through the personal letter of the narrator-protagonist Anna Blume, reporting her bewildering and disorientating experiences in the city while searching for her lost brother, *In the Country of Last Things* constantly confronts one with the intersection of private and public spaces, as her urban experience allows public space to become the stage for private experiences, and private spaces to be unfolded onto public spaces.

David Harvey's discussion of space as a characteristic of post-modernism points out how Michel Foucault conceives of space as the site of social constriction and occasionally the site of processes of liberatory potential: "The body exists in space and must either submit to authority (through, for example, incarceration or surveillance in an organised space) or carve out particular spaces of resistance and freedom—'heterotopias'—from an otherwise repressive world" (213). Harvey goes on to describe how Michel de Certeau argues, contrary to the Foucauldian concept of a "technological system of a coherent and totalizing space," that this is substituted daily by a "'pedestrian rhetoric' of trajectories that have 'a mythical structure' understood as 'a story jerry-built out of elements taken from common sayings, an allusive and fragmentary story whose gaps mesh with the social practices it symbolises'" (214). De Certeau, like Auster, is not unconcerned with the way in which order is transmitted into a repressive technology, but rather seeks to excavate those surreptitious forms created by the marginal, dispersed, tactical, and makeshift creativity of groups or individuals already caught in the nets of "discipline." "Spaces" are more easily liberated than Foucault imagines. Paradoxically, the challenge to the domination of space becomes the invention of new spaces. Within the despotic social and political climate of the city, Anna Blume's letter demonstrates—as political resistors have continually shown during the twentieth century—that the most radical and expansive political gesture against the totalitarian attempt to dominate spatiality is the challenge provided by the creative and imaginative space of the human body. In this respect, Paul Auster's novel is a spatial cartography that explores the manner in which human history is subject to various structures and forms of power that traverse the body and the world, break it down, shape it, and rearrange it—yet always fail to conquer it.

Auster's essay concerning Charles Reznikoff's representation of the city, "The Decisive Moment," might be instructive here: "It seems no accident that most of Reznikoff's poems are rooted in the city. For only in the modern city can the one who sees remain unseen, take his stand in space and yet remain transparent" (*Art of Hunger* 39). Auster's novel, like Reznikoff's poetry, is engaged with the "strange and transitory beauties of the urban landscape" (40). Anna Blume's experience of coming to terms with an otherness, in exile in a foreign land, is exactly reminiscent of Auster's description of Reznikoff's work: "It is exile, and a way of coming to terms with exile that somehow, for better or worse, manages to leave the condition of exile intact. Reznikoff was not only an outsider by temperament, nurturing those aspects of himself that would tend to maintain his sense of isolation, he was also born into a state of *otherness*, and as a Jew, as the son of immigrant jews in America, whatever idea of community he had was always ethnic rather than national" (42). Anna Blume discovers herself to be a constant outsider, looking in on this life in the city, which she always appears to treat as a temporary nightmare until she can find leer brother. Perhaps not accidentally, Blume also crucially announces her Jewish identity during her meeting with the rabbi in the National Library. Displaced into the turmoil of the city, as someone who "had grown up in another place" (*In the Country of Last Things* 106), Anna Blume's ontological, epistemological, and ethnic positions coalesce in her Judaic roots. Amongst Auster's important extended reflections on Judaic roots and culture, is this quotation from Marina Tsvetaeva in *The Invention of Solitude*: "In this most Christian of worlds / All poets are Jews" (95). This persistent exiled consciousness of the writer and the Jew is reiterated by the rabbi, who impresses upon Blume a most "startling" comment: "Every Jew, he said, believes that he belongs to the last generation of Jews. We are always at the end, always standing on the brink of the last moment, and why should we expect things to be any different now?" (*Country* 112). Having lived as if she is the only person left in the world, Blume's meetings with the rabbi reestablish some glimmer of her former self-identity, as she gradually experiences the protective order of the patriarch:

> It was strange what had come over me in the presence of this man, but the more I talked to him, the more I sounded like a child. Perhaps he reminded me of how things had been when I was very young, back in the dark ages when I still believed in what fathers and teachers said to me. I can't say for sure, but the fact was that I felt on solid ground with him, and I knew that he was someone I could trust. (96)

Although the rabbi's allusions to persecutions of the Jewish population in the city echo less savory periods of European history, it is precisely the communal aspect of the rabbi and his disciples that steady Blume at this point of near collapse. The absent father is a persistent theme in Auster's writing, but here is a familiar, solid patriarchal foundation and ethnic security she never experienced in the ever-shifting social sands outside the library, where a sense of *communal* space is at best a vestige shored up by desperation, and at worst nonexistent.

Since we cannot live outside representations of space, and there is no clear dividing line between an authentic *place* and one that may have been constructed along the way, Anna Blume tends to be always negotiating various locales in the city, continuously working to make sense of and articulate both place and event. People are shown to be never simply fixed within a locale, but are active, space-producing *bricoleurs*. Living in complex, contradictory places, one differentiates the pull of events and places. We feel the pull of specific constructions of space or place, and in many ways, are involved in reproducing them on a daily basis; but we can nevertheless alter a vision of strict interpellation with the recognition that discourses are negotiated.

Michel de Certeau has written about the way in which the city is constituted by the "raw material" of "walkers, *Wandersmänner*, whose bodies follow the cursives and strokes of an urban 'text' they write without reading" (124). Auster's sense of the city is similar: many passages are given over to the patterns traced through the city by Blume's walks. Preeminently, walking assumes the imperative of self-preservation: "One step and then another step and then another: that is the golden rule" (*Country* 24). However, just as Reznikoff's poetry was built upon the fundamental experience of *walking* through a city, gauging the topographical and emotional by traversing the landscape on foot, so Anna Blume derives her intimate knowledge of the city from her perambulatory experiences: "The streets of the city are everywhere, and no two streets are the same. I put one foot in front of the other, and then the other foot in front of the first, and then hope I can do it again. Nothing more than that" (*Country* 2). Gradually Blume's journeys assume an epistemological importance, walking being analogous to traveling from one thought to another. Auster's texts constantly fold into one another, and in "The Book of Memory," Auster stresses his conception of the mind's "wanderings" as a walking through a city:

> just as one step will inevitably lead one to the next step, so it is
> that one thought inevitably follows from the previous thought ...
> and so on, and in this way, if we were to try to make an image of
> this process in our minds, a network of paths begins to be drawn,
> as in the image of the human bloodstream (heart, arteries, veins,

capillaries), or as in the image of a map (of city streets, for example, preferably a large city, or even of roads, as in the gas station maps of roads that stretch, bisect, and meander across a continent), so that what we are really doing when we walk through the city is thinking, and thinking in such a way that our thoughts compose a journey, and this journey is no more or less than the steps we have taken. (*The Invention of Solitude* 122)

Journeys are equivalent to mental movements, and walking becomes an actualization of cognition itself. In his poem "White Spaces" Auster seeks "to think of motion not merely as a function of the body but as an extension of the mind" (*Disappearances* 104). He continues on this subject of space, physical movement and mental thought:

I remain in the room in which I am writing this. I put one foot in front of the other. I put one word in front of the other, and for each step I take I add another word, as if for each word to be spoken there was another space to be crossed, a distance to be filled by my body as it moves through this space. It is a journey through space, even if I get nowhere, even if I end up in the same place I started. It is a journey through space, as if into many cities and out of them, as if across deserts, as if to the edge of some imaginary ocean, where each thought drowns in the relentless waves of the real. (107)

Within a single room, the writer can experience "the infinite possibilities of a limited space" (*The Invention of Solitude* 89). Words shape and extend mental and physical spaces. In Auster's novel, the spaces of the city, Blume's mind, and the textuality implode into a space of representation.

What emerges in the novel *In the Country of Last Things* is akin to Lefebvre's argument concerning the dialectical interaction between the space of representation and representational spaces. How is the relation between place and being to be understood? As separate spheres? As interdependencies? As shaped entirely by the forcefulness of the absolute ego? As shaped entirely by the materiality of place? Place as a specific demarcation of space is crucial to the establishment of social order. As Anna Blume gradually discovers, to challenge what that place might be is to challenge something fundamental in the social order.

The city is constantly described as being in a state of perpetual contingency, impermanence, ephemerality, and transience by Anna Blume:

"Slowly and steadily, the city seems to be consuming itself, even as it remains" (*Country* 21–22). When Blume first arrives, it is like "entering an invisible world, a place where only blind people lived" (18). There is no clear sense of how the city has arrived at such a state of decrepitude or collapse, why it is cordoned off, or why it is a no-go zone. It appears in an indefinite future and as an indefinite space, marked by the typicality of New York City and also the indeterminacy of all contemporary urban constructions.[1] It is merely a *space*, a condition in which the author explores, observes, and represents certain states of social behavior. As such a *zone*, it has similarities with Brian McHale's sense that postmodern fiction constructs spaces that allow for experiments, opening up new ontological existences "in a kind of between-worlds space—a zone" (*Postmodern Fiction* 43–58). The city is just such a place and nonplace, in which people are completely indifferent to reality, knowing no logic or negotiation or causality or contradiction, wholly given over as they are to the instinctual play of the desires and the search for survival: The novel's apocalyptic title suggests a world that is disappearing, and there is an incomprehensibility about this knowledge, seemingly lying beyond the limits of the imagination: "I don't expect you to understand. You have seen none of this, and even if you tried, you could not imagine it. A house is there one day, and the next day it is gone" (*Country* 1). The city's organic cycle is repeatedly perplexing and confusing:

> For nothing is really itself anymore. There are pieces of this and pieces of that, but none of it fits together.... At a certain point, things disintegrate into muck, or dust, or scraps, and what you have is something new, some particle or agglomeration of matter that cannot be identified. It is a clump, a mote, a fragment of the world that has no place: a cipher of it-ness. As an object hunter, you must rescue things before they reach this state of absolute decay.... Everything falls apart, but not every part of every thing, at least not at the same time. The job is to zero in on these little islands of intactness, to imagine them joined to other such islands, and those islands to still others, and thus to create new archipelagoes of matter. (35–36)

Life is a process of constructing order out of chaos, an idea that much preoccupies Stillman senior in *City of Glass* in *The New York Trilogy*, with his collection of oddments from the streets of Manhattan. Yet what interests Blume is that a change in one's material circumstances in life in turn alters the value accorded to refuse and rubbish. One person's waste is another person's treasure. In this constant cycle of decomposition and recomposition, the city is represented as a "metonymic site, a zone of spatial contiguity, interdependence, and circulation" (*Postmodern Fiction* 190). Garbage collectors need to look at the world in a new fashion, to think metonymically, where the part forms a new yet different whole. The destruction, collapse and resurrection of identity are crucial factors in the transience of the city, where this new metonymical arrangement causes alternative spatial arrangements to emerge.

Amidst this physical decay, the city inverts one's conventional ideas about life: "It turns your thoughts inside out. It makes you want to live, and at the same time it tries to take your life away from you. There is no escape from this. Either you do or you don't. And if you do, you can't be sure of doing it the next time. And if you don't, you never will again" (*Country* 2). Life in the city is one of black-and-white situations; yet paradoxically, as a result of this stark choice, subjectivity is put under severe pressure—agency is almost a defunct concept. The city is something that has to be carefully negotiated, since it seeks to invade one's very being. Isabel's advice to Blume at one point warns: "Never think about anything, she said. Just melt into the street and pretend that your body doesn't exist. No musings; no sadness or happiness; no anything but the street, all empty inside, concentrating only on the next step you are about to take" (57). In this chameleon-like eradication of any sense of physical, emotional, or mental self, the reader is constantly reminded about how physical space structures social consciousness and activity. "It would have taken a strong imagination to see what was really there, and if anything is in short supply in the city, it's imagination" (61). All people play roles: Isabel and Blume seek to "create the illusion that Ferdinand was a Leaper" (75); Boris Stepanovich invents varying "personal histories" for himself that "were part of an almost conscious plan to concoct a more pleasant world for himself—a world that could shift according to his whims, that was not subject to the same laws and bleak necessities that dragged down all the rest of us" (147); and Samuel Farr's reappearance to pose as a doctor and confessor figure at Woburn House also acts as a self-protective mechanism of distancing the quotidian misery of the city ("It's better not having to be myself... If I didn't have that other person to hide behind—the one who wears the white coat and sympathetic look on his face—I don't think I could stand it" [168]). Constantly acting for her own self-preservation, Blume is similarly forced to change her appearance, "to make feminine things about me less apparent" (60). In order to protect herself, she has to eradicate herself, to feign otherness, to feign masculinity: "It looked so ugly that I didn't recognize myself anymore. It was as though I had been turned into someone else. What's happened to me? I thought. Where am I?" (59-60). Desexed, Blume is also displaced. This alteration of her gender identity is a direct consequence of (and necessity in) her new social space in the city, as she seeks to blend in with her environment. Yet Blume's own contradictory conclusion is that one cannot completely identify oneself with the fabric of the city or afford to succumb to the habitual life of the city: "The essential thing is not to become inured. For habits are deadly" (6). Habit, as Beckett once wrote, is a great deadener, and here it is literally a killer: "Even if it is for the hundredth time, you must encounter each thing as if you have never known it before. No matter how many times, it must always be the first time. This is next to impossible, I realize, but it is an absolute rule" (6). One must constantly practice a "defamiliarization" of life's experiences, preventing oneself from becoming too accustomed to a routine or a familiar place, since this lulls one into a false sense of security.

The city raises phenomenological cognition to the absolute stakes of life and death: "Your eyes must be constantly open, looking up, looking down, looking ahead, looking behind, on watch for other bodies, on your guard against the unforeseeable" (5). Later, when Blume loses her cart, the drastic consequences that a loss of vigilance has upon livelihood are evident: "A moment or two when your attention flags, a single second when you forget to be vigilant, and then everything gets lost, all your work is suddenly wiped out" (82). Blume is obsessive about the problems concerning falling down, reiterating the warning on several occasions: "You must be careful.... Otherwise, you will stumble as you walk, and I need not enumerate the dangers of falling" (21). Consequently, Anna Blume subjects her environment of the city to microscopic scrutiny and finds herself rooted, inbuilt, and constructed by that place. The city is not geographically divorced from the self, but is rather constitutive of the self: geography, topography, and subjectivity are intricately interrelated.

Yet how is such a social space connected to language? Is it a precondition of language or merely a formulation of it? In *The Production of Space*, Lefebvre asks "[t]o what extent may a space be read or decoded? Such a produced space can be read and as such, implies a process of signification. And although there may be no general code of space, inherent to all languages or in language, there appear to have existed specific codes, established at specific historical periods and varying in their effects" (17). What Auster does is to work at the as-yet concealed relations between space and language. The city could be construed as a "logarithm" that contains the structure and texture of all individual urban experiences. The city space in Auster's work acts as both a scene of textual events and a text for individual interpretation. Gradually the city emerges as a text in which, in order to survive, "you must learn how to read the signs" (*Country* 6). Yet even this eternal vigilance is not an adequate and secure mode of existence, since "[b]it by bit, the city robs you of certainty. There can never be any fixed path, and you can survive only if nothing is necessary to you. Without warning, you must be able to change, to drop what you are doing, to reverse. In the end, there is nothing that is not the case" (6). The negation of Wittgenstein's famous phrase of positivist philosophy, from the *Tractatus Logico-Philosophicus*, suggests that the world is a set of unpredictable possibilities rather than a set of finite existents, and that the subject acts in a foundationless, uncertain, and constantly disruptive environment. Blume continues:

> In the city, the best approach is to believe only what your own eyes tell you. But not even that is unfallible. For few things are ever what they seem to be, especially here, with so much to absorb at every step, with so many things that defy understanding. Whatever you see has the potential to wound you, to make you less than you are, as if merely by seeing a thing some part of yourself were taken away from you. (18–19)

Even the phenomenal appearances of things are not reliable, as they defy cognitive apprehension and possess the potential to destroy one's integrity. In this tangled web of comprehension, the conventional Western metaphysical reliance upon the metaphor of sight for truth is undercut, and seeing is *not* believing. The result is that Blume feels that although she can only function as an observer, remaining detached and aloof rather than engaging with the city (where so much remains hidden, secretive, below the surface), this knowledge will always remain partial and inadequate: "There is no way to explain it. I can only record, I cannot pretend to understand.... The facts fly in the face of probability" (22). Any sense of totality of representation or comprehension is constantly undercut, as Blume recognizes that the selective nature of words and the artifice of boundaries prevents totalization: "I've been trying to fit everything in, trying to get to the end before it's too late, but I see now how badly I've deceived myself. Words do not allow such things. The closer you come to the end, the more there is to say. The end is only imaginary, a destination you invent to keep yourself going, but a point comes when you realize you will never get there" (183). Such contingency makes even daily weather predictions, for example, so vital if life is lived outside, resistant to any logical and precise interpretation or syntactic sense:

It would be one thing if the weather could be predicted with any degree of accuracy. Then one could make plans, know when to avoid the streets, prepare for changes in advance. But everything happens too fast here, the shifts are too abrupt, what is true one minute is no longer true the next. I have wasted much time looking for signs in the air.... But nothing has ever helped me. To correlate this with that, to make a connection between an afternoon cloud and an evening wind—such things lead only to madness. You spin around in the vortex of your calculations and then, just at the moment you are convinced it will rain, the sun goes on shining for an entire day. (25–26)

Looking for signs in the air is like building castles in the air—idle fancy, speculative, and groundless. In the maze-like experience of the city, the questions that are asked and the answers that are given appear inappropriate to each other, presenting a confusion of semantic and phenomenological horizons. The goal posts are constantly shifting, causing one to lose one's bearings. The space of the city is also persistently shifting, which in turn causes signs to become unstable:

In spite of what you would suppose, the facts are not reversible. Just because you are able to get in, that does not mean you will be able to get out. Entrances do not become exits, and there is nothing to guarantee that the door you walked through a moment ago will still be there when you turn around to look for it again. That is how it works in the city. Every time you think you know the answer to a question, you discover that the question makes no sense. (85)

Contrary to Wittgenstein's proposition in the *Tractatus* that "[t]he facts in logical space are the world" (5), what is apparently logical constantly turns out not to be the case. Like living inside a kaleidoscope, each turn of the head presents a different set of circumstances and perspectives: nothing remains the same.

Here is the full consciousness of the implications of modern totalitarianism. Totalitarianism appears to be the organization of the bewildered masses who react to their personal incomprehension, the manipulation of their economic weakness, and their spiritual insecurity. Life is organized in the state by accident or whim, such that Anna believes that "[o]ur lives are no more than the sum of manifold contingencies, and no matter how diverse they may be in their details, they all share an essential randomness in their design: this then that, and because of that, this" (*Country* 143–144). Consequently, reality itself is called into question; and thus the basis on which ideas might be verified are themselves unreliable. In the face of this, Auster explores the means by which individuals can challenge or resist such control in this nightmarish existence where received ontologies are disrupted. People develop modes of dealing with the horror, anxiety, and tension that confronts them on a daily basis. Anna Blume records the protocol for speaking about food and how it is necessary for "you to allow your mind to leap into the words coming from the mouths of the others. If the words can consume you, you will be able to forget your present hunger and enter what people call the 'arena of sustaining nimbus.' There are even those who say there is nutritional value in these food talks—given the proper concentration and an equal desire to believe in the words among those taking part" (10). Acutely conscious of the materiality of language, Blume constantly worries away at the issue of representation, and how one's environment shapes writing and narratives. As Isabel slowly dies in Blume's company, Blume reflects upon this interrelationship: "I tremble when I think how closely everything is connected. If Isabel had not lost her voice, none of these words would exist. Because she had no more words, these other words have come out of me. I want you to remember that. If not for Isabel, there would be nothing now. I never would have begun" (79). Narratives and their evocative power are crucial to these characters who are divorced and cut off from their collective pasts. Some use narratives to evoke the good times of previous days, recreating the city as it was: "All this belongs to the language of ghosts. There are many other possible kinds of talks in this language. Most of them begin when one person says to another: I wish. What they wish for might he anything at all, as long as it is something that cannot happen" (10). While Anna Blume confesses her one-time penchant for the power of stories in her childhood, she now recognizes that "the language of ghosts" erects false and nostalgic pictures and is misleading and harmful. Firmly practicing Brecht's dictum that one must not look back to the good old days, but face the bad new ones, Anna Blume refuses to be seduced into playing this narrative game: "Now I am all common sense and hard calculation. I don't want to be like the others. I see what their imaginings do to them, and I will not let it happen to me" (11). Her refusal is a protective mechanism, determinedly fending off the death that inevitably follows the erection of this metaphysical illusion of happiness and peace through narratives of longing (11).

In Auster's focus on Francis Ponge (*The Invention of Solitude* 137–138), Edmund Jabès (*Art of Hunger* 99–106), Louis Wolfson (*Art of Hunger*

26–34), and Paul Celan (*Art of Hunger* 82–94), he is clearly fascinated by their common interest in the complexities of reference, of the relationship between word and thing, and the manner in which they handle words "as if they had the density of objects .... a substantiality that enables them to become a part of the world" (*Art of Hunger* 89). This interest in the materiality of language finds significant expression in the novel. There is Otto Frick's linguistic difficulty, but for whom words "were physical objects, literal stones cluttering his mouth" (*Country* 133). His palindromic play with A-N-N-A and his own name, and his intimate grasp of language as a substance, which makes him "sensitive to the internal properties of words themselves: their sounds as divorced from their meanings, their symmetries and contradictions" (133), endows Frick with a peculiar although intangible strength. In "The Book of Memory" Auster suggests that such wordplay acts as a form of "magic," and concludes that playing with words is "not so much a search for truth as a search for the world as it happens in language" (*The Invention of Solitude* 159–162).

Similarly, Boris Stepanovich's wheelings and dealings on behalf of the Woburn House community is another example of how the world can be altered or felt differently through manipulating the material substance of language at work in referentiality. Owing to his conscious sense of "language as an instrument" (*Country* 146), Boris devises a rhetorical prowess in his speeches, "always looping back and forth between hard sounds and soft, allowing the words to rise and fall as they poured out in a dense, intricately fashioned barrage of syllables" (151). His ability to attach narratives to objects raises them to symbols of value in a market where there is little demand for precious antiques, since "from Boris Stepanovich, you were not just getting a vase, you were getting an entire world to go along with it" (151). With this clear sense of separation between signifier and signified in language, and the concomitant opportunity to control words for profitable ends, narratives and language are frequently described as something about which to be suspicious, since truth and history are quickly muddled: "I have since learned not to take the things I am told too seriously. It's not that people make a point of lying to you, it's just that where the past is concerned, the truth tends to get obscured rather quickly. Legends crop up within a matter of hours, tall tales circulate, and the facts are soon buried under a mountain of outlandish theories" (18). Facts cannot escape fictions, as Blume repeatedly struggles with language to express this inexpressible experience and place, and she constantly finds her narrative straying from a linear progression as it becomes dominated by the sheer existential need to get the information down:

> I know that I sometimes stray from the point, but unless I write down things as they occur to me, I feel I will lose them for good.... Each day brings the same struggle, the same blankness, the same desire to forget and then not to forget. When it begins, it is never anywhere but here, never anywhere but at this limit that the pencil begins to write. The story starts and stops, goes forward and then loses itself, and between each word, what silences, what words escape and vanish, never to be seen again. (38)

Blume's narrative is a series of broken recollections as literal blanknesses and gaps creep into the (non)progression of the events, and the temporal sequence slowly recedes in importance as the novel continues.

There are strong similarities between this novel and Auster's description and meditation upon what occurs in Knut Hamsun's *The Art of Hunger*: the wandering and hunger, maintaining oneself on the edge of death, and the strange effects of disembodiment that this produces within one's consciousness. Auster is particularly intrigued by the experience of living at the edge of one's physical and emotional endurance, of ridding oneself of the weight of the body, of freeing the mind from its corporeal shell, and the concomitant experience of a transcendent mental activity. He argues that in Hamsun's book, "(h)istorical time is obliterated in favor of inner duration. With only an arbitrary beginning and an arbitrary ending, the novel faithfully records all the vagaries of the narrator's mind, following each thought from its mysterious inception through all its meanderings, until it dissipates and the next thought begins. What happens is allowed to happen" (*Art of Hunger* 10). Anna Blume's mental vagaries are the course of *In the Country of Last Things*, and they are not controlled by anything other than the logic of thought and sensation. The erasure of history and information about the city is repeated over and over in Anna Blume's narrative:

> There is so much I want to tell you. Then I begin to say something, and I suddenly realize how little I understand. Facts and figures, I mean, precise information about how we live here in the city. That was going to be William's job. The newspaper sent him here to get the story, and every week there was going to be another report. Historical background, human interest articles, the whole business.... I have no idea how the city keeps itself going ... I can't give you the answers, and I have never met anyone who could. (28)

Her experience of the city occurs in a space without a history: her life is a spatial rather than temporal experience.

In the face of this, *In the Country of Last Things* can be read as a novel about making sense of the postmodern urban environment, a process described by Jameson in terms appropriated from Kevin Lynch as "cognitive mapping" (*Postmodernism, or the Cultural Logic of Late Capitalism* 51–51, 415–417). Blume's inability to overcome the urban alienation in the city overwhelms her, as she desperately tries to enact that process Jameson describes as "the practical reconquest of a sense of place and the construction or reconstruction of an articulated ensemble which can be retained in memory and which the individual subject can map and remap along the moments of mobile, alternative trajectories" (51). For Jameson, the inability to map the urban space is part of a larger problem, the inability to position oneself within the new decentralized communication networks of capitalism. Blume's attempts at such mapping are continually stymied, and her potential to act is consequently vitiated at every turn. Hence, memory becomes increasingly important to Blume, as she constantly finds herself reacting to the effects of mentally constructing the past. Linked as it is to the "language of ghosts," which constantly seduces one into a reconstructed nostalgic period of security and stability, memory as the Wordsworthian store of refreshing images collected and used to sustain one in the future, proves to be equally fallacious for Anna Blume. Instead, memory produces only a blur, since "things themselves passed too quickly.... It was always gone, even before I had it" (*Country* 88). The disappearance of things causes a selective forgetfulness in the general public which "creates difficulties, insuperable barriers against understanding" (*Country* 88). This disintegration of memory coincides with the destruction of language, and whole aspects of the past cease to exist:

> It is a slow but ineluctable process of erasure. Words tend to last a bit longer than things, but eventually they fade too, along with the pictures they once evoked. Entire categories of objects disappear ... words become only sounds, a random collection of glottals and fricatives, a storm of whirling phonemes ... As more and more of these foreign-sounding words crop up around you, conversations become rather strenuous. In effect, each person is speaking his own private language, and as the instances of shared understanding diminish, it becomes increasingly difficult to communicate with anyone. (89)

The gradual obsolescence of language and the entropy of reference causes isolation and the collapse of social interaction. The disappearance of the material realm destroys the realm of representation, and this in turn destroys collective understanding and comprehension. History is slowly erased as a consequence of the erasure of the material existence of objects. Any attempt to resurrect these "lost," "absent" objects or words becomes a form of social insurrection. As one character advises Blume when she asks about the availability of airplanes, "You could get into trouble for spreading that kind of nonsense. The government doesn't like it when people make up stories. It's bad for morale" (87). Hence, memory and history are ultimately part of an imaginative and representative space that is strictly controlled, surveyed, and supervised by the hegemonic power. Narratives, stories and fictions, are treated implicitly as lies and as anti-authoritarian, which need to be firmly edited or suppressed. Narratives are perceived to act as political levers that can pry open alternative spaces, gaps, niches in dominant ideologies. As such, an active "memory" becomes a potent political tool: remembering the past, narrating it, preserves alternative versions of the present circumstances. Blume constantly confronts mechanisms that seek to replace private spaces with public spaces, private narratives and representations with public versions. Yet all the while, she correspondingly finds public narratives and representations collapsing into solipsistic "private languages," which militates against any totalizing orders or ideologies.

Auster's "The Book of Memory" in *The Invention of Solitude* is in part a sustained meditation on the function and action of the architecture of memory. Auster constructs this metaphor of the shape of memory literally, as a defined space:

> Memory as a place, as a building, as a sequence of columns, cornices, porticoes. The body inside the mind, as if we were moving around in there, going from one place to the next, and the sound of our footsteps as we walk, moving from one place to the next. (82)

This passage contains several of the preoccupations of *In the Country of Last Things*—memory, place, walking, the relation of body to mind, texts as spaces. This matrix of ideas is further linked to history in his statement: "Memory: the space in which a thing happens for a second time" (*Invention of Solitude* 83). Memory is here conceived of as a space in which history repeats itself. For this reason, memory has the potential to be a crucial source of political resistance and autonomy. As Auster notes from his reading, Saint

Augustine has observed that memory is a part of the self that paradoxically lies outside the body (88–89); and as such, it functions as a part of the self that challenges the machinery of social control.

Desperate times require desperate remedies, and with the disappearance of a *raison d'être*, religious fervor seems to permeate the social fabric to its core, with the establishment of a variety of fanatical groups that institutionalize a *raison de mourir* as a ritualistic action. The narrative details several of these organizations, such as the "Runners," "Leapers," and members of "Assassination Clubs." Death is transformed into an aesthetic action, in which beauty and the "grand spectacle" dominate as ritualized forms of self-transcendence: "The Last Leap is something everyone can understand, and it corresponds to everyone's inner longings: to die in a flash, to obliterate yourself in one brief and glorious moment. I sometimes think that death is the one thing we have any feeling for. It is our art form, the only way we can express ourselves" (*Country* 13). With the premium placed upon leaving this miserable existence, even death enters into the market economy. Profits are reaped from Euthanasia Clinics, where one can buy one's death on a graded scale of luxury, and where the desire to lead the good life ironically becomes the prelude to death. Paradoxically, joining an Assassination Club where you pay to be killed at some unspecified time, as an alternative mode of death, seems to heighten life: "The effect of all this, it seems to me, is to make one more vigilant. Death is no longer an abstraction, but a real possibility that haunts each moment of life. Rather than submit passively to the inevitable, those marked for assassination tend to become more alert, more vigorous in their movements, more filled with a sense of life—as though transformed by some new understanding of things" (15). In an intriguing fashion, death, rather than functioning as a form of narrative closure, actually spices up the narrative and urges a new opening to life. Such a space of economic deprivation and daily hopelessness causes an inversion of "normal" human values, making the assassin a valuable social asset and death something one longs for, spending a great deal of money and effort upon, rather than seeking to avoid at all costs. Resulting from these sorts of inversions and paradoxes, Blume finds that a strange space emerges within the city, which one is unable to define and comprehend: a space that defies conventional actions; a space that incapacitates all habitual thought:

> Life as we know it has ended, and yet no one is able to grasp what has taken its place. Those of us who were brought up somewhere else, or who are old enough to remember a world different from this one, find it an enormous struggle just to keep up from one

day to the next. I am not talking only of hardships. Faced with the most ordinary occurrence, you no longer know how to act, and because you cannot act, you find yourself unable to think. The brain is in a muddle. All around you one change follows another, each day produces a new upheaval, the old assumptions are so much air and emptiness. That is the dilemma. On the one hand, to accomplish this seems to entail killing off all those things that once made you think of yourself as human. Do you see what I am trying to say? *In order to live, you must make yourself die.* (*Country* 20; italics mine)

The constant push and pull of death on life always tests Blume's sense of self. This sublimation of self occurs repeatedly, and at one crucial point combines a sense of loss felt in the absence of the freedom of sexual expression, and the intense power that emerges in Blume when she is on the verge of murdering Ferdinand, Isabel's crippled and taunting husband. Blume mentions the way in which her body is subjected to sexual pressures as much as physical dangers. During these moments of reflection, she is aware that her mind and body are subjected to "an ache inside you, a horrendous, clamoring ache, and unless you do something about it, there will never be an end to it" (62). In the chaos of her mind every night, she feels battered by her daily existence: "my brain would be in such turmoil, heaving up images of the day I had just spent, taunting me with a pandemonium of streets and bodies" (62). Her release from this is lonely masturbation, a "sad little game," making believe "as if there were two of me and we were in each other's arms" (62). Rather than providing comfort, this merely reinforces her sense of isolation and loneliness, and Ferdinand's "barrage of insinuations and ugly cracks" (63) only adds to her sense of personal degradation. On the night of Ferdinand's attempt at rape, however, sex and murder coalesce, the one acting as a substitute for the other. At the moment that Ferdinand assaults her, Blume places her fingers around his neck in feigned embrace:

Then I began to squeeze, and a sharp little gagging sound came out of his throat. In that first instant after I began to apply the pressure, I felt an immense happiness, a surging, uncontrollable sense of rapture. It was as though I had crossed some inner threshold, and all at once the world became different, a place of unimaginable simplicity. I shut my eyes, and then it began to feel as though I were flying through an enormous night of blackness and stars. As long as I held on to Ferdinand's throat, I was free. I was beyond the pull of the earth, beyond the night, beyond any thought of myself. (65)

"Killing him for the pure pleasure of it" (65), Blume realizes with horror and disgust the sheer power and incredible absence of self brought on by her action. The sexual *frisson* excited by the power to kill is made clear in the metaphors of loss of control, surge, and rapture. The climax is described as freedom, flight, purity, and a release of subjective consciousness from enchainment. The power of taking life becomes equivalent to releasing her own life from the daily torture of her miserable existence. Here is an instance where sexual desire and the desire to kill are linked in a clear bid for release from physical limitations, a concept well-glossed by the narrator in *The Locked Room*: "I had entered my own darkness, and it was there that I learned the one thing that is more terrible than anything else: that sexual desire can also be the desire to kill, that a moment comes when it is possible for a man to choose death over life" (108). Blume retreats from this realization and reasserts her integrity through her resistance to the bestial and immoral behavior inculcated in and exerted upon people by the social structures of the city's exigencies and pressures.

Auster frequently uses death as an image of release and of transcendence: "I suddenly felt I was dead, as dead as Ferdinand in his blue suit, as dead as the people who were burning into smoke at the edges of the city. I became calmer than I had been in a long time, almost happy in fact ... for several months after that I did not feel like myself anymore. I continued to live and breathe, to move from one place to another, but I could not escape the thought that I was dead, that nothing could ever bring me to life again" (*Country* 74–75). Auster has always been fascinated in his fiction with the experience of loneliness and isolation, of being detached from one's social environment, and the disembodied psychological effect this produces in the individual. This occurs most specifically in *City of Glass* where Stillman junior has suffered linguistic and mental dysfunction from isolation, and the detective-narrator Quinn ends up isolating himself to carry out his observations; in *Moon Palace*, where Marco Fogg finds himself living in isolated poverty in his apartment and then in Central Park, during which he tries "to separate myself from my body ... In order to rise above my circumstances, I had to convince myself that I was no longer real, and the result was that all reality began to waver for me. Things that were not there would suddenly appear before my eyes, then vanish" (29–30); and more forthrightly, in *The Invention of Solitude*, where Auster powerfully relates his emotional loneliness after his father's death, and the breakup of his marriage.

In the Country of Last Things widens the screen and amplifies these previously small episodes into the overriding narrative experience: the separation of an individual from conventional social intercourse and the effects that this deprivation and isolation have upon Anna Blume. Magnifying the most obscure and apparently paltry emotions, ideas, and feelings, the novel homes in on society's basic organization, observing the ways in which social structures change, the ways thoughts alter, and the change in social priorities and perspectives:

> Let everything fall away, and then let's see what there is. Perhaps that is the most interesting question of all: to see what happens when there is nothing, and whether or not we will survive that too.
>
> The consequences can be rather curious, and they often go against your expectations. Utter despair can exist side by side with the most dazzling invention; entropy and efflorescence merge. (29)

One is left with a clear description of social determination at work, and a clear demolition of any remnants of human essentialism.

The manner in which the city enforces the abolition of the self in order to survive is reminiscent of Marx's analysis of the workings of capitalism, where the demands of the system of commodity exchange impose a subtle eradication of subjectivity upon the individual consumer. With this metaphorical association, it is no surprise to find that this city is also a space of rampant individualistic competition. Pitting one against another in the outright cut-and-thrust of material acquisition rather than encouraging some form of communal development makes Victoria's project all the more unusual for its existence, despite the "swamp of contradictions" (142) that makes up the politics of welfare at Woburn House. Having been reduced to such abject poverty and desperation as scavengers, people are gullible and easily prey to confidence tricks: "Many of them are duped out of their money before the end of their first day. Some people pay for apartments that don't exist, others are lured into giving commissions for jobs that never materialize, still others lay out their savings to buy food that turns out to be painted cardboard" (7). The city works by a single ethical code—everything is a free-for-all: corruption, extortion, and racketeering function as the sole economic mechanisms. Government, as far as it functions, works best in the city when placed under some form of threat: "Dead bodies and shit—when it comes to removing health hazards, our administrators are positively Roman in their organization, a model of clear thinking and efficiency" (30).

However, as the fabric of society collapses and the social infrastructure disappears, society's ills and problems are exacerbated. Since people are constantly walking, footwear is vital. Blume outlines how people's efforts to keep dry are constantly foiled, and there are innumerable problems of ill health attendant upon this failure (23–24). The disrepair of sidewalks causes additional problems for people wishing to keep themselves dry and their vital shoes in decent condition (25). With predictions about the weather being so crucial to daily life, it comes as no surprise that there are fanatical organizations of belief about this aspect of existence as well. Blume tells us about the Smilers, a sect that believes they can control the weather by personal feeling; and the Crawlers, who feel that the weather will only improve if we abase ourselves beneath the sky. In an imaginative representation, Auster demonstrates how social conditions determine the superstructural beliefs in a society.

Yet the novel goes on to demonstrate how dominant and hegemonic definitions of social space (and time) are perpetually under challenge and always open to modification. In this respect, *In the Country of Last Things* explores the interface between society and the social construction of time and space. The location of place becomes inextricably linked with its position within time: the exploration of situation is also an exploration of temporality. Location is understood as dependent on history or chronology, insofar as the classification of experience is indivisible from what came before and what knowledges were previously sanctioned. This exploration of place and time also embraces the exploration of what constitutes a subject, or how place and temporality constitute subjectivity. As we have seen, ontological interrogations persistently shape *In the Country of Last Things* as Auster reconfigures the relationship between spatial and temporal categories. The notion of subjective identity shifts throughout the text, oscillating between a fairly fixed and locatable entity and a much more fluid and slippery sense of subjectivity. Anna Blume's voice is shaped by her entangled relations with her "lived experience" and the dictates of the boundaries, placements, divisions, and lines of the city's abstract space. This intersection of spaces results in large measure from the cut-and-thrust competition in the marketplace of the city, since it is the market that is especially capable of mediating private desire and public activity.

What finally emerges from Auster's *In the Country of Last Things* is how fragmentation, ruptures, and discontinuities, far from being construed as liabilities and weaknesses, can he transformed into political strengths and opportunities for social resistance. Consequently, this network of pedestrian trajectories and "perambulatory processes" produces an "errancy that multiplies and assembles the city [as] a vast social experience in site deprivation," a series of intersections and interweavings in which "a universe of places haunted by a non-site or by dreamed sites" emerges (de Certeau, "Practices of Space," 139). Place and displacement are bound together, and de Certeau's "insertion strategies" allow for this dialectical movement.

Place, and what escapes articulation and emplacement, become the principal focus. Auster is concerned with unsanctioned histories, those not directly oppressed but occluded. He works between and among endorsed categories of knowledge, and in so doing, he jostles the sequencing of location. Instead of presenting direct causal links or chains for Blume's narratives, the emphasis is placed on establishing loose sets of relations, capillary actions and movements, spilling out among and between different fields. Consequently, Auster is not interested in distancing himself from his locale in order to study it: universalizing the local is perceived as an obscurantist and dangerous thing. Rather than collapsing the local, he opens it up. He looks at the way the local has been constructed, what event is being reproduced in what place and how Blume's subjective experience of the local is circumscribed by the processes of location. The novel is a series of cognitive exercises, attempting to investigate the ongoing production of the world, its structural apparatuses, and how these function to shape one's perception of the world. In this manner, Auster's exploration of place is also a description of the epistemological maneuvers whereby categories of knowledge are established and fixed. Knowledge does not arise in direct correlation to the abolition of the subject's specificity. On the contrary, *In the Country of Last Things* demonstrates that knowledge is deeply complicit with the location of the subject, the "geography of the articulation," the space of the production of discourse.

NOTE

1. Auster has stated that he had a firm sense of historical realities when writing the novel, carrying around in his head the phrase "'Anna Blume walks through the twentieth century'" when writing (3116). See "Interview with Larry McCaffery and Sinda Gregory," in *The Art of Hunger* (269–312).

Works Cited

Auster, Paul. *The Art of Hunger: Essays, Prefaces, Interviews.* Los Angeles: Sun & Moon Press, 1992.

———. *City of Glass.* Los Angeles: Sun & Moon Press, 1985.

———. *Disappearances: Selected Poems.* Woodstock, N.Y.: The Overlook Press, 1988.

———. *In the Country of Last Things.* New York: Viking, 1987.

———. "Interview with Larry McCaffery and Sinda Gregory." In *The Art of Hunger: Essays, Prefaces, Interviews.* Los Angeles: Sun & Moon Press, 1992. Pp. 269–312.

———. *The Invention of Solitude.* New York: Penguin, 1988.

———. *The Locked Room.* Los Angeles: Sun & Moon Press, 1986.

———. *Moon Palace.* New York: Viking, 1989.

de Certeau, Michel. "Practices of Space." In M. Blonsky, ed., *On Signs: A Semiotics Header.* Oxford: Blackwell, 1985. Pp. 122–145.

Harvey, David. *The Conditions of Postmodernity.* Oxford: Blackwell, 1989.

Jameson, Fredric. *Postmodernism, or the Cultural Logic of Late Capitalism.* London: Verso, 1991.

Lefebvre, Henri. *The Production of Space.* Trans. Donald Nicholson-Smith. Oxford: Blackwell, 1991. (Trans. of *La Production de l'espace.* France: Anthropos, 1974.)

McHale, Brian. *Constructing Postmodernism.* London and New York: Routledge, 1992.

———. *Postmodern Fiction.* Basingstoke: Macmillan, 1987.

Wittgenstein, Ludwig. *Tractatus Logico-Philosophicus.* Trans. D. F. Pears and B. F. McGuinness. London: Routledge and Kegan Paul, 1961.

'The End Is Only Imaginary'

O ne prepares, when picking up a novel that promises to be postapocalyptic, to change his critical kit bag. One prepares to find moral guidance and instructions for living in novels of the next world, in a way we've learned it is sophisticated not to find them in novels of this world. The assumption is that whatever horror is contained in the next world may, if we buy the prophecy and the route from here to there, serve to change our current imprudent behavior and steer this unhappy world away from the unhappier one the novelist warns us is ahead. The opening pages of Paul Auster's "In the Country of Last Things" confirm that "last things" denotes an end-of-the-world-as-we-know-it, and one gets ready for those warnings and prophetic detour signs, and then stops. There is entirely too much in these pages about the world as we know it.

A sect of folk in this book is called the Runners: "You set out with your companions on the morning of the appointed day and run until you have escaped your body, running and screaming until you have flown out of yourself. Eventually, your soul wriggles free, your body drops to the ground, and you are dead." This is no bizarre scene to anyone who has watched the lugubrious Iron Man Triathlon on television. And there are instructions for living here, but they are not new or moral: "When you walk through the streets ... you must remember to take only one step at a time.... Your eyes

From *New York Times Book Review* (May 17, 1987). © 1987 by Padgett Powell.

must be constantly open, looking up, looking down, looking ahead, looking behind, on the watch for other bodies, on your guard against the unforeseeable. To collide with someone can be fatal." That is exactly the way Greenwich Village friends instruct this provincial to walk in New York.

The setting, though unnamed, may without dislocation be thought of as New York, and the economy depicted may be termed late service. An industrialist's true nightmare: there are no current manufacturers, and most folk are involved in one form of rude salvage of the broken remnants of "last things." The services are primarily the reclamation of the things and the government collection, for fuel, of corpses and feces. The landscape is a rubble-intense evocation of what could already be parts of the Bronx if buildings there were actually allowed to fall down and remain. The monetary unit is a "glot," and the government—what there is of it—changes hands rapidly. Along with body and waste collection, its main goal is distributing misinformation.

In all, the world is reminiscent of the Great Depression, carried to about, say, the third power, and it is inhabited, mostly, by a race of bag people. One Anna Blume comes into this "grim" (one of her favorite words) scene looking for her brother, William, who, on journalistic assignment from an uncollapsed world to the east (we may assume it is the Old World—and the fallen one the New), has disappeared. The novel is Anna's letter home to an old friend from childhood.

Into this letter, this chronicle of unrelenting travail for Anna Blume, Mr. Auster, author of the highbrow mysteries of "The New York Trilogy," proceeds at a trilogist's pace and with a series of high-novel dares. During an introductory anatomy of the bag world, a summary of how Anna comes to be looking for William and of the horrors confronting her—the very building William was said to be in is gone—we get no real, live characters on stage other than the narrator herself. When we do get some, on page 40 or so, they are doozies: the quintessence of bag people, precisely the denizens we might lazily expect following Anna's anatomy of her bag world. Moreover, they are Isabel and Ferdinand—Ferdinand carves tiny ships that go into bottles, a "lilliputian fleet of sailing ships and schooners," and certain historic and mythic contours are set up. Anna Blume is become a latter-day Columbus in a world anything but New.

Ferdinand just happens to be reminiscent of Louis-Ferdinand Celine as well. "'The smaller the better,'" he says to Anna one night, "bragging about his accomplishments as an artist. 'Some day I'll make a ship so small that no one can see it.... They'll write a book about me, I'll be so famous. Then you'll see what's what, my vicious little slut.'" Anna concludes, "One non sequitur after another, rushing out of him like some poison that had accumulated in his blood." That he inhabits the very kind of world Celine seemed to prophesy is not lost on us.

These are daring touches, and they let us drop all notion of having to suffer a didactic, finger-wagging account of how we ruined ourselves. Not Mr. Auster's game at all. What did happen? "Collapse" is the entire explanation offered—late in the book—again, the worst word conceivable for the free-enterprise believer, yet nowhere is there a suggestion that a socialist order has prevailed. As if to further not let us worry on this score, Mr. Auster keeps on offering novelistic dares.

He will try to surprise with the obvious, and he will advance the story with the madly (but somehow not maddeningly) coincidental. The boldness of these maneuvers—rather like the big lie—allows them to work. After searching for months for one Samuel Farr, who assumed her brother's journalistic post, Anna, fleeing riot police, runs "into a door that opened" before her. In this anonymous building, on the ninth (top) floor, she finds Sam Farr, falls in love with him, marries him, conceives (not done anymore, we are told); then, attempting to escape some men who would put her on a meat hook and freeze her, she jumps out of another building, aborts, convalesces, takes a job admitting convalescents (more or less) to the hospital of her recovery and, one day, interviews for admission someone strangely familiar to her: Samuel Farr, presumed dead in a fire that razed the library in which they lived at about the time Anna was diving out the window to avoid the meat hook boys. These are heavy chords that Mr. Auster gets away with playing because they are not, one feels, the main music; in fact, some of the large action here may satirize narrative action itself.

The main music, the game perhaps, is linguistic, even though Anna Blume is a most regular, most unexperimental, most conventionally "elegant" writer. Upon disposing of Ferdinand, who somewhat mysteriously dies: "We had to create the illusion that Ferdinand was a Leaper.... The dead Ferdinand was standing between us, wobbling like some giant windup toy—hair blowing in the wind, pants sliding down his hips, and that startled, horrified expression still on his face. As we walked him toward the corner of the roof, his knees kept buckling and dragging, and by the time we got there both his shoes had fallen off." She notes early that as objects disappear, the language used to identify them soon follows. Anna confronts a grimmer and grimmer degeneration each day and yet tries to generate more words from it. From nothing, something: she is the last manufacturer in the New World; she is, again, a Columbus, sending back not what she wanted but something to show for it all.

Mr. Auster seems most interested in this problem of confronting a limited thing with talk that shall not be, or cannot be, limited: "I've been trying to fit everything in, trying to get to the end before it's too late, but I see now how badly I've deceived myself. Words do not allow such things. The closer you come to the end, the more there is to say. The end is only imaginary, a destination you invent to keep yourself going, but a point comes when you realize you will never get there. You might have to stop, but that is only because you have run out of time. You stop, but that does not mean you have come to the end. The words get smaller and smaller, so small that perhaps they are not even legible anymore. It makes me think of Ferdinand and his boats, his lilliputian fleet of sailing ships and schooners." It is an asymptotic approach of expression to the nothing it finally defines, an infinite series of effables toward the ineffable. It is not simply objects that are disappearing. Human things are on the wane too. Mr. Auster offers Anna nothing in the way of hope and wants her to make a generous, human account of it anyway. In light of this aim, if indeed it is Mr. Auster's, it is telling that (Louis–) Ferdinand is bumped off early, and that Anna, facing a world ever bleaker than Celine's, remains resilient, plucky, apologetic for uncivilized behavior necessary to survive, and hopeful yet. She promises to write more of her continuing search for William. If in the beginning there was only the Word, she wants to say that in the end It will still be.

KATHARINE WASHBURN

A Book at the End of the World:
Paul Auster's In the Country of Last Things

T ransparent, straightforward as speech, and almost entirely innocent of
the formal conundrums and cross-referenced allusions for which his *New
York Trilogy* is noted, Paul Auster's *In the Country of Last Things* would appear
at first glance to take a sharp turn in a new literary direction. Auster's novel,
like the long visionary epistle that ends Doris Lessing's *The Four-Gated City*,
is written in the shape of a document cast into the void, mailed to some sort
of dead letter zone at the end of the world. This, too, is a fictional account
of an apocalypse, but where Lessing's Martha Quest is prolix, doctrinaire,
and relentlessly literal, the voice of Anna Blume maintains through 182 pages
the discipline of a rare sanity contemplating extreme derangement,
observing, reporting, and never escaping into the ease of the oracular or the
comfort of the grand historical explanation.

A young woman has sailed across the ocean, leaving one continent,
where civilization is evidently still intact, for another in a terminal stage of
collapse and ruin. Although the text makes no such proposal, we are tempted
to substitute the maps of first Europe, then America to chart her voyage. In
search of her missing brother, William, Anna discovers she will require all
her wits to survive in the rubble of a city governed by assassins, profiteers,
and thugs. Years later she writes in a blue notebook of the failure of her quest
and describes the history of her wanderings to an unnamed person, some old

From *The Review of Contemporary Fiction*, 14, no. 1 (Spring 1994). © 1994 by The Review of
Contemporary Fiction.

lover, old friend, or even her former self, still safe in the civility and reason of an older order on the other side of the sea. Anna's lost brother was sent across the same ocean on a journalistic mission, to report what he found in a city where all social and material structures have sunk into that debris which is the central image of this book. His reports soon cease, and it is one of the small ironies Auster folds into his story that it is Anna, in fact, who will send the last dispatch from a universe of "last things."

What Anna finds in a country whose darkened shoreline warns her at her approach of a disaster beyond words—Hawthorne's "City of Destruction" provides the novel's epigraph—is a nightmare place where no children are born, a *univers concentrationnaire* whose inmates toil at the collection of garbage and corpses, where mayhem has replaced the rule of law, where nothing, save for a solitary madman's construction of a miniature fleet confined in glass bottles, is manufactured. Its beggared inhabitants scrabble in the ruins for the shards of material goods, the "last things" which give them their final employment in a brutal, half-criminalized salvaging and recycling operation. There is an official currency, measured in "glots," but Auster, who wears his wide reading lightly, is no doubt playing with a Dickensian trope for the breakdown of industrial society by conjuring up a swarm of Golden Dustmen trafficking in the night soil and corpses which convert into the fuel which still runs the engine of this debased and exhausted world.

Anna Blume never finds her brother and spends her days roaming the blasted landscape of a city which, like Eliot's *Unreal City*, becomes a score of dying cities in the West. No departure is possible from this place: the city, under some last, mad, military directive, is expending its final resources in building a seawall to repel invaders, an echo of a similar enterprise undertaken by Thucydides' Athenians near the end of the Peloponnesian War which ultimately destroyed them. This city, where governments change with the same speed, incomprehensibility, and hostile force as its unpredictable weather, mirrors other cities, other dark times, as it tunnels through twentieth-century history: the Warsaw Ghetto, the Siege of Leningrad (without any redeeming heroic purpose), postearthquake Managua, the last days of Berlin, and, above all, New York City in the present.

Herein lies the enormous irony of Auster's tale. Once more, as in the three volumes of *The New York Trilogy*, it's all done with mirrors. This time, the game is played with, if anything, greater cunning and obliqueness behind the same screen of lucid and uncompromising prose. *In the Country of Lost Things* is occupied not with a future dystopia but with a hellish present. Its citizens are no more inhabitants of the future than Swift's Houyhnhnms are native to some unmapped mid-Atlantic island. They belong to the here and now, to its ethical, spiritual, and cultural chaos. The broken objects and decayed relics they dig up from rutted streets and collapsed buildings to trade at considerable sums for a marginal existence are emblematic of a society which has not only ceased to invent and produce but which, for nearly two decades, has inflated the value of real property, objects of art, and fetishistic junk alike. Where productivity and invention fail, any artifact from the recent past becomes a work of art. Where even memory fails, becoming an atrophied faculty of human intelligence, the desire for sensation and novelty is quickly gratified by a highly accelerated recycling of goods, whether damaged or sound. Auster's description of this process gives the word *collector* an almost sinister ring, just as his "Leapers," a group of elective suicides who jump from high buildings, suggest, through a familiar historical association, the shaky financial structure of our own economy.

Some of these correspondences converge in such an inescapable fashion on life in the present in New York City that *In the Country of Last Things* supplies a phantom unit to what is, in effect, Auster's New York Tetralogy. "A house is there one day, and the next day it is gone. A street you walked down yesterday is no longer there today." A bomb crater, a vanished neighborhood, a demolished building unite in the unstable urban landscape of an American city. Few readers will miss these implications, or, when they encounter the book's description of the howling "Runners" who hurl themselves down the filthy streets of Auster's metropolis, running blindly until they attain their end—death by exhaustion—will ever contemplate an urban creature loping along, senses sealed through his electronic apparatus, eyes glazed and vision straining at a distant nullity, in quite the same way.

Part of the book's bleak entertainment lies in the discovery of these manifold and dense connections between the fictional city and present reality. These remain, however, suggestive rather than coercive. Auster parodies the breakdown of law by unionizing his muggers: they organize themselves as "Tollists," patrolling random streets, extorting a fee from every passerby unable to anticipate the presence of their barriers. The vacancy rate in the city is at zero, and streets and subways swarm with sleepers from an underclass of paupers, criminals, and lunatics, although a level of society called "the rich" still coexists with it.

In this climate of endless scarcity, there is continuous talk of food, obsessive reminiscence of meals once eaten, the preparation of meals which might be eaten, the verbal evocations of perfect menus and the sensations they bestow. The speakers in Anna Blume's astonished narrative are, in fact, half-starved, but their preoccupation with food, like the onanistic rush of the Runners, mimics still another cultural vagary of the last decade: the urban sophisticate's absorption in restaurants and cuisine. The parallels become uncanny. Where are we, if not in New York, near the end of the century, in an entrepreneurial capital where nothing indigenous is grown or generated? Children appear twice: one a corpse and the other an unborn fetus. (Anna's pregnancy ends in miscarriage.) Zero Population Growth is at its zenith. And corpses, which can be mined for gold teeth and burned for fuel, have some residual value.

Anna sees and records this world, her pluckiness and intelligence marking her for independent survival, although several calamities make her a candidate for rescue. Losing the shopping cart on which her trade as a licensed scavenger depends, cast out in the streets once more after the death of her dubious protectors, she wanders to the library (a beleaguered monument to high culture in which books must be burned for warmth) where she finds her brother's old colleague Samuel Farr. They fall in love and winter over in the library until Anna, literally barefoot and pregnant, is lured into a shop where corpse-merchants assault their victims. Diving through a window to safety, she's found by the head of a charitable hostel, a woman named Victoria whose rescue operation will end in defeat. Nursed back to health, restored to sanity by salvaging, this time, the sick and starving and through a somewhat unconvincing lesbian relationship with Victoria, she watches the city burn, smolder, and die around them through another frightful winter. Farr rejoins them, and a small pack of survivors prepares an escape from the city. Rejecting various exit points, all treacherous and uncertain, they choose a gate which leads—in hope? in despair?—past the westernmost barrier of the city. (The promise of safety outside the city seems small, and the western exit, in all the indices of folklore and mythology, is synonymous with death.) Although the close of the novel is ambiguous, Anna's doom seems imminent. The blue notebook will fall into the immense detritus of her world.

Closing the book, we think of Emmanuel Ringelbaum's memoir of the Warsaw Ghetto, buried in the earth and dug up for another generation. Anna's book, however, can address itself to no such hope, for in her catalog of loss the words which would serve her purpose and make intelligible her story are consigned to a rubbish heap from which they will not rise again. When Anna learns that there can be no return voyage by sea to her own country, she alludes to airplanes and learns that not only have airplanes been absent from this country for some time but the very word is extinct. Oceania has always been at war with Eastasia. *There are no more bicycle wheels left in the world*. Memory of the past is fading and Anna in *In the Country of Last Things* is one of its rare agents: perhaps this accounts for her name, borrowed from an obscure poem of Kurt Schwitters which celebrates an eponymous "pale Anna Blume." Auster's Anna, however strong and unfaltering her powers of observation, is a wan ghost of the past astray in an intolerable present.

Auster's naming of his characters, however, points to one of the few flaws in his careful composition. There's a tendency to seed this book, as in his earlier volumes, with Significant Names, without any commitment to integrate them. "Ferdinand and Isabella," "Samuel Farr," and "Mr. Frick" summon associations that come too easily, shortcuts to the unfolding of a narrative scheme which Auster's tine prose is well equipped to avoid. The true force of the book lies in its oblique aim. the feminine narrator has managed an elegant trick of distance without relinquishing the power to move us, and the book does not suffer through the numerous comparisons to be made with the tone and the urgency of Anne Frank's *Diary of a Young Girl*. The strain of recording the gaze of the utterly normal on the totally insane is immense, and that Anna abides her author's severe economy, telling her personal story in precisely the same cadences she employs to detail the wreck of Western culture, is no small achievement.

Auster has succeeded with Swiftian guile and ferocity in constructing a world of demolished things which we are forced, immediately and painfully, to recognize as our own. The antecedents of such fables of an intolerable present, given life by removal to another place, another time, would comprise a long and honorable list. Among these, Orwell's *Nineteen Eighty-Four*, springing from an altogether different literary tradition, is considered to be grounded in the reality of the postwar England in which he wrote it. Here, coming in from a different angle, is an oblique history chronicle of a great city "after the storm," its fall as unaccountable to its narrator as it is to us.

STEVEN WEISENBURGER

Inside Moon Palace

In the 1960s it was obvious, to the point of appearing to be "the natural order," that language was with the people. Not so. The people it turned out were infinitely more unsettled than originally supposed. They were sick of the body, and many of them longed for the public body, for age, wisdom, and strong authority. The disgust with the political process and the wish for simple clarity also reflected a distrust of the Outside, a rejection of the metaphysical and a new desire for the comforting routine of the interior.

—Andrei Codrescu (184)

This epigraph is lifted from Andrei Codrescu's 1989 essay "The North American Combine: Moloch and Eros," first published in the magazine *Columbia*. Columbia University is also the alma mater of Marco Stanley Fogg, narrator of Paul Auster's *Moon Palace*, a 1989 novel saturated with references to 1492 and Cristoforo Columbo, to the systematic westwarding domination of the Outside after him, and to the crisis of that modern ethos during the late 1960s. Codrescu critiques the faith of many sixties radicals in a "natural" and presumably regenerative "Free Speech" whose daisies, chucked against Moloch, would jam the gears like monkey wrenches. Such a belief, he argues, naively disregarded how the plots of mastery and violence crisscrossed discourse; thus, when the frustrated radical turned inside, it was

From *The Review of Contemporary Fiction*, 14, no. 1 (Spring 1994). © 1994 by Steven Weisenburger.

only to replay old dramas of authority. *Moon Palace* partly figures that cultural crisis in the terms of genealogy and inheritance. Now, there is no evidence of descent, Codrescu to Auster, and the contemporaneous appearance of their two texts remains simple coincidence, yet worth remarking because chance and coincidence name the other half of those forces shaping Auster's narrative figuration.

A *useful* coincidence, then. As though it were an extended narrative meditation on Codrescu's argument, *Moon Palace* is preoccupied with the problem of the Inside. Its action unfolds through a series of quests for natural language, fathers, authority, and history, always occurring within claustrophobic interiors. These spaces—apartments, bedrooms, and caves— are sites for what Codrescu aptly defines as a "comforting routine," a degenerative obsession for origins and power that is dimly backlighted, throughout *Moon Palace*, by oblique references to the historical 1960s: the occupation of administration offices at Columbia, the Apollo moon landing, and the Kent State massacre. Such moments unfold just beyond Fogg's threshold or on television screens suspended in fogs of barroom smoke, in either case seemingly without embodiment, much less a connection to Fogg's intellectual preoccupations.

The novel insists otherwise. M. S. Fogg defines himself as a glitch "in the national machine," a text (or MS, as he notes [7]) whose actions are "living proof that the system had failed, that the smug, overfed land of plenty was finally cracking apart" (61). The deteriorating social body thus finds its analogy in Fogg's body, as well as in the body of his story, itself a conventionally chronological quest narrative whose recurring figure is the bodily self sliding irrevocably, like the story itself, towards the Zero: towards bankruptcy, starvation, and death; towards "The End." Yet Fogg's degenerative descents are also always checked and redirected by moments of coincidence, by glitches demonstrated in the text of the novel through characters' recognitions of the errant potentials in representational texts themselves. Such recognitions of errant coincidence are staged against the recuperation of Fogg's genealogy. For Marco himself this process of discovery unfolds through accidents so farfetched, so apparently contrived, that Gary Indiana (for example) uses them to flog Auster for writing a dryly "theoretical" and "mechanical" plot. It is mechanical, in the reading proposed here, but for purposes that need to be differently reckoned, though from the same details of story which the critics thrashed.

What is that story? In brief, Marco's relation of his mother's untimely death (she's run over by an errant bus), his adolescence spent with an eccentric uncle, and Uncle Victor's death which leaves the youth seemingly without family, are events that set the stage for a series of extraordinary coincidences and accidents. Marco pays for his education at Columbia by gradually spending his mother's legacy and by selling off 1,492 books inherited from Uncle Victor. On graduating in 1969 he's forced out of his claustrophobic apartment and into vagrancy, whereupon in a near visionary state induced by malnourishment he watches Neil Armstrong's moon walk, foretold (he reflects) at the end of "Passage to India," Whitman's ode to Columbus and Manifest Destiny. Rescued from starvation and disease that autumn, Fogg recovers and finds a lover in a Chinese woman named Kitty Wu, also an orphan. He answers a newspaper ad that leads to his becoming the companion for a wealthy eccentric, blinded by old age. This man's identity, "Thomas Effing," then turns out to be a fifty-four-year ruse, as Marco discovers in transcribing the man's orally narrated autobiography.

In 1916, as artist Julian Barber, he experienced a series of misfortunes while on a painting expedition in the Utah desert. Accident gave him the opportunity to abandon a frigid wife and contrive both a new self as well as a new fortune during the Jazz Age stock-market boom. Subsequently, though, Effing discovers that before departing for Utah he had conceived a child with his former wife, Elizabeth, which child the woman's brother had reared after she succumbed to insanity during childbirth. On Effing's death Marco contacts this heir, an obese professor of history named Solomon Barber, who turns out (in the novel's most extreme coincidence) to have been Emily Fogg's teacher and onetime lover, therefore Marco's father. This recognition comes almost simultaneously with Marco's frustrated paternity (Kitty, over his vigorous objections, gets an abortion) but is not the novel's end. Visiting Emily Fogg's grave with his newfound father, Marco accidentally tips Solomon Barber into an open grave, which fall eventually kills him, an absurdly oedipal twist that sends Marco westward, into the lunar, Southwestern landscape where Effing's identity switch occurred, a site of seemingly limitless Gatsby-like potential. Effing's cave, however, has been recently inundated by the waters of Lake Powell. Thus failing that quest and robbed of all but some $400, Fogg resumes his linear, westwarding trajectory and walks from Lake Powell to the Pacific shore at Los Angeles. There the novel ends, a "full moon, as round and yellow as a burning stone" shining over his shoulder (307) while he gazes over the Pacific—watery trench formed by the cataclysmic tearing free of the moon sometime in geological prehistory. The reconstruction of Fogg's genealogy, now inscribed under the aegis of geologic or cosmic forces, stands complete.

Marco begins his tale in New York, with "no evidence" of paternity and thus "a blank" (4) where his genealogy should be. It ends in Los Angeles, having filled that gap through a quest for paternal origins, a quest Marco never in fact intended but one that readers (like Marco) rather systematically and authoritatively reconstruct. We do so, I want to argue, for quite powerful reasons of genre, and the result may well be graphed, as follows:

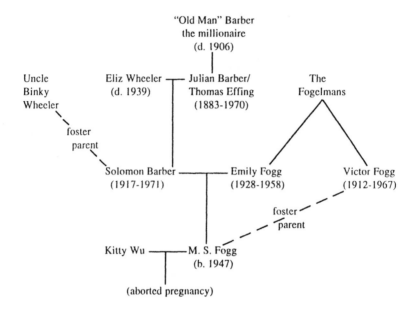

One point of reproducing Marco's heritage like this is to stress its profoundly ingrown effects. This genealogy simply fails to exfoliate in any "natural" way. Instead it collapses inward on Marco and thus approaches a near erasure or zeroing-out in the abortion Kitty demands over his objections. In addition, Marco's genealogy stresses the insanity, absence, and abortiveness of its maternal side as much as the alienated, unstable, and obsessive (yet equally successful) features of his recuperated paternal side: its putative beginning, in the nineteenth-century wealth of Effing's robber-baron father, "old man" Barber (146); then the successive degradation of that wealth through three generations, until Marco loses the last of it to unknown highway thieves somewhere in southern Utah in 1971; and the logic of this, indeed its progression from the lunacy traced on Marco's maternal side, to the rationality of his father, Sol. In all such details one recognizes a narrative so obviously symbolical, so antirealistic (to borrow John Kuehl's terminology), it's a wonder that critics like Indiana (or Kornblatt, for Sven Birkerts's intelligent review of the novel was exceptional) would so slavishly flog it for violating realistic conventions. Clearly, one aim of Auster's technique is to push those conventions over the top, into a kind of metafictional counterpractice.

Among the naturalizing conventions of narrative, none is more basic than "the genealogical imperative." Years ago Robert Nisbet described how the complex of causal propositions—the *proteron hysteron* sequences subtending narrative itself—achieve their clearest figuration in genealogy. The belief, as Nisbet puts it, "that events give birth to events" (352), or that in narrating a genealogy one merely uncovers causalities in natural events rather than artificially imposing them, commits realistic writing to a potent set of secondary assumptions. Chief among these is the assumption of an "inside" force or dynamic of event sequences which it is the narrator's "natural" function to represent (359). Another is the assumption of some inherent determinism of which the novelistic mimesis, in all the formalist complexity of its plot orderings, stands as the privileged model.

Patricia Tobin has further analyzed the ways that these assumptions also serve to legitimize state authority, by equating "the temporal form of the classical novel—the conceptualized frame within which its acts and images find their placement—with the dynastic line that unites the diverse generations" (6–7). Perhaps more than any other convention, the genealogical metaphor thus limits a narrative fiction to the mimesis of a supposedly homogenous time and to the principal alibi for that linear, developmental temporality, "the subject" or hero. Most recently, Elizabeth Ermarth stresses these epistemological affiliations (22–24) and, working from Kristeva's 1979 essay "Women's Time," equates the disposition towards linear and teleological temporality with a linguistic disposition to propose and summarize (rather than to play and multiply), thus with the "obsessional time" of psychoanalysis: a zeal for mastery over temporal process that is itself "the true structure of the slave" to official power (44–41). These relations of temporal structures to ideology are deeply embedded.

In modernist fictions, such as *The Rainbow* or *Go Down, Moses*, genealogy subtends a range of assumptions about origins, degraded modern society, and traces of man's primitive potency in the "blood." Faulkner and Lawrence valorize that power in differently inflected but ideologically similar (reactionary) myths. By contrast postmodernist fiction, such as *J R* or *Gravity's Rainbow*, deploys a range of discontinuous and chance events to subvert genealogical, "historical" time. Edward Bast's inwardly collapsing family tree, like the diminution of an originary, Puritan self in Slothrop ("last of his line, and how far fallen," notes Pynchon), are principal figures reconstructed by any reading of these two novels. Yet in both novels such monuments to genealogy and dynastic history teeter above the increasingly quake-fractured ground of postmodern events. Undermined by the entropic and negentropic rhythms of Gaddis's narrative or by the stochastic flux into which Pynchon's subject (Slothrop) disappears, causal history tumbles aside; it is too fragile, too limited, to fully do contemporary work. It cannot function as a reality principle for postmodern theaters of action. The more open the perceptible universe is to fluctuation and coincident innovation, the less *useful* are metaphors of genealogy and progressive growth.

Moon Palace opens with references to a dramatic expansion of that perceptible universe in the Apollo moon shot. Moreover, it quickly begins to plot the characters' loss of a continuous and coherent genealogy as the occasion for degenerative obsessions. Always staged inside—in Fogg's apartment or Effing's house—it is also figured as a stepwise, seemingly absolute consumption or divestiture. Attending Columbia, Fogg runs through his inheritance, as well as his uncle's 1,492 books, and gradually divests himself of things and conveniences. Knowing that "the process could not go on forever" (27), Marco recognizes that "the mind cannot win over matter" (29) but presses on in any case, nearly consuming his body through starvation. Sol Barber literally eats "his way to the brink of oblivion" (242) after his disastrously discovered intercourse with Emily Fogg, which loss of a beloved has (he erroneously thinks) cut short any hope for genealogical extension. His eventual death is also phrased as a long, slow rallentando into the grave the financial cost of which, ironically, further diminishes the inheritance of a son and heir he never knew he fathered. Analogously, Barber/Effing authors a new identity without any conception of Elizabeth's conception. Then, painting from the threshold of his Utah cavern in 1916, Effing runs through his tubes of pigment and his available canvases, and moreover consumes the available scenery itself, "as though he could feel the landscape vanishing before his eyes" (171). These are Marco's words, as conventional a "foreshadowing" of the old man's actual blindness as readers could want, but understood here as the 20-20 hindsight commanded by determinist temporality. Yet Effing's calculated diminution of his fortunes and his vitality towards the zero-point of death has a further twist: he accurately predicts the date of his demise, on 12 May 1970 (after Kent State, American soldiers were "Pulling Out of Cambodia," notes the *New York Times*, and Marco's team, the Chicago Cubs, grabbed a 4-to-3 eleventh inning victory over the Braves on Ernie Banks's 500th home run: more coincidental tidbits from the annals of time). Yet any such predictive, millennialist inscriptions of The End, the informing desire of modernist temporality, is exactly what Auster's narration always counters. In the midst of the first, long drift towards starvation in 1969, Marco already glimpses the possibility of his own release from determinist time. "Causality was no longer the hidden demiurge that ruled the universe," he recalls thinking, for "down was up, the last was first, the end was the beginning" (62). That echo of Eliot, though, is a calculated deception. The narrative never proposes a metaphysical leap out of time.

What then is the alternate mode of temporality that *Moon Palace* imputes to events? In the desert, having exhausted his food supplies, paints, and canvas, Barber/Effing recognizes that a phase of his existence has concluded "with the speed and force of a book slamming shut." He feels it also as the conclusion of a sentence, a death sentence, in fact. Precisely at this moment, however, "his life suddenly veered in a new direction" (181). The Greshams, a band of outlaws, show up to reclaim the booty on which Effing has been surviving in his cave. He kills them, and twenty thousand dollars of stolen money found in their saddlebags places him at the doorstep of a new existence, "trying to imagine what he would do next" (182). This instance strikingly implicates the structures of imaginative discourse, especially narrative discourse, in the fashioning of temporality: what seemed foreclosed and predetermined, a *sentence*, veers randomly off on unforeseen trajectories. Over and over again this is the rhythm of events in *Moon Palace*. Each time characters approach a "dead end" or "period" (289) concluding any particular "sentence," then chance and contingency take over. Thus even as Marco slowly starves in Central Park, the charitable gifts of total strangers alter his daily course, and it seems to him as though each miraculous gift is "always the last miracle. And because it was the last, I was continually being thrown back to the beginning" (59). This amounts to saying that any conception of events as "plot" (with beginning, middle, and end) must be ceaselessly reinvented on the basis of contingent potentials. In this view, the "sentence" or "period" is supplanted by the "phase."

There are strong analogies for such a reading in current science. Ilya Prigogine and Isabelle Stengers, for example, discuss how the lineal trajectories of classical dynamics have given way to new models of "dissipative" processes defined by phasal rhythms. In their descriptions, the "end" of any process requires, not theories of finality or closure (as with entropy), but instead those of "translation" or phasal "fluctuation." Now, in a complex multilevel environment of life processes beyond prediction or "control" in any classical sense, the "end" of one phase must be conceived as the probabilistic fluctuation into the "beginning" of still another. These ceaseless, sustaining, negentropic fluctuations do indeed bring "order out of chaos," in Prigogine and Stengers's phrase; they also resist mechanical description and depend entirely on stochastic formulae for any modeling of them. The element of chance, then, emerges (if we must) as *the* definitive law in the rhythm of nature, particularly in the ceaseless production of novel states.

Such concepts sharpen the edge of Marco's statement in the first paragraph of *Moon Palace*, about how he "eventually" came to see "chance as a form of readiness, a way of saving myself through the minds of others" (1). Going inside *Moon Palace* means readying oneself for such chances. It also means being undeceived about the ethics of such chances. After all, the prospects for self-renewal "through the minds of others" would seem to involve conventional standards of empathy or compassion with presumably stable subjects, an ethos where humanistic intentionality remains intact. Marco, for example, is saved from starvation because of the dogged efforts of Kitty Wu and Zimmer, an old friend. But this is not always the case. Barber's several shifts of phase in the desert are enabled by brutal violence: first, the prior murder of the cave-dwelling hermit whose stockpiled foods allow Effing to survive and paint; then Barber's murder of the outlaws whose fortune in money and bonds enables his full assumption of a new identity as "Effing." Traditional hierarchies of value have nothing, necessarily, to do with such chance transitions. In a still greater extension of these problems, Auster puts historiographic representation on the same uncertain ground by disclosing that Sol Barber's nationally acclaimed scholarly "histories" are the phantasmatic products of his own lack of, or quest for, a father, itself a phasal process whose markers are his three books, each a hallmark of determinist thought.

Moon Palace submits representational art to the same critique, and its principal instances are taken from American landscape painting. So in a long, rambling discourse to Marco, at the virtual center of the novel, Effing criticizes the nineteenth-century realists, Thomas Moran and Albert Bierstadt in particular, for their complicity with structures of domination and control: "Manifest Destiny! They mapped it out, they made pictures of it, they digested it into the great American profit machine. Those were the last bits of the continent, the blank spaces no one had explored. Now here it was, all laid out on a pretty piece of canvas for everyone to see. The golden spike, driven right through our hearts!" (149). This sounds romantic, but Effing insists not ("I didn't hold with any of that romantic bullshit") and instead stakes his claim to difference from these painters on the basis of painterly versus linear technique: "The line didn't interest me. Mechanical abstraction, the canvas as the world, intellectual art—I saw it as a dead end" (150). In fact Effing regards the modernists who hung about Stieglitz's gallery at 209 Fifth Avenue—John Marin, Charles Demuth, Man Ray—as merely the unwitting inheritors of nineteenth-century realism, an extension of that dead-end path.

By contrast, Effing's exemplary artist is the obscure nineteenth-century painter Ralph Albert Blakelock (1847–1919). So vital is Blakelock's work to this novel, and particularly Blakelock's 1885 canvas *Moonlight*, that any reading of Auster will have to take account of the Blakelock image as a standard of aesthetic, moral, and ideological values. Marco sees *Moonlight* at Effing's behest, putting himself before it in the Brooklyn Museum after being urged "to enter the landscape before you. See if you can't begin to enter the mind of the artist who painted the landscape" (135). Effing's enjoinder presumes on aesthetic texts as intersections of "inside" and "outside," as well as on a vigorous response to them, one goal of which is to reconstruct intention. But Marco himself realizes the difficulty of this, mainly in the contingencies of "noise"—those voices of other viewers that "imposed themselves" in the museum gallery despite his attempts to "shut them out" (136). Persisting, he nonetheless recognizes in *Moonlight* a "landscape of inwardness and calm" so opposite to the rantings of his "mad employer" (137) that he must put Effing out of mind as well. In short he must also unwittingly (for he doesn't yet know the full facts) deny the genealogical imperative of his own grandfather.

What follows in *Moon Palace* is a reading of *Moonlight* that Auster originally published (with slight variations) in a 1987 issue of *Art News*. For our purposes the significant aspect of it is Auster's reading of the canvas as an antirepresentational text, one whose mimetic details (the disklike moon centered over a lake, a stream dividing the landscape in two, the left bank and its Indian teepee, the right with a large tree and solitary horseman) are significantly undone by Blakelock's painterly brushstrokes and, still more important, by his apparently lunatic disregard for realistic color: an underwash of green pigment shows "beneath the cracked glazes" (138) and suffuses the moonstruck figures in a weirdly serene hue. Marco (like Auster, in the magazine piece) therefore recognizes that any reading of the canvas must involve "wild, symbolic judgments," as well as Blakelock's intention of "painting an American idyll" (139), a "memorial" for "a vanished world" of cross-cultural contacts between Native American and Eurocentric culture. What most troubles him (and Auster) is the loss of a unique chance, the loss of a contingent but symbolically rich ground for innovative cultural contact, a chance he sees as having been destroyed under the wheels of an obsessively lineal narrative of progress and destiny.

If this is the ideological center of *Moon Palace*—and I believe its placement in the text says so, just as Blakelock's moon appears in "the precise mathematical center" (137) of his canvas—then there are further

consequences for reading. One of them is that with few exceptions Blakelock himself has existed as an absence or unrecognized chance, his place on the genealogy of American art acknowledged only in "a few articles here and there, a couple of old catalogues, nothing much" (140), as Marco notes. (And he's right. Excepting the Whitney and Stuurman catalogues, and Vernon Young's fine essay, there's little else on Blakelock, and Auster derived most of his details about the painter's life from Lloyd Goodrich's introduction to the 1947 Whitney exhibition.) In sum, Blakelock neatly instantiates the critique of genealogy implied throughout the novel. He's the lunatic offspring omitted from available "histories."

Moreover the instance of Blakelock stresses the subversion of representational values following from that critique. The genealogical ethos represents value, most obviously, in terms of inheritance: specifically by way of properties or monetary sums. Before he was finally locked up, Auster notes, the impoverished Blakelock had insanely tried to exchange his own, hand-painted money. Yet *Moon Palace* also seems initially obsessive about such things: in Marco's inheritances from his mother, Uncle Victor, Effing, and Solomon Barber, Effing's from his father and various illicit sources; Barber's from Effing, and so forth. Dead center in the text, however, is the image of Ralph Albert Blakelock dressed as an Indian brave and attempting to exchange those bills, a man gone lunatic, Effing claims, because of stresses brought on by eight starving children and unscrupulous art dealers, people like Effing's father, whose name (Barber) he is given the *chance* to renounce. Auster's reading of Blakelock's *Moonlight* focuses, then, on the *gaps* of a realistic representation. Marco says that the moons in Blakelock's paintings always resemble "holes in the canvas, apertures of whiteness looking out onto another world" (141). He means not windows, in the conventional mimetic sense, but gaps or "apertures" of specific media, in all their contingency. Their potential function, once one has gotten inside, is paradoxically to open on the unrecognized and novel Outside, on a range of social and ideological matters.

This reading of the Blakelock scenes in *Moon Palace* also spins us back to prior moments when the novel has been concerned with representational discourse. At one point, responding to another of Effing's enjoinders—this time that he supply the blind old man with a verbal picture of the sights around them—Marco considers the immensity of it all. There are, for instance, "the accidents and losses" of temporality itself, the mutability of natural being, in which "inanimate things were disintegrating, [and] all living things were dying"; but most of all there is the absolutely unstable ground of things seen from the standpoint of physical phenomena: "the unceasing explosions of matter, the collisions, the chaos boiling under the surface of all things" (122). At first, Marco errs on the side of overdetermination. In "a mad scramble to leave nothing out" he builds wild Whitmanian catalogues and piles "too many words on top of each other, and rather than reveal the thing before us, they were in fact obscuring it." Marco soon recognizes that, if the object is to "help him [Effing] see things for himself," then "the more air I left around a thing, the happier the results" (123). He learns to exult in the gaps. Rejecting Emerson's idealist doctrine, in *Nature*, that "words are signs of natural facts," Marco revels in the errancy of representational discourse rather than in its finality. In the acausal spaces between words and things which determinist, genealogical figures cannot abide are chances for innovation.

A further recognition of this argument in *Moon Palace* occurs when we realize how the Chinese restaurant for which the novel is titled exists, practically, as a gap or absence. Marco eats three meals there, we're told; yet the restaurant exists mainly as a name, without descriptive passages or traits of any kind. "Moon Palace" remains, literally, just its sign, first glimpsed from Marco's dingy little room during the political upheavals of the 1960s. Being inside *Moon Palace* means, then, inhabiting this representational gap or error. It means rejecting our "wish for simple clarity" in the dissimulated authority of dynastic power and its narratives. It means recovering, through the contingencies in texts, "apertures" on that complex Outside of which Andrei Codrescu has written.

WORKS CITED

Auster, Paul. "'Moonlight' in the Brooklyn Museum." *Art News* 86.7 (September 1987): 104–05.

———. *Moon Palace*. New York: Viking, 1989.

Birkerts, Sven. Rev. of *Moon Palace*. *The New Republic* 27 (March 1989): 36.

Codrescu, Andrei. *The Disappearance of the Outside*. Reading: Addison-Wesley, 1990.

Ermarth, Elizabeth Deeds. *Sequel to History: Postmodernism and the Crisis of Representational Time*. Princeton: Princeton University Press, 1992.

Gebhard, David, and Phyllis Stuurman. *The Enigma of Ralph Albert Blakelock, 1847–1919*. Santa Barbara: The Art Galleries, University of California–Santa Barbara, 1969.

Kornblatt, Joyce Reiser. "The Novelist Out of Control." Rev. of *Moon Palace*. *New York Times Book Review*, 19 March 1989, 9.

Kristeva, Julia. "Women's Time." 1979. Trans. Alice Jardine and Harry Blake. *Signs* 7.1 (1981): 31–53.

Kuehl, John. *Alternate Worlds: A Study of Antirealistic American Fiction*. New York: New York University Press, 1989.

Indiana, Gary. "Pompous Circumstance: Paul Auster Indulges Himself." Rev. of *Moon Palace*. *Village Voice*, 4 April 1989, 45.

Nisbet, Robert. "Genealogy, Growth, and Other Metaphors." *New Literary History* 1 (1970): 351–64.

Prigogine, Ilya, and Isabelle Stengers. *Order Out of Chaos: Man's New Dialogue with Nature*. 1979. New York: Bantam, 1984.

Tobin, Patricia D. *Time and the Novel: The Genealogical Imperative*. Princeton: Princeton University Press, 1978.

Whitney Museum of American Art. *Ralph Albert Blakelock: Centenary Exhibition*. Introd. Lloyd Goodrich. New York: Whitney Museum, 1947.

Young, Vernon. "'Out of the Deepening Shadows': The Art of Ralph Albert Blakelock." *The Arts* 32.4 (October 1957): 24–29.

Doubles and more doubles

Moon Palace, a strange and arresting new novel by Paul Auster, follows a flurry of outre offerings by this prolific American author.[1] Though barely in his forties, Auster is already well known for his writings in a variety of fields—translations of Frenchmen from Mallarmé to Sartre; original poetry, including the collections *Unearth* (1974) and *Wall Writing* (1976); a poignant memoir entitled *The Invention of Solitude* (1982); and the recent novel *In the Country of Last Things* (1987). Perhaps Auster's best-known productions, however, remain the novels of his *New York Trilogy*, which received considerable attention—and no small amount of critical acclaim—on their small-press publication in 1985 and 1986. Indeed, though *Moon Palace* is not a part of the trilogy, its thematic ties to these three novels are very strong, and a brief discussion of them may serve not only to provide some necessary background to Auster's most recent effort but to illuminate the distinctive and ever-developing literary vision that informs all four books.

On one level, the works of the *New York Trilogy* may be said to fall into a category of which many of us are justifiably suspicious: they're mysteries about Mystery, stories about Storytelling; like many a contemporary writer, Auster is hung up on the meaning of language, the enigma of naming, the philosophy of signification. The identity crisis suffered by Quinn, the mystery novelist-turned-detective who serves as the protagonist of *City of*

From *The New Criterion* 7, no. 8 (April 1989). © 1989 by Bruce Bawer.

Glass, is typical: Quinn (a) writes under the name of William Wilson, (b) finds himself taking on characteristics of his private-eye hero Max Work, and (c) is hired to do detective work because he has been mistaken for a sleuth named (yes) Paul Auster. Quinn's client identifies himself as Peter Stillman, but tells Quinn bluntly: "Peter Stillman is not my real name. So perhaps I am not Peter Stillman at all." Quinn's assignment is more in the line of, say, Thomas Pynchon or Don DeLillo than of Raymond Chandler: he is asked to shadow a linguistics professor whose obsessive search for mankind's Ur-language has led him to lock his son in a closet.

Ghosts, the second novel of the trilogy, also depicts one man hiring another to follow a third; the story's aggressively abstract nature is reflected in the fact that all its characters are named for colors: White, Black, Blue, and so forth. As for the detective protagonist of the third novel, *The Locked Room*, he doesn't have a name at all. Since boyhood he has been widely confused with a friend, an unpublished writer named Fanshawe; when Fanshawe suddenly disappears without explanation, the nameless detective takes over Fanshawe's life—wife, son, manuscripts, and all—and for some time thereafter struggles with his (and the wife's) feelings about the maybe-dead, maybe-not-dead writer.

The recurring elements in these novels are striking: detectives search out the truth about some bizarre circumstance or other, only to be unprepared for what they find; unexpected coincidences, correspondences, and connections abound; characters recognize each other as twins, as *Doppelgängern*, and act upon that recognition in remarkable fashion. In all of the *New York Trilogy* novels, very little is what it seems to be; as Auster puts his bemused gumshoes through their unsettling, often surreal paces, the purportedly stable and well defined melts before one's eyes, while the supposedly chaotic proves to conceal startling patterns, bonds, and similitudes. Among other things, Auster would seem to want us to come away from his trilogy with a newfound appreciation of the unpredictability of life and the relativity of identity, and with a stubborn reluctance to take anything for granted in the world around us. "What you finally learn from life," observes a character in *The Locked Room*, is "how strange it is. You can't keep up with what happens. You can't even imagine it." In a similar vein, *The Invention of Solitude* opens with the following sentence from Heraclitus: "In searching out the truth be ready for the unexpected, for it is difficult to find and puzzling when you find it." To be sure, no reader who has dipped into the so-called metafiction of William Gaddis, John Barth, and company will find Auster's surprises particularly surprising; plots such as those proffered in the *New York Trilogy* are everyday fare in the works of these academic novelists. And in their hands, make no mistake, such material typically makes not for "meta-novels," which take the form a step beyond itself, but for belabored, pretentious para-novels that betray nary a trace of human interest, narrative drive, or suspense.

Such is far from always the case with the *New York Trilogy*. Yes, such stratagems as Auster's naming of the characters in *Ghosts* after colors are tiresomely contrived, and his introduction of himself into the *dramatis personae* of *City of Glass* is too precious by half; at their best, however, these novels effectively tell suspenseful and compelling stories even as they productively contemplate the act (and art) of storytelling. Aside from Auster's native gifts for character, dialogue, and narrative, what saves these books from being self-indulgent and pseudo-intellectual exercises is that Auster's preoccupation with words and their relations does not derive from an empty allegiance to the fashionable idea that language is only about itself; rather, his preoccupation manifestly flows from a keen interest in the nature of physical reality, and an equally intense compulsion to define, as precisely as possible, the nature of the subtle and intricate nexus between the outer world of observable phenomena and the inner world of the endlessly observing, generalizing, and denominating human mind. To read these books in sequence is to get the impression that Auster is groping, intelligently and sincerely, toward an original and well-focused literary vision; indeed, Auster himself has said that the novels of his trilogy "are finally the same story, but [that] each one represents a different stage in my awareness of what it is about."

Moon Palace might be said to represent yet another stage in that awareness—which is to say that it constitutes an even more accomplished attempt to capture, in fictional terms, the vision toward which Auster is reaching in his trilogy. The novel's protagonist is Marco Stanley Fogg, whose appellation alone will probably be the subject of a dissertation someday. Not only do Fogg's given names recall two of the great world travellers in history (Marco Polo and Henry Stanley), and not only does he share his last name with a dashing globetrotter from literature (Jules Verne's Phileas Fogg), but his initials also happen to be the abbreviation for the word manuscript—which is Auster's way of reminding us that Fogg is a literary creation, a man who exists only on paper. Fatherless at birth, and orphaned in childhood, Fogg is an eighteen-year-old undergraduate at Columbia University in the spring of 1966 when he suffers the loss of his Uncle Victor, "my only relative, my one link to something larger than myself." This death sends Fogg into a nihilistic tailspin; irrationally resolving to abandon himself to "the chaos of the world" in the hope that "the world might ultimately reveal some secret harmony to me, some form or pattern that would help me to penetrate myself," he lives out his college years as a virtual hermit, doggedly reading his way through his uncle's thousand-volume library and letting his finances dwindle to nothing. By the time graduation rolls around, Fogg is homeless, bookless, and penniless; he spends several weeks as a Central Park vagrant, only to be rescued by a Chinese girl named Kitty Wu who has decided that they are spiritual twins. For reasons that are never made clear (can't he get anything better with a Columbia degree?), Fogg accepts a low-paying job as the companion and biographer of a rich, eccentric octogenarian named Thomas Effing, a sometime painter with his own story of youthful self abandonment, isolation, and rebirth. Like Fogg's, Effing's name is not without meaning: when, decades ago, he threw over his former life as Julian Barber, he coined a crude moniker for himself (f—ing, get it?) that reflected his frustrations over the botch he'd made of his life. It is through Fogg's relationship with Effing that the world ultimately accords him a glimpse of "some secret harmony, some form or pattern" that helps him to penetrate himself—though (as is far from unusual in Austerreich) the glimpse comes too late for him to derive as much from it as he might otherwise have done; perhaps too late, even, for him to come away with anything more than a sense of frustration over lost possibilities.

The first thing that must be said about *Moon Palace* is that our hero's quest for secret harmony is far more cogently charted than in any of the novels of the *New York Trilogy*. Largely, perhaps, because Auster has grown more adept at translating his preoccupations into the language of action and form, *Moon Palace* feels more assured than its predecessors, and has a satisfying sense of closure that they lack. Even more than those books, it is (to borrow Geoffrey O'Brien's description of *City of Glass*) a well-choreographed "dance of doppelgängers," an intellectually engaging meditation on self and other, solitude and society, mind and matter—and, not least of all, on art as "a method of understanding, a way of penetrating the world and finding one's place in it." It is certainly more realistic than the *New York Trilogy*—which is to say that the series of far-fetched coincidences upon which its resolution depends occur in a context that, in every other respect, seems thoroughly congruent with the world as we know it. The novel's prose, meanwhile—lean, fluid, vigorous, and delightfully lucid—marks (if anything) an advance in sophistication over the more hard-boiled, staccato manner of the earlier fiction. But then, Auster's style has from the beginning been his greatest strength.

Perhaps *Moon Palace*'s most signal virtue, in comparison with the *New York Trilogy* novels, lies in the roundness of its two principal characters. It is a testament to Auster's imaginative powers that Fogg's behavior, though at times wildly illogical and inexplicable, feels credible and consistent almost without exception, and that this often less-than-admirable character manages to provoke in the reader an impressive level of interest and sympathy. As for Effing, though at times he seems a bit too much of a standard-issue crazy old coot, the blind, wheelchair-bound old man is on the whole a lifelike and highly colorful creation, and Fogg's relationship with him is light years more vivid, complex, and believable than Fogg's perfunctorily evoked romance with Kitty (who, alas, remains stubbornly one-dimensional throughout). As in the *New York Trilogy*, moreover, the island of Manhattan is itself a major and full-bodied presence. In contrast to the expertly rendered tableaux of busy, upscale metropolitan nine-to-fivers that are offered up in, say, Tom Wolfe's *Bonfire of the Vanities* and the novels of Louis Auchincloss, Auster concentrates here on a different, but no less real, New York: that of the isolate, the outsider, the midday wanderer in the streets.

Then there's the moon, which at times seems to crop up on every page of *Moon Palace*. Why? Because Auster is concerned with Fogg's—and, by extension, with every individual's—need for a "link to something larger" than himself, for "a way of penetrating the world and finding one's place in it," and the moon is symbolically useful in this regard. As Effing explains to Fogg, "[Y]ou can't fix your position on the earth without referring to some point in the sky. Something to do with triangulation, the technique of measurement .... A man can't know where he is on the earth except in relation to the moon or a star." At the Brooklyn Museum, Fogg studies *Moonlight*, a painting by Ralph Albert Blakelock, and wonders "if Blakelock hadn't painted his sky green in order to ... make a point of showing the connection between heaven and earth. If men can live comfortably in their surroundings, he seemed to be saying, if they can learn to feel themselves a part of the things around them, then perhaps life on earth becomes imbued with a feeling of holiness." It is the universal need for this sense of connectedness that Auster seeks most urgently to communicate in *Moon Palace*, and the moon, with its modest but steady presence, serves his symbolic purposes well. (A transfiguring sense of one's connectedness to humanity does not, after all, announce itself glaringly like the sun, but, like the moon, waits quietly to be discovered and appreciated; moreover, moonlight is *reflected* light.)

Yet it must be said that the references to the moon proliferate here to the point of distraction, and even (at times) to the point of ludicrousness: Uncle Victor's band is called the Moonlight Moods; Fogg's favorite Chinese restaurant is the *Moon Palace*; a fortune cookie at the *Moon Palace* reads: "The sun is the past, the earth is the present, the moon is the future." The novel begins with a mention of the Apollo 11 moon landing, and ends with Fogg staring up at the full moon as it finds "its place in the darkness." It's all rather overdone. Potentially even more problematic are Effing's bizarre life story—which, as dictated to Fogg by Effing, occupies most of the middle third of the novel—and the astonishing connections which that story ultimately brings to light. "Our lives are determined by manifold contingencies," Fogg observes at one point, and as *Moon Palace* advances, one flagrant contingency after another reveals itself. Auster perpetrates coincidences which in most novels would be deemed impermissibly contrived; and it is admittedly true that at the moment when one suddenly realizes where all the pieces of Fogg's puzzle fit, one balks at the flagrant improbability of the whole thing, and may even be tempted to fling the book across the room. But then one finds oneself accepting Auster's coincidences—partly because (like the absurd-but-gripping reversals in John Fowles's novel *The Magus*) they're the point of the story, and partly because Auster drops them into place with such unflinching, brazen finesse. Even more significantly, perhaps, one recognizes that Auster *understands* coincidences—that, in other words, he has taken note of and reflected seriously upon the sense of harmony, of magic, and even of transcendence that a striking coincidence can inspire, and has brought these reflections to bear upon his story.

To reveal the specific nature of the coincidences in *Moon Palace* would be equivalent to giving away the name of the killer in *The Murder of Roger Ackroyd*. So I won't do it. But I will say that at the heart of *Moon Palace*, as well as of all three *New York Trilogy* novels, lies a complex and powerful obsession—an obsession, namely, with the theme of fathers and sons, with the notion of family as an indispensable means of connection with the world beyond oneself, and with the sense of alienation and directionlessness that can be the lot of the solitary and fatherless. Something of a key to this obsession may be found in *The Invention of Solitude*, an account of Auster's too-early loss and too-late discovery of his father, an enigmatic man whose memory seems to have become, after his death, the chief motive force in Auster's creative consciousness. Beyond a shadow of a doubt, this brief memoir establishes that Paul Auster's work in the novel constitutes, in essence, a remarkable transmutation of private grief into public art. *Moon Palace* testifies that he is accomplishing that transmutation with ever-increasing skill.

NOTE

1. *Moon Palace*, by Paul Auster; Viking, 397 pages, $18.95.

ALIKI VARVOGLI

Exploding Fictions

*L*eviathan is, ostensibly, Auster's most realistic novel to date. The narrative adheres to the basic principles of realist writing, and the world the characters inhabit is, not predominantly, the world of the text, or the realm of metaphor, but a representation of contemporary America. Narrated by Peter Aaron, *Leviathan* tells the story of Aaron's friend Benjamin Sachs. The narrative begins six days after Sachs is found dead, and it moves backwards to trace the beginning of the friendship between the two men and the extraordinary events that led up to his violent death. Sachs was a pacifist who chose to go to jail rather than fight in Vietnam. Through a series of unusual events and coincidences Sachs killed a man; although he was never arrested, he tried to atone for his crime, and when he found out that the dead man was a terrorist he decided to carry on his work. In a symbolic gesture, he began to blow up replicas of the Statue of Liberty until one of his attacks went wrong and he was killed by one of his own bombs. The story unfolds against a realistic background, and the chronology is established with reference to historical events: in the second chapter, for instance, Aaron recalls a meeting with Sachs which took place in a restaurant: '*The New York Times* was spread out on the Formica table in front of him, and he seemed engrossed in what he was reading ... This was early 1980, the days of the hostage crisis in Iran, the Khmer Rouge atrocities in Cambodia, the war in Afghanistan' (*Lev* 90).

From *The World That is the Book: Paul Auster's Fiction.* © 2002 by Aliki Varvogli.

At the same time, however, this is a novel in which the categories 'fiction' and 'reality' collapse into one another as the world and the book become indistinguishable.

If, as Paul Auster has remarked, all his novels are really the same book, *Leviathan* is another version of *The Locked Room*. Both narratives involve a quest for a missing writer in the course of which the narrator, a writer himself, confronts the problem of gaining access to another person's self, and trying to turn the events of another man's life into a coherent narrative. Aaron, like the narrator of *The Locked Room*, becomes an investigator, and both novels attest to Auster's continuing interest in reconciling the role of the detective with that of the artificer. The narrator who sets out to find his missing friend has to confront his own limitations as a seeker of truth, as a writer, but what he achieves is not an insight into his friend's 'true self'. Instead, he is confronted with the realisation of the unavailability of truth or objectivity. The only truth each narrator arrives at is the truth of the story he has created in the process of his investigation. Benjamin Sachs, the missing protagonist of *Leviathan*, could be described in the words that the narrator of *The Locked Room* uses to describe Fanshawe: 'he was there for you, and yet at the same time he was inaccessible. You felt that there was a secret core in him that could never be penetrated, a mysterious center of hiddenness. To imitate him was somehow to participate in that mystery, but it was also to understand that you could never really know him' (*LR* 210). Like Fanshawe, Sachs 'absents himself' for a long time, and the narrator writes about him in an attempt to understand him. In the process, Aaron becomes another detective figure trying to piece together the fragments of another man's life, only to be confronted by absence and gaps where he had hoped to find answers. Sachs, like Fanshawe, becomes a symbol of the unknowability of human nature, of the impossibility of gaining access to another person. In *City of Glass* Quinn decided, like a latter-day Don Quixote, to live the adventures of his own books, only to find himself imprisoned in another kind of fictional room; in *Leviathan*, Sachs gives up writing in order to become a terrorist and urge America to change its ways. He steps into the real world only to find that he cannot escape his own self-mythologising.

Despite these parallels, there are obvious differences between the two texts. *The Locked Room* is more self-conscious and, towards the end, the writer shows complete disregard for realistic conventions. The book not only ends with the protagonist 'answering the question by asking another question', but it also sends the readers back to the first story in *The New York Trilogy*, thus placing all three stories primarily (though not exclusively) inside the realm of the text. If *The New York Trilogy* can be read as the image of a labyrinth, *Leviathan* becomes a garden of forking paths. The recurring imagery of explosions and fragmentation indicates dispersal which does not, as I shall be arguing, result in annihilation, be that the annihilation of self, of signification, or the possibility of being saved by fiction or representation. *Leviathan* is populated by more realistic characters than any of Auster's previous books, and it appears to be more conventional than anything he has written before it. Yet the reader acquainted with Auster's *oeuvre* will recognise some familiar devices. Peter Aaron, the narrator, shares his initials, and some biographical details, with Paul Auster: he has written a novel called *Luna* (Auster's *Moon Palace*), his wife is called Iris to Auster's Siri, his first wife Delia (Auster's Lydia), and the two protagonists meet in Nashe's Tavern, whose proprietor we last saw involved in a car crash at the end of *The Music of Chance*. Brian McHale uses the phrase *retour de personnages* to refer to the authorial practice of having characters reappear in a series of novels.[30] In the case of writers such as Balzac or Trollope, the device is used to heighten the effect of realism and to reinforce the illusion that characters exist outside the text, living and growing older between novels. In postmodernist texts, on the other hand, the device is deliberately exaggerated to create confusion and impart a sense of indeterminacy; it is a defamiliarising technique aimed at drawing attention to the fictionality of the text and undermining traditional notions of delineation of character, while it is also an expression of uncertainty and indeterminacy. When a writer names a character, it does not follow that he has any insight into this person's 'real life', and the person does not have a real life anyway because he or she is a creation of the author. Auster brings together characters from 'real life' as well as from other novels, but what this achieves is not so much to underpin the narrative as to stress that the world of the novel is an alternative reality, a more self-conscious fiction. This blurring of the line that ought to separate the 'real' from the invented also relates to the way Auster chooses to address the question of politics, how he writes about contemporary society and the writer's role in it.

As in previous novels, chance dominates the plot. Aaron and Sachs are brought together when a snowstorm prevents anyone from going to their reading. Later, Sachs ends up killing Reed Dimaggio because he receives a lift from a young man, while Aaron inadvertently helps the FBI to identify the body of Benjamin Sachs by mentioning that someone had been impersonating him and signing his books. A lost address book leads Maria Turner to her old friend Lillian Stern, who turns out to be the murdered man's ex-wife. Once again, coincidence is not used as a mechanical device to drive the plot; it gives the author the opportunity to ask questions about free will, and to explore the extent to which one can be said to have control over one's own life. This is especially apt in a novel that deals with a writer's decision to give up writing and 'step into the real world': can he ever escape the plots he weaves himself, and does he not escape into another plot made by the author and the narrator of the book?

The political aspect of the novel is stressed through a series of references to political events, but the emphasis lies more heavily on writing, as the book self-consciously refers to texts which either deal explicitly with politics or have acquired a strong political resonance. Auster explains that the title *Leviathan* is a reference to Hobbes, 'the State as a monster which devours people', but also a reference to 'the monster of consciousness', Sachs, who devours himself in the process of fulfilling his mission.[31] The novel's epigraph is taken from Emerson: 'every actual state is corrupt', he writes in 'Politics', and, in consequence, 'good men must not obey the laws too well'.[32] A similar view is expressed in 'Resistance to Civil Government', which is instrumental in shaping Sachs's attitudes and beliefs, where Thoreau proposes a model of passive resistance against unjust governments. Echoing Emerson, he writes: 'under a government which imprisons any unjustly, the true place for a just man is also in prison'.[33]

Leviathan is dedicated to Don DeLillo, whose 1991 novel *Mao II* charts similar territory, dealing as it does with a reclusive writer who reluctantly agrees to re-enter the public arena in order to save a poet taken hostage by terrorists in Beirut. The writer, Bill Gray, initially decides to come out of hiding and have his picture taken by Brita Nilsson, a photographer whose project involves taking pictures of famous writers. They have long sessions together, during which they talk about their art while she takes pictures, much as Sachs in *Leviathan* talks to the artist Maria Turner. Bill Gray tells Brita Nilsson:

> There's a curious knot that binds novelists and terrorists. In the West we become famous effigies as our books lose the power to shape and influence. Do you ask your writers how they feel about this? Years ago I used to think it was possible for a novelist to alter the inner life of the culture. Now bomb-makers and gunmen have taken that territory. They make raids on human consciousness. What writers used to do before we were all incorporated.[34]

The proximity of this view to Sachs's own beliefs about the role of the writer in society may emphasise the affinity between the two characters, but *Leviathan* is more fruitfully read as a response to, or in dialogue with, *Mao II* rather than as a recapitulation of similar thematic concerns or discursive strategies. DeLillo anchors his debate in the contemporary world; placing his characters against a background dominated by the intrusiveness of the media, and the tyranny of a visual culture in the service of consumerism. As Bill Gray notes, 'In our world we sleep and eat the image and pray to it and wear it too.' Moments of historical crisis or catastrophe are experienced as televised events in the novel, while the title reference to Andy Warhol's multiple portraits foregrounds the book's preoccupation with proliferating, self-generating images.

The Statue of Liberty replicas in *Leviathan* can be said to have a similar *function*, but whereas DeLillo is preoccupied with postmodern consumerist culture, Auster negotiates his writer's position in the world by invoking, as I have already indicated, the spirit and the rhetoric of nineteenth-century American writing. In doing so, he places Sachs's dilemmas and actions in a context that has few similarities with DeLillo's. Bill Gray wants to stay out of the limelight partly because he condemns the all-pervasiveness of the image as consumerist event, whereas Benjamin Sachs's withdrawal from the world is continuous with the Thoreauvian tradition of individuality and resistance. His subsequent bombing mission, and its accompanying rhetoric, are negotiated through references not only to Thoreau, but also to Hawthorne and Melville. As a result, it can be argued that Aaron (and ultimately his creator) asks that Sachs's career be read with reference to those American writers whose work engaged with questions relating to prophecy, apocalypse and ultimately the sense of betrayed promise. At the same time, Auster's narrative technique involves Aaron telling another author's story, trying to do him justice, but ultimately betraying him, metaphorically because he cannot write about someone else without writing about himself, and literally because he unwittingly helps the FBI to identify Sachs's body. In this respect, the book's very process of enunciation is inextricably bound up with its historical and political project.

Even though Auster's intertextual practice places the novel in a political context, Aaron's narrative also tells a different story. The first replica of the Statue of Liberty does not explode until thirty pages before the end of the novel, and Sachs's transformation from writer to terrorist is only explained in the last twenty pages of the book, from the moment he finds out that Dimaggio was some sort of political activist and decides to carry on his work, until one of his bombings goes wrong and he ends up dead. The bulk of the narrative is taken up by the story of how Sachs killed a man and set out to atone for his crime, and the lives he touched—and was in turn transformed by—in the course of his personal odyssey.

In his much-quoted, but always relevant, 1961 essay 'Writing American Fiction', Philip Roth argued that 'the American writer in the middle of the twentieth century has his hands full in trying to understand, describe, and then make *credible* much of American reality ... The actuality is continually outdoing our talents, and the culture tosses up figures almost daily that are the envy of any novelist.'[35] This was written before the Vietnam war, before the first man walked on the moon, and long before the arrest of the Unabomber. For his part, Auster has claimed that he wants to write books 'as strange as the world we live in', and that he sees this as a political act. He recently told an interviewer: 'We cannot escape politics! I belong ... to the first group [of American citizens]—those who think that we live together in society and that we are all interdependent. In this sense, yes, every work of art, whether consciously or not, is a political act.'[36] As a declaration of political commitment, this statement sounds vague and detached, and it points to Auster's continuing interest in the personal rather than the political. Philip Roth concluded his essay with the remark that the 'communal predicament' is distressing, more so to the writer than to other people. 'And it may be that when this situation produces not only feelings of disgust, rage, melancholy, but impotence too, the writer is apt to lose heart and turn finally to other matters, to the construction of wholly imaginary worlds, and to a celebration of the self, which may, in a variety of ways, become his subject, as well as the impetus that establishes the parameters of his technique.'[37] Paul Auster's fiction occupies the middle ground between writing that is primarily interested in the 'communal predicament', and writing that concerns itself with the construction of 'wholly imaginary worlds'. If he explores the political, he does so by way of the personal. Moreover, his world is not one of negation; the world of *Leviathan* may be fragmented, but there is no evidence of a total breakdown, be that the breakdown of the individual, of society, of meaning, or of narrative. As in his previous novels, Auster seeks a pattern—one that may not necessarily exist in the world around him, but one which may emerge from his narrative and, in Hawthorne's phrase, 'be shaped into a figure'. In this respect, *Leviathan* can be said to chronicle a quest for meaning; not a universal, all-encompassing pattern, but something on a smaller and more personal scale. The novel charts Peter Aaron's search for his friend, and Benjamin Sachs's quest for redemption and for his role as a writer in contemporary America. Auster deals with the political by aestheticising it, and if *Leviathan* contains many references to real historical and political events, it is equally made up of other texts, and the question of writing and representation is as important as that of politics.

There are two books within *Leviathan*: one is *The New Colossus*, Sachs's first novel, and the other is *Leviathan*, written by Peter Aaron using the title of the book Sachs never completed. *The New Colossus* functions as a mirror image of *Leviathan* (Auster's *Leviathan*), while it could also be read as a comment on Auster's own earlier fiction. 'As every reader knows, *The New Colossus* is a historical novel, a meticulously researched book set in America between 1876 and 1890 and based on documented, verifiable facts. Most of the characters are people who actually lived at the time, and even when the characters are imaginary, they are not inventions so much as borrowings, figures stolen from the pages of other novels' (*Lev* 37). The cast of characters in the novel includes Emerson, Whitman, Hawthorne's daughter Rose, and fictional characters such as Raskolnikov, Huck Finn, and Ishmael. It is curious, then, that in a novel of such overt literariness the 'dominant emotion was anger, a full-blown, lacerating anger that surged up on nearly every page: anger against America, anger against political hypocrisy, anger as a weapon to destroy national myths' (*Lev* 40). Like the Auster of *Leviathan*, Sachs addresses questions pertaining to historical fact in terms of other books, fictional characters and writers; from Sachs's formative reading of Thoreau to the writing of his own historical novel, his attitude stems from reading. Time, however, renders Sachs's novel almost obsolete:

> The era of Ronald Reagan had began. Sachs went on doing what he had always done, but in the new American order of the 1980s, his position became increasingly marginalized ... Almost imperceptibly, Sachs came to be seen as a throwback, as someone out of step with the spirit of the time. The world had changed around him, and in the present climate of selfishness and intolerance, of moronic, chest-pounding Americanism, his opinions sounded curiously harsh and moralistic. It was bad enough that the Right was everywhere in the ascendant, but even more disturbing to him was the collapse of any effective opposition to it. The Democratic Party had caved in; the Left had all but disappeared; the press was mute. All the arguments had suddenly been appropriated by the other side, and to raise one's voice against it was considered bad manners. (*Lev* 104)

If Sachs and his work can be read as an image of Auster and his novel, two things are happening in this passage. It can be read as an 'apology' on the author's part, a way of signalling an awareness of the political climate, and thus seeking to preempt criticisms of the novel for its perceived lack of involvement. At the same time, as Sachs and his work are framed by Aaron's narrative, the marginalised author and his writings are saved, recovered: the fiction they become part of becomes a justification, and also a vindication, of Sachs's perceived failings.

The image that dominates *Leviathan* is that of the Statue of Liberty, a conceit which works on various levels. Sachs's first visit to the statue at the age of six is recounted early on in the narrative. Aaron points out that Sachs was prone to self-mythologising, and this incident is a good example of how Sachs linked personal experience with the world around him. Two things happened during that visit, and Sachs ascribes to them what may seem a disproportionate significance. First, he recalls how his mother made him wear a pair of 'terrible short pants with the white knee socks', whereas he wanted to wear jeans and sneakers, especially since he was going to meet two boys his own age. This trivial episode is now remembered as a formative experience in Sachs's career: 'Even then, the irony of the situation didn't escape me. There we were, about to pay homage to the concept of freedom, and I myself was in chains. I lived in an absolute dictatorship, and for as long as I could remember my rights had been trampled underfoot' (*Lev* 33). After that visit, Sachs became 'master of his own wardrobe': 'I felt as if I'd struck a blow for democracy, as if I'd risen up in the name of oppressed peoples all over the world' (*Lev* 33). During the ascent inside the Statue, his mother and her friend suffered from vertigo, and as a result they had to go down the stairs sitting down. '"It was my first lesson on political theory," Sachs said, turning his eyes away from his mother to look at Fanny and me. "I learned that freedom can be dangerous. If you don't watch out, it can kill you"' (*Lev* 35). Aaron recognises the fact that the statue must have held some secret attraction for Sachs, and he also points out that Sachs's novel contained numerous references to the Statue of Liberty: 'If not for Sachs's novel ... I might have forgotten all about it. But since that book is filled with references to the Statue of Liberty, it's hard to ignore the possibility of a connection' (*Lev* 35). The same, of course, is true of Aaron's own narrative and Auster's novel, in which the statue becomes the scene of conflict and is, in a sense, the key to Sachs's development: the statue is associated with the formative childhood experience, the crisis he suffers, and the answer he finds to his predicament. It is therefore significant that, as soon as the statue makes its first appearance in the narrative, Sachs is seen to weave plots around it, using it as a landmark for his own development.

Sachs's second encounter with the Statue of Liberty is equally important, as it marks the beginning of a phase that transforms him forever. On 4 July 1986 Sachs attended a party to celebrate the one hundredth anniversary of the Statue of Liberty. The circumstances led Aaron and Sachs's wife, Fanny, to recall Sachs's childhood incident, but no sooner had that descent been recalled than Sachs fell from the fire escape. Both the cause and the effects of this accident remain a mystery to Aaron, and they become an emblem of his own ignorance: 'This is the thing I'm still struggling to come to terms with, the mystery I'm still trying to solve. His body mended, but he was never the same after that. In those few seconds before he hit the ground, it was as if Sachs lost everything. His entire life flew apart in midair, and from that moment until his death four years later, he never put it back together again' (*Lev* 107). The circumstances of his death confirm this, as he is blown to bits, his body burst into dozens of small pieces, and it is left up to Aaron to put the pieces back together, even when he knows that Sachs can never be whole again.

The theme of the Fall is a recurrent one in Auster's fiction. The Fall of Man is the shaping force of Stillman's argument in *City of Glass*, and it concerns not only humankind's fall from grace but also the fall of language. Theological and linguistic connotations give way to personal tragedy when Stillman ends his life by jumping off a bridge. In *In the Country of Last Things*, Anna Blume jumps out of a window to escape her persecutor; the fall becomes a means of struggle for survival in a brutal world where the protagonist can only rely on her own resources to preserve her humanity. Nashe's story in *The Music of Chance* is introduced with these words: 'Without the slightest tremor of fear, Nashe closed his eyes and jumped' (*MC* 1). What he jumped into was an adventure that would change his life for ever. In *Moon Palace*, Solomon Barber falls into a freshly dug grave, and Fogg loses his father the moment he has found him. The fall therefore represents loss, but at the same time it is seen as a necessary stage in each character's development, an unburdening that can lead to recovery.

With his accident, Sachs falls out of his social milieu; by refusing to talk to his friends as he is lying on a hospital bed, he becomes a stubborn recluse who wants to sever his ties with the outside world. Like a latter-day Transcendentalist, he withdraws from the outside world in order to contemplate in isolation:

> Something extraordinary had taken place, and before it lost its force within him, he needed to devote his unstinting attention to it. Hence his silence. It was not a refusal so much as a method, a way of holding on to the horror of that night long enough to make sense of it. To be silent was to enclose himself in contemplation, to relive the moments of his fall again and again,

as if he could suspend himself in midair for the rest of time—forever just two inches off the ground, forever waiting for the apocalypse of the last moment. (*Lev* 119–20)

Yet it is not only the Transcendentalist practice of withdrawal from society that is ironically echoed here. Auster is also returning to the story of Jonah in the belly of the fish, which had excited his imagination *in The Invention of Solitude*. In 'The Book of Memory', he imagines Jonah inside the great leviathan, and he writes:

> In the depth of that solitude, which is equally the depth of silence, as if in the refusal to speak there were an equal refusal to turn one's face to the other ... —which is to say: who seeks solitude seeks silence; who does not speak is alone; is alone, even unto death—Jonah encounters the darkness of death ... And when the fish vomits Jonah onto dry land, Jonah is given back to life, as if the death he had found in the belly of the fish were a preparation for new life, a life that has passed through death, and therefore a life that can at last speak. For death has frightened him into opening his mouth ... In the darkness of the solitude that is death, the tongue is finally loosened, and at the moment it begins to speak, there is an answer. And even if there is no answer, the man has begun to speak. (*IoS* 125–26)

Like Jonah, Sachs experiences death in his self-imposed linguistic prison. When Sachs recovers from this spell of intense introspection, he decides to trade words for action: 'The idea of writing disgusts me. It doesn't mean a goddamned thing to me anymore ... I don't want to spend the rest of my life rolling pieces of blank paper into a typewriter. I want to stand up from my desk and do something ... I've got to step into the real world now and do something' (*Lev* 122). 'And even if there is no answer, the man has begun to speak': despite his decision, Sachs has no specific plans for accomplishing his mission. He gives up writing for a while, and he turns down a number of commissions from editors, but later he starts working on a new novel, which he calls *Leviathan*. He is only a third into it when fate intervenes and forces him to 'step into the real world'.

Taking a break from the composition of his new novel, Sachs goes for a walk and gets lost in the woods. He is offered a lift by a young man, and they meet another car that blocks their way. In a twisted reenactment of the murder of Laius, Sachs kills the aggressor, after the latter has killed the

young man. This sets in motion a whole series of events that will determine
Sachs's passage from guilt to redemption, and lead to the discovery of what
he sees as his vocation. Going through the dead man's possessions, he finds
out that his name was Reed Dimaggio, and that he carried in the car large
quantities of explosives and a big sum of money. The first person that he
confides in, Maria Turner, turns out to be acquainted with the victim, and
Sachs sets out to atone for his crime by giving the money to the man's ex-
wife, an old friend of Maria's. A large part of the narrative is then devoted to
the relationship that develops between the two, but this is not the happy
conclusion to the story. During his stay with Lillian, Sachs does not learn
much about his victim until he decides to look into his room. There, he finds
Dimaggio's dissertation, a reappraisal of the life and works of anarchist
activist Alexander Berkman. One thing Sachs learns from it is that terrorism
'had its place in the struggle, so to speak. If used correctly, it could be an
effective tool for dramatizing the issues at stake, for enlightening the public
about the nature of institutional power' (*Lev* 224). This, in turn, leads him to
a comparison between himself and his victim, and he comes to the
conclusion that 'I'd sat around grumbling and complaining for the past
fifteen years, but for all my self-righteous opinions and embattled stances, I'd
never put myself on the line. I was a hypocrite and Dimaggio wasn't, and
when I thought about myself in comparison to him, I began to feel ashamed'
(*Lev* 225). Although he does not realise it, Sachs cannot escape from the
world of books, and it is ironic that, despite the fact that he felt 'a lot of anger
towards America', it is a dissertation that forces him to reappraise his own
position as a writer. Even at this late stage in his awareness of his role in
society, his first impulse is to write something about Dimaggio, 'something
similar to what he had written about Berkman'. However, for reasons he
cannot comprehend, he cannot perform the task and his inability to do so is
the only indication that this is not his true vocation, not the way to step into
the real world and do something. Once again, the answer to his problem
comes from a book. Taking refuge in a bookshop to avoid an old
acquaintance in the street, he buys a copy of his own book; he spends a lot of
time just gazing at the cover, and it is then that he experiences an epiphany:

> The Statue of Liberty, remember? That strange, distorted
> drawing of the Statue of Liberty. That was where it started, and
> once I realised where I was going, the rest followed, the whole
> cockeyed plan fell into place ... I would be using it [Dimaggio's
> money] to express my own convictions, to take a stand for what I
> believed in, to make the kind of difference I had never been able

to make before. All of a sudden, my life seemed to make sense to
me. Not just the past few months, but my whole life, all the way
back to the beginning. It was a miraculous confluence, a startling
conjunction of motives and ambitions. I had found the unifying
principle, and this one idea would bring all the broken pieces of
myself together. For the first time in my life, I would be whole.
(*Lev* 227–28)[38]

This is how Sachs justifies his decision to blow up replicas of the Statue of
Liberty. In his newly found zeal, he is 'less like a political revolutionary than
some anguished, soft-spoken prophet' (*Lev* 217), accompanying his
explosions with messages that read 'Wake up, America', or 'Democracy is not
given. It must be fought for every day.' However, the unifying principle that
Sachs thinks he has discovered is just a fiction (he has created, a synthesis of
his various encounters with the Statue of Liberty, whose value, in turn, is
symbolic rather than intrinsic. Like Rousseau, who thought that hitting a
tree with a stone could determine the course of his life, Sachs seizes on this
arbitrary connection in an attempt to find an answer to his dilemmas.
However, as in previous novels, arbitrary connections do not amount to a
postmodernist loss of faith. Instead, they lead to a sense of personal recovery.
   Leviathan opens with the image of a man who has been blown to pieces,
and the subsequent narrative chronicles the attempt of the dead man's best
friend to put the pieces back together by telling the story of how this man
came to blow himself up by the side of a road in northern Wisconsin. This
in effect reverses Hobbes's procedure in his *Leviathan* (1651), where he
begins with the image of an artificial body in its entirety and then goes on to
analyse its parts. In his introduction, he writes: 'For by Art is created that
great LEVIATHAN called a COMMON-WEALTH, or STATE, (in latin,
CIVITAS) which is but an Artificial Man.'[39] Auster borrows Hobbes's main
conceit, the image of the artificial man, a construct which has parts
corresponding to nature but which is 'of greater stature and strength', but he
uses it not so much for its political implications as for the way in which it can
be seen as a metaphor for the act of writing, and what that writing reflects of
people's lives. Writing thus becomes an attempt to find a pattern, to put
together the fragments. The novel is an artificial body whose parts
correspond metaphorically to real life, just as Hobbes's body has
'soveraignty' for a soul, magistrates for joints, reward and punishment for
nerves. This move from Hobbes's analysis to Aaron's (and Auster's)
attempted, but not quite accomplished, synthesis is indicative of a more
general trend in contemporary writing which rejects the grand, totalising

narratives of the past in favour of internalisation and subjectivity. Paul Auster as the author of the novel puts together the fragments of his limited knowledge while, within the text, Peter Aaron does so too, by putting together the parts of his friend's shattered life; the fiction he creates he calls *Leviathan* in homage to his friend's unfinished novel of the same name. Sachs's work in progress is curiously absent from the text. Whereas *The New Colossus* is described in detail, Aaron says little of *Leviathan*. Tantalisingly, he does remark that this was the book he had always imagined Sachs could write, but he goes on to add that 'as it stands now, the book is no more than the promise of a book, a potential book buried in a box of messy manuscript pages and a smattering of notes' (*Lev* 142). Aaron's own novel, though coherently narrated and complete, is equally fragmented to the extent that the writer confesses the limitations of his own perception and acknowledges the impossibility of turning another man's life into a story that could correspond to that man's 'real' life.

Leviathan tells the story of Benjamin Sachs and his transformation from writer to terrorist, but it is also the story of Peter Aaron. At the beginning of his narrative, Aaron promises to confine himself to verifiable facts, but his promise is as questionable as that of the narrator in *City of Glass* who claims to have refrained from any interpretation. Peter Aaron is aware of his limitations as observer and writer: 'I can only speak of the things I know, the things I have seen with my own eyes and heard with my own ears ... I have nothing to rely on but my own memories ... I don't want to present this book as something it's not. There is nothing definitive about it. It's not a biography or an exhaustive psychological portrait' (*Lev* 22). However, he often presents his own theories concerning his friend, and he also records 'facts' he has not been able to verify. Above all, what emerges from his narrative is the realisation that writing about someone else's life is a process of fiction-making. Lives do not unfold in a linear sequence and effects cannot always be traced to a single cause. Inevitably, then, the novel is the portrait of two artists, Sachs and Aaron, whom Auster himself thinks of as two sides of the same coin.[40] At the same time, both characters are given biographical details which belong to the real, extratextual Paul Auster. In this complicated relationship, the boundaries between self and other are constantly blurred, and it is no accident that impersonation and representation play a big part in the novel.

The recurring Austerian theme of imagining the self as other is reflected here in the character of Maria Turner, who is herself based on a real artist, Sophie Calle, whom Auster thanks for 'permission to mingle fact with fiction'.[41] Maria Turner is an artist whose work defies traditional categorisation. 'Her subject was the eye,' writes Aaron, 'the drama of watching and being watched, and her pieces exhibited the same qualities one found in Maria herself: meticulous attention to detail, a reliance on arbitrary structures, patience bordering on the unendurable' (*Lev* 63). Among other projects, Maria hires a detective to watch her and write reports of her movements. When she studies these reports, she feels 'as if she had become a stranger, as if she had been turned into an imaginary being' (*Lev* 63). Later, she takes a job as a stripper and invites a friend to take pictures of her to 'satisfy her own curiosity about what she looked like' (*Lev* 65). Conversely, she herself takes pictures of strangers and composes imaginary biographies. Although Peter Aaron has a limited understanding of what happened the night Sachs fell from the fire escape, he knows that Maria Turner was somehow involved in it. Sachs's version of the story is that he was tempted by her, and chose to fall rather than give in to that temptation. But if she was the cause of his accident, she was also the agent of his partial recovery. Although at the time it was assumed that the two were no longer in touch, Aaron later found out that they met regularly, spending every Thursday together as part of a loosely defined project of Maria's. During those meetings they would sometimes talk, and Maria would tape their conversations, while at other times she would take pictures of him, occasionally dressing him up in costume, or she would follow him in the streets. Aaron thinks that these projects saved Sachs from himself:

> When Sachs came to visit her in October, he had withdrawn so far into his pain that he was no longer able to see himself. I mean that in a phenomenological sense, in the same way that one talks about self-awareness or the way one forms an image of oneself. Sachs had lost the power to step out from his thoughts and take stock of where he was, to measure the precise dimensions of the space around him. What Maria achieved over the course of those months was to lure him out of his own skin ... They say that a camera can rob a person of his soul. In this case, I believe it was just the opposite. With this camera, I believe that Sachs's soul was gradually given back to him. (*Lev* 129–30)

Maria enables Sachs to exit his solipsistic world by allowing him to see himself in representation, to reestablish a sense of identity in relation to others. With his narrative, Aaron saves his friend in a similar way.

It is chance that brings the two men together. An author who is due to give a reading alongside Sachs cancels at the last minute, and Aaron is invited to take his place. However, a snowstorm forces the cancellation of the event, and when Aaron arrives at Nashe's Tavern, the only people there are the bartender and Sachs. The two writers spend the evening drinking in the bar, talking about their lives and their work. By the end, Aaron has had so much to drink that he begins to see double: 'Whenever I looked at Sachs, there were two of him. Blinking my eyes didn't help, and shaking my head only made me dizzy. Sachs had turned into a man with two heads and two mouths' (*Lev* 22). With the recounting of this episode, the effect is twofold: Aaron introduces the theme of the double, while he is also giving a warning. Not only during this initial meeting but throughout their friendship, and when he finally sits down to write the story of his friend, Aaron will be unable to focus clearly. All he can hope to achieve with his story is to give his partial, fragmented perception of a man whose personality is multiple, and whose actions and ideas are contradictory. There are numerous disclaimers in Aaron's narrative, especially when he writes of events related to the time prior to his own meeting with Sachs. No sooner does he give some information about Sachs's family than he adds that 'I doubt that I'm trying to make a specific point about this. These kinds of partial observations are subject to any number of errors and misreadings' (*Lev* 29–30). When, following his accident, Sachs withdraws from his friends, Aaron writes: 'Knowing what I know now, I can see how little I really understood. I was drawing conclusions from what amounted to partial evidence, basing my responses on a cluster of random, observable facts that told only a small piece of the story' (*Lev* 126). The same holds true for Aaron's narrative 'now'; the evidence remains partial, and the process of representing his friend forces Aaron to look at himself as well. The final irony of the novel is that Aaron, who is racing against time to give his side of the story before the FBI can identify his friend's body, actually helps them to solve the case by mentioning that someone has been impersonating him: that person turns out to have been Sachs himself.

In conclusion, despite the ostensible realism of the text, *Leviathan* asks the same questions that Auster's previous novels had raised. The lines that ought to separate the text from the world are constantly blurred: Sachs's appreciation of books leads him to the decision to give up writing and involve himself actively in the world. His story survives because another author writes it down from his own limited perspective, thus putting Sachs back into a book. That book, Aaron's narrative, helps the FBI to identify Sachs, thus putting the writer back into the extratextual world. And just before Sachs dies, another writer who had been imprisoned steps into the real world: Vaclav Havel becomes president of Czechoslovakia (*Lev* 237). The activities

of writing and reading, far from producing a clear distinction between the 'real' and the textual, emphasise their interconnectedness. As Valery Hugotte observes, 'if Auster's novels are at heart literary because of their erudition and their implicit allusions to certain literary traditions, they do not cease equally to affirm their relation to life'.[42] If Blue were to get out of the room that is the book, he would find himself in another book, the world which is known through its representations.

NOTES

30. McHale, *Postmodernist Fiction*, pp. 57–58.

31. Wajsbrot, 'Paul Auster, l'Invention de l'Ecriture', p. 82.

32. Ralph Waldo Emerson, 'Politics' (1844), in *The Collected Works of Ralph Waldo Emerson*, ed. Joseph Slater and Douglas Emory Wilson (Cambridge, MA, and London: Belknap Press of Harvard University Press, 1983), III, p. 122.

33. Henry David Thoreau, 'Resistance to Civil Government' (1849), in *The Reform Papers*, ed. Wendell Glick (Princeton, NJ: Princeton University Press, 1973), p. 76.

34. Don DeLillo, *Mao II* (London: Vintage, 1991), p. 41.

35. *Commentary*, 31 (March 1961), pp. 223–33. Reprinted in *The Novel Today: Contemporary Writers on Modern Fiction*, ed. Malcolm Bradbury (London: Fontana Press, 1977), p. 29. Auster expresses a similar idea by using a quotation from Jules Verne as the epigraph to *Moon Palace*: 'Nothing can astound an American'.

36. De Cortanze, *La Solitude du labyrinthe*, p. 98.

37. In *The Novel Today*, ed. Bradbury, p. 42.

38. The cover of *Moon Palace* depicts the Statue of Liberty seen from many different angles.

39. Thomas Hobbes, *Leviathan*, ed. A.D. Lindsay (London: J.M. Dent, 1962), p. 1.

40. De Cortanze, *La Solitude du labyrinthe*, p. 67.

41. Fact and fiction were further mingled when Sophie Calle mounted an exhibition in which she recreated the art described by Auster in the novel. Sophie Calle, *Double Game* (London: Violette Editions, 1999).

42. 'Paul Auster ou l'art de la fugue', p. 57.

LINDA L. FLECK

From Metonymy to Metaphor:
Paul Auster's Leviathan

L *eviathan* is a novel begun by chance. The narrator, Peter Aaron, decides
to reconstruct, to the best of his ability and beginning on July 4, 1990, the
tale of his friend and fellow writer Benjamin Sachs, who was born on the day
the atom bomb was dropped on Hiroshima and was himself blown to
smithereens about forty-five years later. A bomb he had been making to blow
up a scale replica of the Statue of Liberty went off in his hands on the side of
a Wisconsin road. Aaron, who had read about the incident in the paper,
learns with certainty of his friend's demise from FBI agents attempting to
ascertain the victim's identity. Aaron's New York City home telephone
number had been found in the man's wallet, which had somehow survived
the explosion intact; the FBI managed to track Aaron down at the summer
home of Sachs's ex-wife in Vermont. In response to the agents' questions,
Aaron plays dumb. He is fairly certain the FBI will eventually solve the riddle
of the man's identity, but he writes,

> as far as I'm concerned, the longer it takes them the better. The
> story I have to tell is rather complicated, and unless I finish it
> before they come up with their answer, the words I'm about to
> write will mean nothing. Once the secret is out, all sorts of lies
> are going to be told ... and within a matter of days a man's

From *Critique: Studies in Contemporary Fiction* 39, no. 3 (Spring 1998). © 1998 by the Helen
Dwight Reid Educational Foundation.

reputation will be destroyed.... [S]ince he's no longer in a position to defend himself, the least I can do is explain who he was and give the true story of how he happened to be on that road in northern Wisconsin.... If by some chance the mystery remains unsolved, I'll simply hold on to what I have written, and no one *will* need to know a thing about it. (2–3)

Of course the fact that we are reading the text means that the FBI has succeeded in solving the mystery, and the novel comes to an abrupt halt when Agent Harris cracks the case, thanks to Sachs's having impersonated Aaron in upstate New York. In between the chance event that sets the narrative in motion (the arrival of the FBI) and the chance event that brings it to a close (their return), there is the "rather complicated" story, filled with chance events, that makes up the body of the text. The "true story" of how Sachs happened to be on a road in Wisconsin is part "I-witness" narrative, based on what Sachs observed to Aaron and what Aaron observed of Sachs (although what Aaron sees with his own eyes does not always correspond to the "truth"), and part "other-witness" narrative, based on the accounts, sometimes conflicting, sometimes unreliable, of those close to Sachs. Even the title, *Leviathan*, turns out to belong not to this book but to an unfinished novel by Sachs about which we are told next to nothing except that it had the makings of a masterpiece. Sachs had been working on it at the Vermont house where the FBI agents located Aaron.

Shortly before dusk on a mid-September day, Sachs decided to go for a short walk in the woods. Like a latter-day fairy tale hero, he became lost in the forest, spent the night there, and emerged the following morning miles from home. A truck happened by. The driver, named Dwight, a bat-toting first baseman on a local softball team, offered Sachs a ride and took a shortcut back through the woods. Suddenly they come upon a man leaning against a parked car in the middle of the road. Dwight assumed the man needed help. The man, a history professor named Dimaggio, shouted then shot at Dwight, who dies. Sachs does in Dimaggio with Dwight's bat and never writes another word. Aaron's *Leviathan* exists because Sachs's does not.

The entire text would appear to be written under the banner of metonymy, figure of contiguity and contingency, of displacement and difference. Commenting on a passage from *Swann's Way* in which Proust privileges the "necessary link" that ties the "little concert" of buzzing flies to the summer over "a human tune ... heard perchance" during the same season, de Man remarks:

the preference is expressed by means of a distinction that corresponds to the difference between metaphor and metonymy, necessity and chance being a legitimate way to distinguish between analogy and contiguity. The inference of identity and totality that is constitutive of metaphor is lacking in the purely relational metonymic contact: an element of truth is involved in taking Achilles for a lion but none in taking Mr. Ford for a motor car. (14; quotation from Proust 13)

The music of chance, title of another Auster novel, runs through all of the writer's works and Auster's predilection for metonymy over metaphor is incontrovertible. And yet, I would argue, it is not irreversible. For in Auster there is chance and there is chance. One evinces the radical contingency of the Ford motorcar; the other is rooted in a quest for "an element of truth" and is akin to what the Surrealists termed *le hasard objectif*, objective or *necessary* chance. When the "it happened this way" is transformed into the "it had to happen this way," when the contingent is turned into the necessary, we have moved from the world of metonymy to that of metaphor, with its "inference of identity and totality."

When, one might ask, does that occur? Lacan says that it happens in love or that love makes it happen:

> All love, existing on but *ceases not to be written* [Lacan's formula for the contingent], tends to shift the negation to *does not cease to be written* [his definition of the necessary], does not cease, will not cease. (*Séminaire XX* 132)

In a necessary, necessarily metonymic move, love displaces the not of contingency, makes it be not. Negating the iron law of contingency, it opens up the realm of metaphor and meaning; it takes two arbitrary points on a line and makes them into a circle, makes them make a circle.

When, one might ask, does that occur in Auster, in *Leviathan*? As in Lacan, it happens in and because of love. For the story of Sachs is not the only one in the novel. There is also the narrative of the narrator, Peter Aaron, drawn from the life story of Paul Auster. Sachs's life ends in tragedy; Aaron's reads like a fairy tale. After a number of trials and tribulations, he meets the woman of his dreams and lives happily ever after. The encounter with Iris—Auster's wife's name spelled backwards—leads to love, which, in turn, transforms the contingent into the necessary, the tragic into the comedic. Aaron's fairy tale follows the appropriate paradigm, the "U-shaped pattern" that "recurs in literature as the standard shape of comedy" (Frye, *Great Code* 169). Sachs's, on the other hand, does not. Sachs's emergence from the dark wood ends in murder rather than marriage, and his entire tale corresponds to the inverted-U structure of tragedy, including the fall of the tragic hero from "the top of the wheel of fortune" (Frye, *Anatomy* 206), which, in *Leviathan*, takes the form of a literal fall on July 4, 1986, the centennial of the Statue of Liberty.

The sudden plummet from a fire escape, the "moment of dizziness, when the wheel of fortune begins its inevitable cyclical movement downward" (*Anatomy* 213), occurs in the third and central chapter of the novel. The first had portrayed Sachs at the height of his powers, happily married to Fanny, writing easily and quickly "as if he had found a secret passageway that ran straight from his head to the tips of his fingers" (54). The second related the ascension narrative of Aaron and its intersection with the story of Sachs. For it is thanks to an affair with Sachs's wife Fanny that Aaron learns that he is capable of love: "If not for her, I never would have been in a position to meet Iris, and from then on my life would have developed in an altogether different way" (98). As for their actual encounter, it takes place at an exhibition, hence, in Aaron's view, "under [the] influence" of the artist Maria Turner, of "Maria as the reigning spirit of chance" (113). The two adjuvants in Aaron's tale will become agents of catastrophe in Sachs's. Maria will be present on the fire escape when Sachs plunges four stories to the ground, saved from almost certain death by a clothesline that breaks his fall. Subsequent to the murder of Dimaggio, Fanny too will assume the role of unwitting agent of catastrophe. Realizing that he needed to talk to someone about the disaster on the Vermont dirt road, Sachs "knew that person had to be Fanny" (174). Though he and his wife had been separated for a time, Sachs did not expect to find Fanny in bed with another man. Stunned, he beats a hasty retreat and turns instead to Maria who, unlike Fanny, happens to know Dimaggio, "the one fact powerful enough to turn an ugly misfortune into a full-scale tragedy" (179).

The division of the text into five parts—or acts—certainly conforms to the structure of a full-scale tragedy. The question remains as to the mode in which we should read this tragedy and the novel as a whole. As Frye has pointed out, a comedy is capable of enclosing a tragedy (e.g., Job, the Bible, Dante's *Commedia*) but not the reverse (*Anatomy* 215). And yet it is precisely this reverse situation that obtains in *Leviathan*. Moreover, the tragedy and comedy contained herein are inverse mirror images of each other. The actors in both dramas are the same, playing the role of adjuvants in the one, agents of catastrophe in the other. The protagonists are likewise linked, not just as friends and fellow writers but by virtue of the fact that Sachs impersonates Aaron, literally appropriating his *autograph*. One of Auster's favorite lines is Rimbaud's "*je est un autre*." Are we to read Sachs's story with the "I" of Aaron or against it, that is, in the mode of radical otherness and contingency? The latter would correspond to Frye's category of tragic irony, the sixth and final stage of tragedy governed by the figure of Sparagmos—ripping apart, Sachs blown to bits—whereas the former would fall into the third of Frye's stages, where "tragedy ends in triumph" (Sachs's death as the equivalent of the dissolution of Oedipus at Colonus), where tragedy is or may be inscribed within a larger comedic context (220–21). And if, as Frye also argues, the tragic hero's fall represents a fall from freedom, something once again rendered literal in the novel, how are we to interpret Sachs's fall? As we have seen, it transpires in full view of Lady Liberty, but it is also tied to a climb that Sachs, his mother, and another family made up the statue in 1951, when visitors were still allowed into the torch. As Mrs. Sachs relates the event,

> when you looked down through the arm, you felt like you were three hundred miles up in the air. It was pure nothingness all around, the great void of heaven.... It was the worst panic I ever felt in my life. (38–39)

"It was my first lesson in political theory," Sachs replies. "I learned that freedom can be dangerous. If you don't watch out, it can kill you" (39). In the light of that comment—reminiscent of Hegel's assertion that absolute freedom is terror—are we to regard Sachs's fall as a fall from freedom into chaos or rather as a fall from abstract freedom (freedom as its own opposite) into a subterranean exploration of the concept of liberty itself? Finally, how are we to read Sachs's relationship to the leviathan, which is another way of saying how are we to read *Leviathan* itself? Opposed in Hobbes to the other monster from Job, the behemoth, the leviathan figures a positive relinquishing of freedom for the sake of the common welfare and security. It may also be read as a symbol of disorder. "What this power looks like," Frye maintains, "depends on how it is approached." It may be seen as "an unimaginable horror" but also as "a source of energy that man can put to his own use" (*Words with Power* 285). The leviathan and the Statue of Liberty prove to be one and the same thing and the manner in which the leviathan of freedom is approached leads to very different readings of the novel. In what follows, I want to sketch out two possible interpretations of Sachs's tale, one written in the language of Sparagmos, of metonymy bereft of metaphor, the other rewritten in the language of Eros, of metonymy pushed into metaphor.

"Why ask why?" and "Just do it" are two advertising slogans that have passed over the airways in recent years. The product of what Jameson terms the cultural logic of late capitalism, they aim to convince the consumer to purchase their product, but they also rehearse something approaching the spirit of the metonymic postmodern age. A refusal (or mere "why bother") to ask why, to search for a reason for things, is an acceptance of the radically contingent and the formula for action that flows from it: Just do it—for no reason, just because. Contained within this injunction is an approach to abstract freedom that, in Gide's day, went by the name of *l'acte gratuit*. Gide, along with the later Surrealists, was fascinated by the concept and wrote a "sotie," *les Caves du Vatican* that featured Lafcadio "just doing it," in this case, pushing a man off a train into the void. *Leviathan* contains its own *acte gratuit*: Dimaggio shoots Dwight, end of discussion. There neither is nor can be an explanation or justification for this act. It just is. It is pointless, indeed impossible, to ask why.

In stark contrast to Dimaggio as the embodiment of pure contingency, Sachs is presented throughout the novel as someone who relentlessly asks why, who seeks "unifying principle[s]" (256), who attempts to piece things together into a whole. As such, he would appear to be the consummate metaphorical man, operating within the orbit of necessity. That said, it is possible to step back from what Sachs *says* and examine what he produces, what he does (as well as what is done with what he does), and how he ends up: as a heap of fragments most postmodern. By virtue of the era in which he lives, Sachs may be seen as having been drawn into what Jameson has described as "the postmodern force field," with its (over)emphasis on space and spatial logic and its deprivileging of time and temporal logic. To the extent that "the subject has lost its capacity actively ... to organize its past and future into coherent experience, it becomes difficult enough to see how the cultural productions of such a subject could result in anything but 'heaps of fragments' and in a practice of the randomly heterogeneous ... and the aleatory" (25). Among Sachs's cultural productions there is *Leviathan*, which is itself a fragment, a part of an unfinished book whose contents are never revealed. There is also *The New Colossus*, Sachs's only published novel, on whose cover there is a "strange, distorted drawing of the Statue of Liberty" (255) that is simulated—or more precisely "simulacrumed," the simulacrum being "the identical copy for which no original has ever existed" (Jameson 18)—on the cover of Auster's *Leviathan*.[1] Aaron discusses *The New Colossus* at some length. Although the historical period covered is shifted back a few decades, it recalls Doctorow's *Ragtime*. In the vertiginous logic of the postmodern, *The New Colossus* would be the nonidentical, imaginary copy of an original that does exist.

The extant original, too, is discussed at some length—by Jameson. Aaron's view of Sachs as a serious writer with a genuine concern for history mirrors Jameson's view of Doctorow. That admiration notwithstanding, Jameson goes on to read *Ragtime* as "a postmodern artifact." Quoting the interpretation of Linda Hutcheon (61f) that assigns "something like a political 'meaning'" to the text, he writes:

> Hutcheon is, of course, absolutely right, and this is what the novel would have meant had it not been a postmodern artifact. For one thing, the objects of representation, ostensibly narrative characters, are incommensurable and, as it were, of incomparable substances, like oil and water—Houdini being a *historical* figure [like Emerson and Bartholdi, for example, in *The New Colossus*], Tateh a *fictional* one, and Coalhouse [i.e., Kleist's Michael Kohlhaas] an *intertextual* one [like Ishmael and Raskalnikov, among others, in *The New Colossus*].... [A] seemingly realistic novel like *Ragtime* is in reality a nonrepresentational work that combines fantasy signifiers from a variety of ideologemes in a kind of hologram. (22–23)

Several pages later, Jameson concludes that "if there is any realism left here, it is a 'realism' that is meant to derive from the shock of ... slowly becoming aware of a new and original historical situation in which we are condemned to seek History by way of our own pop images and simulacra of that history, which itself remains forever out of reach" (25). Read along the lines of Jameson's assessment of *Ragtime*, Mr. Metaphor's *New Colossus*, which Aaron compares to "a pinball machine, a fabulous contraption with blinking lights and ninety-eight different sound effects" (42), is transformed into a jumble of postmodern factoids groundlessly grounded in an historicism devoid of historicity.

As the novel progresses, Sachs increasingly loses interest in writing, indeed he loses the very ability to write. The direct conduit from mind to hand that resulted in the vertiginous pinball machine of *The New Colossus* gives way to vertigo itself:

> Every time I picked up a pen and tried to start .... my head would spin, and I'd feel as though I was about to fall. Just like the time I fell off the fire escape. (253–54)

Then, as Sachs himself puts it, "something strange happened" (254). He ducks into a used bookstore to avoid being seen by an acquaintance and discovers a copy of *The New Colossus*. He purchases the book and later finds himself staring at the blurry image of the Statue of Liberty on its cover. She will, as it were, transmit to him a message, determine his course of action—the abandonment of writerly pursuits and the embrace of direct, political intervention. In a quintessential metaphorical move, Sachs declares:

> All of a sudden, my life seemed to make sense to me.... I had found the unifying principle, and this one idea would bring all the broken pieces of myself together. For the first time in my life, I would be whole. (256)

"'The original bomb child'" (25) embarks on a career as a bomber of a different sort, a bomber who makes sure that no one is harmed, who harms nothing but the symbol of the United States in an effort to remind America of its failure to live up to its ideals, to its Hegelian Idea. That, at any rate, is what Sachs, a.k.a. the Phantom of Liberty, believes himself to be doing. But what he in fact does from a postmodern perspective is to blow up shrunken replicas, mere simulacra of the Statue of Liberty. In addition, his attempt to engage in old-fashioned political action would appear to fall victim to late capitalism's seemingly infinite power of co-optation. As Jameson argues, "we all ... dimly feel that not only punctual and local countercultural forms of cultural resistance ... but also even overtly political interventions ... are all somehow secretly disarmed and reabsorbed by [the] system" (49). In Sachs's case, the reappropriation takes the form of T-shirts and buttons "on sale in novelty shops," of call-in shows on the radio, even of striptease acts in which Lady Liberty is seduced and disrobed by the Phantom (263). Sucked into the media and the market, Sachs's action is reduced to nothing or, more precisely, to mere exchange value. Meant to wake up the market, it becomes a part of it. And Sachs will only exit the market when he dies, a death to be read not as a form of destiny (Sachs's life under the sign of the bomb) but as an arbitrary point on a line, as an irrevocable ripping apart (Sparagmos) without meaning. It just is. Why ask why?

As for the *Leviathan* authored by Peter Aaron and signed by Paul Auster, it would be the nonidentical copy of an original that will never exist. Because an original like Sachs can no longer exist. We are confronted here with the leviathan of freedom as horror, as the freedom to do *anything* and thereby the freedom to *do* nothing. The clock within the space of the postmodern goes tick, tick, tick but is never allowed to go tick, tock. For the *sense* of an ending is here no more (Kermode, *Sense of an Ending* 44–45).

There is but tomorrow and tomorrow and tomorrow—in "a gulag or perhaps a shopping mall" (Jameson xi).

Like Humpty Dumpty, Sachs had a great fall. "In those few seconds before he hit the ground, it was as if Sachs lost everything. His entire life flew apart in midair, and from that moment until his death four years later, he never put it back together again" (120). With that assertion, Aaron would seem to endorse the preceding version of Sachs's tale (or some variation thereupon); he would appear to give the lie to Sachs's claim that he had found the guiding thread to and through his own life. Perhaps it is vain to attempt to put the broken pieces of Sachs back together again, to look for unity where there are only fragments. Even Frye contends that although "a tragedy may contain a comic action, it contains it only episodically as a subordinate contrast or underplot" (*Anatomy* 216). It is no doubt possible, but nevertheless difficult, to regard Aaron's story as a mere subplot in Sachs's. Sachs and Aaron are inverse mirror images of each other and participate in the logic of Lacan's *stade du miroir*, but something funny happens to the mirror stage on its way through *Leviathan*. In Lacan, it is always the ego that is fragmented, whereas the other, or ideal ego, appears as unified (the baby, with limited motor control, admires the seeming control and unity of its own reflection). In *Leviathan*, the situation is reversed: The ego and the other have switched places. And that role reversal inspires me to read Sachs's tragedy as an episode within Aaron's comedy rather than vice versa. That would make of Sachs a Job figure to whom something is restored (the title, after all, has its source in the Book of Job) rather than a creature who loses everything once and for all. It might be wiser simply to revise the foregoing assessment of postmodernism, to retrace my steps through the text, erasing Jameson's reductive remarks and replacing them with the more positive comments of a Linda Hutcheon. But I shall leave that operation to another. Instead, I shall perform a full-blown "premodern" reading of the work complete with references to the author and a happy ending of sorts.

Aaron, in the second chapter of the novel, remarks that "some thoughts are too dangerous, and you mustn't allow yourself to get near them" (89); in the last, that "some stories are too terrible, perhaps, and the only way to let them into you is to escape" (258). The thought in question is his own; the story, that of his alter ego Benjamin Sachs, with which he has been entrusted, which he fears could "go on and on, secreting its poison inside [him] forever" (272). Aaron speaks of the necessity of distance, of escape, and suggests a need for resolution. Auster *qua* Aaron "speaks of himself as another in order to tell the story of himself" (*Invention of Solitude* 154). Auster *qua* Sachs speaks of himself as another in order to return to a tale already told, the

Portrait of an Invisible Man; that is, the story of the father, of the self as father, which, once ended, "will go on telling itself" (67). In the penultimate segment of *Portrait of an Invisible* Man—penultimate also in the sense of the "inexplicable penultimate" in Mallarmé's prose poem, "The Demon of Analogy"—Auster cites Kierkegaard's famous line pertaining to the realm of spirit, where "he who is willing to work gives birth to his own father" (68). *Leviathan* is another such effort at parturition, one accomplished at a distance, through the looking glass, by way of the character Benjamin Sachs, who will be made to carry the burden of Auster's past, who will allow Auster "to relieve some of the pressure" not only of "hidden memories, traumas, [and] childhood scars" (*Art of Hunger* 285), but of an all too accessible adult memory and trauma—the sudden death of his father, which resulted in an inheritance that allowed him to go on writing. As Auster puts it: "It's impossible to sit down and write without thinking about it. It's a terrible equation, finally. To think that my father's death saved my life" (295–96). To see how the novel stages this terrible equation, together with the inexplicable penultimate of giving birth to one's own father, of delivering him from "the belly of the whale"; of rescuing him, in short, like Pinocchio "sav[ing] his father from the grip of death" (*Invention of Solitude* 89, 134); it is first necessary to wend one's way through the demon of analogy at work in *Leviathan*.

Let me begin with a brief aside. I am fully aware that *Leviathan* is a work of fiction. Because it is a structured narrative the operation in which I am about to engage, the importation of extratextual elements into the text itself, has a chance of demonstrating that, as Auster/Sachs says in *Leviathan* and Auster/A. says in *The Book of Memory*, "everything" is "connected to everything else" (231; 76, 159). Both Sachs and A. are referring to the world, to the world as "our beloved codex," to borrow Frank Kermode's phrase. Just like Kermode, Auster sometimes attempts to read the world as a book, "divining congruences, conjunctions, opposites; extracting secrets from its secrecy, making understood relations, an appropriate algebra." Also like Kermode, Auster sometimes admits that both world and book "are hopelessly plural, endlessly disappointing"; that "we stand alone before them, aware of their arbitrariness and impenetrability, knowing that they may be narratives only because of our impudent intervention, and susceptible of interpretation only by our hermetic tricks" (*Genesis of Secrecy* 145). Of course all of this concerns me as much as Auster. But having allowed world and book to remain true to their incomprehensible selves in the preceding section, here I shall travel back and forth between them, endeavoring to endow at least one of them with meaning.

"Absence," Auster writes in *Portrait of an Invisible Man*, was "the fundamental quality of his [father's] being" (6), and the presence of Auster's father in *Leviathan* is first made felt through his very absence in the tale Auster has Aaron recount concerning his own life. In January 1979, when Auster's father died of a massive heart attack, Aaron, like Auster, found himself virtually penniless, down on his luck. Out of the blue, Aaron, like Auster, receives a sum of money. But it comes not in the form of a bequest but of two grants from literary foundations. There is, however, another windfall in the book, one intimately bound up with death, and which it falls to Sachs to "inherit." Following the double murder in the Vermont woods, Sachs discovers more than $160,000 in a bowling bag in the trunk of Dimaggio's car. Like Nashe's windfall in *The Music of Chance*, which allowed Auster "to explore the implications" of the one he had received upon his father's death, this one is tied to "the question of freedom" (*Art of Hunger* 319). In *Leviathan*, the Statue of Liberty is present to pound in the point, and it is with reference to Lady Liberty that Auster once again transfers a personal memory away from Aaron and onto Sachs. "He remembers visiting the Statue of Liberty with his mother and remembers that she got very nervous inside the torch and made him go back down the stairs sitting, one step at a time" (*Invention of Solitude* 169), which is exactly what Sachs's mother will have the boy do. Sachs's fall will occur while Fanny and Aaron are laughing "at the idea of falling through the Statue of Liberty.... It was as if uttering the word fall had precipitated a real fall" (122). And a real fall broken by a real clothesline there was—in Auster's father's life. Sam Auster fell off a roof in Jersey City and came away "from the accident with only a few bumps and bruises" (*Art of Hunger* 354). As did Sachs. Just as Sachs's father is an "Eastern European Jew" (27), so too is the father of Sam Auster. In 1919, while the seven- or eight-year old Sam lay in bed in an adjoining room, Harry Auster, Sam's father, was shot to death by his estranged wife, Sam's mother, over a woman named Fanny—like the woman named Fanny in the novel who becomes Aaron's lover and Sachs's ex-wife. After that trauma, Sam Auster remained forever aloof, detached, seemingly apart from the world, including the world of his own son. At the end, "he had no wife, no family that depended upon him, no one whose life would be altered by his absence." In sum, and this is what most disturbs Paul Auster, his "father had left no traces" (*Invention of Solitude* 6). Sachs will find himself in the same situation at the end of *Leviathan*. Absent some eighteen months, childless and spouseless, the *Phantom of Liberty* exits the world blown to smithereens, almost literally without a trace. Sachs, it is clear to see, is Auster's father, but he is also Auster himself. He is the son as the father and the father as the son.

Occupying both roles, alternately and simultaneously, the prankster Sachs (33)—like the prankster Collodi, author of *Pinocchio* (*Invention of Solitude* 163)—will allow Auster to save his father's life in the realm of spirit just as his own was saved by his father's actual death.

Sachs "went out for a walk one afternoon in the middle of September, and the earth suddenly swallowed him up" (159). Which is to say, he entered the belly of the leviathan, for "only one who descends to the underworld saves the loved one" (Kierkegaard 57; qtd. in *Invention of Solitude* 68). It all comes back to the incident in the Vermont woods, which forms the traumatic kernel of the novel and revisits the traumatic kernel of Sam Auster's life. The characters present are Dwight McMartin, an amateur baseball player whose gesture of kindness will result in his own death; Reed Dimaggio, whose very name is synonymous with baseball; and Sachs, who will kill Dimaggio with a baseball bat. Baseball is omnipresent here, and for Auster "the power of baseball" is none other than "the power of memory. Memory in both senses of the word: as a catalyst for remembering his own life and as an artificial structure for ordering the historical past" (*Invention of Solitude* 116). The idea of a man named Dimaggio being done in with a baseball bat is less irony or comic relief than it is artifice, designed to give narrative shape to events past. As in the Book of Job, it is the just man who will be punished, and the occurrence will remain incomprehensible to those involved (neither Job nor his friends know about God's wager with Satan to test Job's faith). But just as the frame narrative in Job supplies the *reader* with the key to Job's plight, here the presence of baseball provides a clue to the incident's connection with the biographical past. Transferred into the realm of baseball, onto a baseball diamond of sorts where the players move around the bases, trade places like so many changes at bat, Dimaggio's action and its aftermath remain at once inexplicable and explainable in terms of the power of memory.

Reed Dimaggio alternates between the role of Sam's mother—who not only shot and killed her husband but wreaked havoc in the life of her son—and Sam himself, the source of the windfall. The victim Dwight occupies the place of Harry Auster within the family romance recreated here. And Sachs represents Sam, the innocent bystander unable to prevent the crime that will alter his own existence, as well as Paul, the one who receives the money. But Sachs likewise commits a murder of his own, attempting to stop Dimaggio in a gesture too late to save Dwight's life but rife with consequences for his own. That "dangerous supplement" opens the door for a renewed quest in search of an invisible man—Dimaggio *qua* Sam Auster. Returning to the site of the original crime, the foundational drama within his father's life, Auster revisits a source of trauma within his own: "the curse of the absent father" (*Invention of Solitude* 117). It is necessary to seek him out once more, once more through the person of Sachs.

Like the discourses on retributive justice that form a large part of the Book of Job, much of the remainder of *Leviathan* is concerned with the question of retribution. Consistent with the many mirror-image reversals in the novel, here Sachs's friends protest his innocence (and thereby occupy the place of Job), whereas Sachs himself insists upon his necessary guilt, the stance of Job's friends. (And that guilt is necessary if he is to pursue and fill in the contours of an invisible man.) The remainder of Sachs's life will be consumed in an effort to make amends, to right the balance upset in this tragedy. He will go to California where Dimaggio's ex-wife Lillian and daughter Maria live. He will attempt literally to *pay* for his crime by giving Lillian daily installments of $5,000 from the money found in Dimaggio's car. He will become a surrogate father to Dimaggio's daughter, a lover to his former wife. He will read his dissertation on the anarchist Alexander Berkman and try to write a book about Dimaggio's life:

> I planned it as an elegy, a memorial in the shape of a book.... It would be an enormous project ... that would take me years to finish. But that was the point somehow. As long as I was devoting myself to Dimaggio, I would be keeping him alive. I would give him my life, so to speak, and in exchange he would give my life back to me. (253)

The memorial in the form of a book will of course be written—but not by Sachs. As we have seen, he finds himself unable to write. Every time he sets pen to paper, he finds himself falling off the fire escape, returning to the moment of the fall:

> First I realized that I was falling, and then I realized that I was dead.... [T]hough I was technically still alive, I was dead, as dead as a man who's been buried in his grave. (130–31)

From that moment forward, Sachs's entire journey transpires in the zone Lacan refers to as "between-the-two-deaths," two deaths bound up in *Leviathan* with the father. Sachs's second death will occur in a final effort to merge with Dimaggio, who had the makings of a bomb in the trunk of his car, whom Sachs believes to have been a political activist "brave enough to put his ideas to the test" (252). *Believes to have been.* For again like the reader of the Book of Job, the reader of *Leviathan* knows something that Sachs does not know—that Dimaggio may not have been a political activist at all, but rather an agent working for the FBI or the CIA. In other words, the reader knows that it will never be possible to know who Dimaggio truly was, that "each fact is nullified by the next fact, that each thought engenders an equal and opposite thought." That is what Auster wrote about his father in *Portrait of an Invisible Man* (61). That is what Auster tells us about his father *qua* Dimaggio in *Leviathan*.[2]

The book seemingly ends in tragedy, irrevocable and irredeemable. Lacan draws upon tragedy, Sophocles's *Antigone*, to elaborate his concept of between-the-two-deaths. But what the notion in fact concerns is the subject who does not give way on his or her desire—the ethical imperative of psychoanalysis. For Antigone, that access to desire takes place within the context of a sacrifice that Lacan compares to an anamorphosis in which "a most beautiful image of the Passion appears in the beyond of the mirror, whereas something rather disjointed and disgusting surrounds it" (*Séminaire VII* 318). In *Leviathan*, the father *qua* Sachs follows his desire to the end of desire itself even as he sacrifices himself so that the son might live. The dissolution of Sachs *qua* Auster, however, means something altogether different, though it too involves "the beyond of the mirror." Just as "Job's egocentric perception has disappeared along with its objective counterpart, the leviathan," at the end of the book of Job (Frye, *Great Code* 197), at the conclusion of the work entitled *Leviathan*, the ego as other, *le stade du miroir*, has vanished. From a Lacanian perspective, that corresponds to the end of analysis, the *Wo es war, soll Ich werden*, the moment when the ego/other (the *Ich*) moves into the beyond of the mirror, locus where the *subject* (the "S," the *es*) at last has "the floor and enter[s] into a relation with the true Others" (*Séminaire II* 288). The subject *qua* subject here addresses the "absolute Other. Absolute, meaning that he is recognized but not known" (*Séminaire I* 148). That, I would argue, is how Auster saves the father, not through cognition—he remains as mysterious as ever—but through *recognition*, the very essence of comedy. "This end is about reintegration and concord, I would even say reconciliation" (*Écrits* 524). This end represents a radical shift from metonymy to metaphor, a pendular swing from the metonymic pole that is bound up with lack "to the other, metaphorical pole of the signifying quest," where the subject is called upon "to become that which I [the speaking subject] am, to come into being" (517). In his seminar on Freud's technical writings, Lacan, as was his wont, turned to literature, to a poem by Angelus Silesius, to deliver the essential message of metaphor:

Contingency and essence
*Man, become essential: for when the world passes
The contingent falls away and the essential remains.*

This is indeed what the end of analysis is about, a twilight or imaginary waning of the world, and even an experience bordering on depersonalization. *It is then that the contingent falls away*—the accidental, the trauma, the snags of history. *And it is being that comes to be constituted then.* (258)

Lacan, I think, would have appreciated Auster's use of metaphor, for the example he always gave to illustrate the workings of the trope was culled from Hugo's poem, "Booz endormi," revolving around the "paternal mystery" and "accession to paternity" (*Écrits* 508). When Lacan finally gave his long-delayed seminar on the Name of the Father, "the passage he chose was that of the sacrifice of Isaac by Abraham, a story of salvation, of someone saving someone from the grasp of death" (Schneiderman 55). Of course, Kierkegaard's *Fear and Trembling* is also a reflection on the story of Abraham and Isaac, one that gave rise to his famous maxim about giving birth to one's own father. And when a man who left no traces is made to leave traces in the shape of a book, when he is delivered in this way from the clutches of death, then, in the words of one of Auster's favorite poets, Marina Tsvetayeva,

It may be that a better way
To conquer time and the world
Is to pass, and not to leave a trace—
To pass, and not to leave a shadow
on the walls ... (qtd. in *Invention of Solitude* 95)

NOTES

1. To be precise, the blurred image of the Statue of Liberty appears on the cover of the paperback edition whereas it figures on the spine of the hardcover edition.

2. This also applies to the father *qua* Sachs, whom Aaron will describe at one point in the novel as "an emblem of the unknowable itself" (164).

WORKS CITED

Auster, Paul. *The Art of Hunger*. 1992. New York: Penguin, 1993.

———. *The Invention of Solitude*. 1982. New York: Penguin, 1988.

———. *Leviathan*. 1992. New York: Penguin, 1993.

De Man, Paul. *Allegories of Reading: Figural Language in Rousseau, Nietzsche, Rilke, and Proust*. New Haven: Yale UP, 1979.

Frye, Northrop. *Anatomy of Criticism*. Princeton: Princeton UP, 1957.

———. *The Great Code: The Bible as Literature*. 1981. New York: Harvest/HBJ, 1983.

———. *Words with Power*. 1990. New York: Harvest/HBJ, 1992.

Hutcheon, Linda. *A Poetics of Postmodernism*. New York: Routledge, 1988.

Jameson, Fredric. *Postmodernism, or, The Cultural Logic of Late Capitalism*. Durham: Duke UP, 1991.

Kermode, Frank. *The Genesis of Secrecy*. Cambridge: Harvard UP, 1979.

———. *The Sense of an Ending*. 1966. Oxford: Oxford UP, 1968.

Kierkegaard, Soren. *Fear and Trembling*. Trans. Alastair Hannay. London: Penguin, 1985.

Lacan, Jacques. *Écrits*. Paris: Seuil, 1966.

———. *Le Séminaire I: Les Écrits techniques de Freud*. Paris: Seuil, 1975.

———. *Le Séminaire II: Le Moi dons la theorie de Freud et dans la technique de la psychanalyse*. Paris: Seuil, 1978.

———. *Le Séminaire III: Les Psychoses*. Paris: Seuil, 1981.

———. *Le Séminaire VII: L'Ethique de la psychanalyse*. Paris: Seuil, 1986.

———. *Le Séminaire XX: Encore*. Paris: Seuil, 1975.

Schneiderman, Stuart. *Jacques Lacan: The Death of an Intellectual Hero*. Cambridge: Harvard UP, 1983.

STEVEN G. KELLMAN

Austerity Measures:
Paul Auster Goes to the Dogs

"We're not dogs after all," insisted Paul Auster in a 1990 interview. "We're not driven solely by instincts and habits; we can think, and because we think, we're always in two places at the same time."

For *Timbuktu* (Henry Holt, 1999), the ninth novel published under his own name, Auster sets himself the challenge of representing a dog's-eye view, the perspective of a mangy, middle-aged mutt who can indeed think and who even undergoes out-of-body experiences that situate him in two places at the same time. "Part collie, part Labrador, part spaniel, part canine puzzle," Mr. Bones has a "grasp of Ingloosh [that] was as good as any other immigrant who had spent seven years on American soil." Because he lacks the appropriate laryngeal equipment, he cannot speak the language very effectively, but the pensive woofer can reason, remember, and dream. He can also ponder mortality and his prospects for attaining that blissful afterlife, "an oasis of spirits," that his favorite master called Timbuktu.

At the outset of *Timbuktu*, Mr. Bones is suffering "pure ontological terror" over the imminent demise of Willy G. Christmas, the drifter who has been his constant companion throughout most of the cur's seven earthly years. Much of that time has been spent on the road, in adventures that might recall *Travels with Lizbeth* (1993), Lars Eighner's picaresque account of sharing the homeless itinerant life with his faithful canine. Willy was once

From *Hollins Critic* 37, no. 4 (October 2000). © 2000 by Hollins University.

William Gurevitch, the Brooklyn-born son of Holocaust survivors who adopted the "lifelong philosophy of embracing trouble wherever he could find it." Trouble embraced William too ardently, forcing him to drop out of Columbia University and into the psychiatric ward of St. Luke's Hospital. When Santa Claus appears on a TV screen and exhorts him personally to transform his life, he changes his name and resolves to become a peripatetic saint. Auster has pronounced *Don Quixote* his favorite book, and there is more than a little trace of Cervantes' Knight of Mournful Countenance in the psychotic Luftmensch who sallies forth with Mr. Bones. To another interviewer, Auster, who specialized in the Renaissance during his graduate study at Columbia University, characterized the Elizabethan novel *The Unfortunate Traveler* as "one of my very favorite books." He paid tribute to its author, Thomas Nashe, by choosing Nashe as the name for the protagonist of his own 1990 book, *The Music of Chance*, and by returning to the picaresque in several of his novels, including *Timbuktu*. Ill-shod Willy G. Christmas is not the only one of Auster's motley tramps to undertake a bootless quest.

Mr. Bones fondly recalls the roving times he shared with Willy, but the hardships of vagrancy finally wear his human companion down. Dying, Willy makes his way to Baltimore, intent on bequeathing his manuscripts— seventy-four notebooks that include the unfinished epic *Vagabond Days*—to his old high school English teacher. When Willy expires just outside the Edgar Allan Poe house, Bones is left to make his way in a world that is perilous to a solitary *Canis familiaris*. He takes up first with a loving, lonely boy named Henry Chow, until Henry's forbidding father threatens to turn the dog into dinner at the family's Chinese restaurant. After fleeing into northern Virginia, Bones is adopted into an affluent suburban household and basks in the bourgeois comfort that seems to him a betrayal of Willy's principled penury. Should the dog who walked with a raffish, demented poet end his days as a well-heeled pet?

Books about dogs can of course boast a distinguished pedigree. The category includes not only ethological studies by Roger A. Caras, Jeffrey Moussaief Masson, Elizabeth Marshall Thomas, and Mary Elizabeth Thurston but also an enormous litter of kiddie lit—Fred Gipson's *Old Yeller*, Eric Knight's *Lassie Come-Home*, and Albert Payson Terhune's *Lad: A Dog*, among much else. It numbers J. R. Ackerley's loving tribute to his Alsatian, *My Dog Tulip*, Jacqueline Susann's surprisingly untrashy memoir of her French poodle, *Every Night Josephine*, and *A Dog's Life*, Peter Mayle's further take on Provence as seen by his dog Boy. In *The Heart of a Dog*, Mikhail Bulgakov anticipates organ transplants and satirizes Soviet presumptions to engineer human souls. In an early, virtuosic chapter of *Anna Karenina*, Leo Tolstoy presents the proceedings through the eyes of Levin's hunting dog, Laska, and in *The Call of the Wild* and *White Fang*, Jack London uses canine protagonists to dramatize life as a struggle. Twenty-one years after becoming a Woolf, in 1912, even the former Virginia Stephen contributed to the genre; her *Flush* is no ode to indoor plumbing but rather a biography of Elizabeth Barrett's cocker spaniel. A wag might note how often serious literature has gone to the dogs.

Timbuktu is no shaggy dog story, nor does it sentimentalize its portrait of an orphaned pet. Neither does the novel infantilize either its protagonist or its reader. In creating a thinking beast, one who thinks incessantly about celestial transfiguration, Auster is able to dramatize the mind–body problem, the tenuous connection between spirit and matter that is a preoccupation of much of his other fiction as well. In the grownup Mr. Bones, Auster has created an Everyman who happens to be canine, a furry philosopher who craves companionship but recognizes solitude as the fundamental condition. "What he has," explained Auster, "is what all dogs have: a purity of emotion and an intensity of attachment that all of us human beings respond to because we feel these things as well." A feeling for the illusoriness of intense attachments has also been a constant in Auster's protean career. However ardent his allegiances, Mr. Bones—who becomes "Cal" to one master and then "Sparky" to the next—discovers that ties do not bind very long, that contingent events shape and reshape our evanescent lives. Willy is a reminder that we are all tramps in ash-time.

In the prose poem *White Spaces* that he wrote in 1978, Auster ponders how to render into words the music of chance, how to create a text that will subvert itself and its author with the deconstructive recognition that things might well have been other than they are. The poet expresses: "The desire, for example, to destroy everything I have written so far. Not from any revulsion at the inadequacy of these words (although that remains a distinct possibility), but rather from the need to remind myself, at each moment, that things do not have to happen this way, that there is always another way, neither better nor worse, in which things might take shape." Two personal experiences in particular impressed Auster with the randomness of existence: In July, 1961, he saw lightning strike and kill a fellow summer camper, and later, during the Vietnam War, a high lottery number happened to spare him from the perils of the military draft. In *Smoke*, the 1995 film that Wayne Wang directed from a Paul Auster screenplay, Augie Wren (Harvey Keitel) is an impresario of coincidence, the imaginatively generous proprietor of a cigar shop that is the locus of serendipitous meetings among a ragtag cast.

The conception of alternatives is of course the motive of all fiction, but in Auster it also becomes the matter. It has been both topic and problem of the haunting stories he composes about individuals forced to confront a crisis over the instability of identity. "*Un coup de dés jamais n'abolira le hasard*" (A toss of the dice will never abolish chance"), famously proclaimed Stéphane Mallarmé, whom Auster has admired and translated. The function of the novelist, according to an interview Auster gave in 1990, is to be the amanuensis of enigmatic encounters: "The unknown is rushing in on top of us at every moment," he contended. "As I see it, my job is to keep myself open to these collisions, to watch out for all these mysterious goings-on in the world."

The unpublished Willy is Auster manqué, and during one winter of frenetic activity, he attempts to produce the first work of art designed expressly for canine sensibilities, a laboriously assembled collage of aromas that he calls "A Symphony of Smells." Auster himself offers no such experiment in trans-species aesthetics. *Timbuktu* is human art, a laboriously assembled collage of words about an anthropomorphic hound. Mr. Bones is a device to explore the range of human possibilities, and he has less in common with Rin Tin Tin than with men in Auster's other books, including, like Willy, the author himself.

A dog's-eye view defamiliarizes even an ordinary city street, and by adopting the vantage point of a canine mind, Auster is able to suggest the uncanny. "I believe the world is filled with strange events," he told an interviewer in 1987. "Reality is a great deal more mysterious than we ever give it credit for." In *City of Glass*, the protagonist, Quinn, writes mystery novels, but all of Auster's characters, including Mr. Bones, live them. "What I am after, I suppose," confessed Auster in 1990, "is to write fiction as strange as the world I live in." It is for that reason that he scorns critical fastidiousness over verisimilitude; if life is fraught with flukes, it makes no sense to fault a plot for seeming to be implausible. Despite its fanged and growling narrator, Auster would count *Timbuktu* as realistic.

The word *cynic* is derived from the Greek term for dog, and in providing a dog's take on the United States in the final years of the twentieth century, Auster, a poet and novelist who has likened poetry to still photography and prose to filming with a movie camera, offers the reader low-angle shots. It is true that the horizontal Mr. Bones looks up to humans, particularly Willy, but, traveling close to the ground, he is also always seeing the underside of everything. No one is a hero to someone else's dog. More generally, Mr. Bones, who struggles to reduce the world to English words, assists Auster in his continuing efforts to expose the futility of articulation.

"In the impossibility of words, / in the unspoken word / that asphyxiates, / I find myself," the reader finds Auster writing in a 1976 poem called "Interior."

In the spare, ascetic poetry that he abandoned in favor of prose during the 1980s, Auster challenges the inadequacy of language. "Each syllable / is the work of sabotage," he writes in a 1974 volume whose title, *Unearth*, exposes the poet in the act of undoing. *Disappearances* is the appropriate name that Auster, the self-erasing author, gave his collected poems, in 1988. The vatic voice that Auster projects while trying to write a poetry that cannot be written persists in the fiction, especially the ontologically astringent *New York Trilogy* but also Bones's leveling prose in *Timbuktu*.

Moreover, Auster's investment in other poets is often an extension of his own preoccupation with rhetoric that negates itself. What interests him in the poetry of Laura Riding is "its will to seek its own annihilation." About Giuseppe Ungaretti, he writes: "Ungaretti's poetic source is silence, and in one form or another, all his work is an expression of the inexhaustible difficulty of expression itself." In George Oppen, Carl Rakosi, and Charles Reznikoff, he discovers lessons in how to speak what cannot be spoken. Auster is fascinated by Edmond Jabès's struggle to create "a poetics of absence," and he insists that the poems of André du Bouchet "cannot be truly felt until one has penetrated the strength of the silence that lies at their source. It is a silence equal to the strength of any word." Though its style is not nearly as hermetic as that of Auster's earlier works, even *Timbuktu*, narrated by a voice that cannot truly speak, from a vantage point beyond earthly communication, acknowledges and defies the imperatives of the ineffable. It is a book that straddles realms, between the *hic et nunc* that Mr. Bones presently inhabits and the no-place to which Willy has already gone and Bones aspires: "Where the map of this world ends, that's where the map of Timbuktu begins," explained the departed traveler.

In several autobiographical efforts, including the 1997 *Hand to Mouth: A Chronicle of Early Failure* and a 1982 memoir—and meditation on memory—called *The Invention of Solitude*, Auster presents himself as insomniac before the American Dream, a connoisseur of worldly nonachievement who cherishes the challenge of inhabiting social margins. As an undergraduate at Columbia University, he even devised and tried to bestow a Christopher Smart Award to reward failure, to recognize the person who, like Smart himself, "had done the least with the most," but the honor had no applicants. In *The Art of Hunger* (1991), a collection of occasional essays roughly united by an interest in "an art that begins with the knowledge that there are no right answers," he would even elevate gauntness into an aesthetic principle. Born in 1947, Auster grew up in the suburbs of Newark, New Jersey, in a middle-class family that made him feel "an internal émigré, an exile in my own house." His parents' divorce exacerbated the adolescent Auster's alienation. Immediately after high school, he headed for Europe and later spent his junior year in Columbia's Paris program. After receiving an M.A. in Comparative Literature, Auster shipped off as a utility man on a tanker that worked the route between the North Atlantic Coast and the Gulf of Mexico. In 1971, he returned to Paris and remained in France until 1974, subsisting on odd jobs that included operating the switchboard for the Paris bureau of the *New York Times*, translating a variety of texts, including the Vietnamese Constitution, and doctoring movie scripts. It was not until his father's death, in 1979, that a modest inheritance freed him to concentrate on longer literary projects. Similarly, in what is probably Auster's best-known novel, *The Music of Chance*, a sudden, unexpected bequest from his long-estranged father frees Nashe to set out on the open road and submit his life to the tyranny of happenstance. Sudden windfalls also play a crucial role in *City of Glass* (1985) and *Moon Palace* (1989). And in *Timbuktu*, Willy G. Christmas does not know what to do with the ten thousand dollars he suddenly receives after his mother's death except to give it away. For Quinn, looking for coherent explanations in *City of Glass*, "nothing was real except chance," and chance itself is fantastic.

Auster describes the early years on his own as "a state of never-ending panic," in which he was never far from starvation, so anxious for funds that he struggled to design and market a baseball card game that no one ever bought. Out of desperation, he even tried, and failed, to teach. When he concocted a hopeless potboiler, *Squeeze Play*—under the pseudonym Paul Benjamin—in 1982, it barely sold a few hundred copies. Yet for all the angst and agony of life on Grub Street, Auster posits deprivation as a literary virtue. The unkempt characters who ramble through his novels lead transient lives, but then so do his readers, even if settled in the temporary comfort of an easy chair. Though Franz Kafka never ranged very far beyond his native Prague, Auster hails him as a fellow wanderer, a confederate of Mr. Bones, Willy, and the American author himself. "He moves from one place to another, and dreams continually of stopping. And because this desire to stop is what haunts him, is what counts most for him, he does not stop. He wanders."

In Auster's Kafkaesque allegory *In the Country of Last Things* (1987), Anna Blame abandons the security of home to suffer foreign hardships, a *picara* rootless and resourceful in a distant, devastated land. In *Mr. Vertigo* (1994), Walt Rawley is a vivid contrast to his genteel English namesake; an orphaned urchin, Rawley departs the streets of St. Louis for the highways of America and a barnstorming career exhibiting his gifts of levitation. "Once you throw your life to the winds," declares Marco Stanley Fogg, who narrates *Moon Palace* and sleeps in Central Park, "you will discover things you had never known before, things that cannot be learned under any other circumstances. I was half-dead from hunger, but whenever something good happened to me, I did not attribute it to chance so much as to a special state of mind."

Auster's books are fictions of austerity, sparely told tales about ontological fundamentalists, characters who regard embellishment as an obstacle to the special state of mind that in their author's universe approximates enlightenment. A lean and hungry look might alarm Caesar, but it pleases Auster, who called his collection of essays *The Art of Hunger*. In the title piece, Auster asserts a personal literary credo while describing Knut Hamsun's achievement in his 1890 novel *Hunger*: "It is first of all an art that is indistinguishable from the life of the artist who makes it. That is not to say an art of autobiographical excess, but rather, an art that is the direct expression of the effort to express itself. In other words, an art of hunger: an art of need, of necessity, of desire." Announcing, and displaying, his elective affinities with Hamsun, Kafka, Beckett, Celan, Hawthorne, Jabès, and other verbal minimalists, Auster—whose name is Latin for the South Wind— throws life and art up to be buffeted by the cruel and cleansing air.

Willy G. Christmas is a logomaniac, and as he lies dying in Baltimore he delivers a rambling, insane, and inspired monologue that in effect voids his cluttered mind of all its memories and passions and reduces him to a vacant corpse. (Onomastically, Bea Swanson, the retired teacher who draws him to Baltimore, emphasizes that much of *Timbuktu* is Willy's swan song). Among much else, he recalls his college roommate at Columbia, "a guy named Anster, Omster, something like that—who had gone on to write a number of so-so books...." Recounting an anecdote that Anster/Omster once told, about a dog who learned to type, Willy insists on the honesty of his source: "In all the years we were friends, I never knew him to make up stories. That's one of his problems, maybe—as a writer—not enough imagination—but as a friend he always gave it to you straight from the horse's mouth."

Auster's playful self-reference here, an imaginative attack on his own failure of imagination, recalls other cameo appearances by the author in his fictions. In *City of Glass*, which begins with a case of mistaken identity, between the protagonist, Quinn (a pseudonym Auster once employed when publishing book reviews), and a writer named Paul Auster, Quinn even visits

Auster and shares lunch with him in his New York apartment. *Ghosts* (1986), which follows *City of Glass* and precedes *The Locked Room* (1986) in what Auster calls *The New York Trilogy*, begins on February 3, 1947, the author's birthdate. A writer named Paul Benjamin—the *nom de plume* under which Auster published his hapless crime caper *Squeeze Play*—is played by William Hurt in the adaptation of Auster's screenplay *Smoke*. Though not "an art of autobiographical excess," Auster's art of hunger is "indistinguishable from the life of the artist who makes it"—as that life is refracted through the coy words of a cunning author.

For any writer, the entire oeuvre constitutes a cumulative opus, one that draws obliquely on the life of its creator. But Auster makes the links among works and between art and life overt and problematic. In his memoir, *Hand to Mouth*, Auster recalls H. L. Humes, the homeless, charismatic crackpot he befriended while attending Columbia. Like Willy G. Christmas, Humes was wont to orate in endless, breathless riffs that mingled malarkey with sagacity. Intent on undermining American capitalism, Humes one day began handing out fifty-dollar bills to strangers. It is an anecdote that Auster duplicates in *Moon Palace*, where Thomas Effing, an eccentric old blind man—whose housekeeper is named Mrs. Hume—employs Marco Stanley Fogg to wander the streets of New York dispensing to passersby twenty thousand dollars' worth of fifty-dollar bills. Similarly, Willy, the "loudmouthed crank, a nihilist, a besotted clown" who would be a saint, gives away every nickel of the ten thousand dollars in insurance money he receives for the death of his mother.

In *Mr. Vertigo*, narrator Walt Rawley notes that: "... *dog* and *god* are the same word spelled backwards and forwards," a quip that Auster recycles in *Timbuktu* as a witticism ("Just turn around the letters of the word dog, and what did you have?" asks Willy) and as a central theme. A spark of divinity inhabits Mr. Bones; but his own name is a mocking reminder of the meager scaffolding we each provide to house the spirit. In another jest from *Mr. Vertigo*, Walt Rawley explains that while they were on the road performing levitations, his mentor Master Yehudi assumed a stage name: "Buck was the alias he'd chosen. Timothy Buck for himself and Timothy Buck II for me, or Tim Buck One and Tim Buck Two. We got some good laughs out of that, and the funny thing was, it wasn't a whole lot different from Timbuktu where we were, at least as far as remoteness was concerned." To a Brooklyn dog, Timbuktu, a Mali town abutting the Sahara, might seem the *ultima thule*. But the point of *Timbuktu* is that paradise is never very remote for Mr. Bones. The entire novel is an interrogation into road directions. Is Timbuktu, "an oasis of spirits," best attained by settling in with Polly and Richard Jones, affluent suburbanites who offer all the creature comforts a pet could want, or by following mobile, madcap Willy and setting out, tattered, for the territory ahead?

Ultimately, Auster answers No! in thunder to bourgeois complacency. He celebrates Willy's "noisy, fractious disdain for Everything-That-Was" even as he himself commands wider respect and, in his second marriage—to novelist Siri Hustvedt—evidently thriving as husband and father, no longer lives from hand to mouth. Yet it is easy to see how Auster would be fascinated by the voice of a meditative quadruped who is torn between bohemia and the bourgeoisie. And in Willy G. Christmas, he found a surly rebel against a cosmic order that, at least according to the narrator of *The Locked Room*, lacks any meaningful order: "Lives make no sense," argues the fictional writer, a friend of a man named Fanshawe who unaccountably disappeared. "A man lives and then he dies, and what happens in between makes no sense." For Willy, reflecting on the death of his father when he was only twelve, revelation is abrasive: "The more wretched your life was, the closer you were to the truth, to the gritty nub of existence." Using a testy, unkempt vagabond and his companion mongrel, Auster gropes again toward the gritty nub of existence.

Auster has claimed that his original plan was to use Mr. Bones and Willy G. Christmas as minor characters in a much larger work, but the narrative tail ended up wagging it all. Veteran actors know better than to appear with a dog, lest the fuzzy creature steal the show. Begun in 1993, *Timbuktu* took five years to complete, while its author was distracted by new activities in film. With *Blue in the Face* (1995), a cinematic whimsy that he and Wayne Wang shot in six days as an impromptu sequel to their collaboration on *Smoke*, he added co-director to poet, playwright, essayist, translator, and novelist on a formidable list of accomplishments. In Harvey Keitel's storyteller Augie Wren, Auster continued his metafictional investigations into the possibilities of fiction.

Though he is no literary Jerry Lewis, Auster has long been taken more seriously in France, and other parts of Europe, than in the United States. *Leviathan* won France's prestigious Prix Medicis Étranger, and a three-day symposium on Auster's work held at the University of Provence has not been matched in his native country. *Lulu on the Bridge*, a film starring Harvey Keitel, Mira Sorvino, Gina Gershon, Willem Dafoe, and Vanessa Redgrave, that he both wrote and directed, was first screened at Cannes in 1998 and, though shown commercially and acclaimed in France and elsewhere throughout Europe, was unable to find a theatrical distributor in the United States before finally being released directly onto video in 1999. The story of a jazz saxophonist, Izzy Maurer (Harvey Keitel), who finds a magic stone and falls in love with a young actress named Celia Burns (Mira Sorvino), *Lulu on the Bridge* is another Auster fable about coincidence, identity, and imagination. French enthusiasm for the author of *The New York Trilogy* can be explained in part as reciprocation for his own Gallic interests. Auster lived for several years in France, translated French poets, including André du Bouchet, Jacques Dupin, and Stéphane Mallarmé, and edited *The Random House Book of Twentieth-Century French Poetry* (1982). In his preface to that anthology, he argues for the enormous influence that the French have exerted on the history of English and American literature, extensive enough that their poetry "can be read as a chapter in our own poetic history."

Yet Auster acknowledges disparities, and his own narrative aspirations align him more directly with the terse French *récit* than with the expansive Great American Novel. In *City of Glass*, it is the Gallic quality of literary economy that his protagonist Quinn finds so appealing about mystery novels: "In the good mystery there is nothing wasted, no sentence, no word that is not significant.... Everything becomes essence; the center of the book shifts with each event that propels it forward. The center, then, is everywhere, and no circumference can be drawn until the book has come to its end." In part because of his apprenticeship in poetry and in part out of his respect for European minimalists—like Beckett and Mallarmé—who mistrust their own verbal medium, Auster is a maestro of silences and spaces. "I want my books to be all heart, all center, to say what they have to say in as few words as possible," he told an interviewer in 1990. "This ambition seems so contrary to what most novelists are trying to accomplish that I often have trouble thinking of myself as a novelist at all."

When American readers think of contemporary novelists, Auster does not come instantly to mind. His exquisite metafictional mysteries have been caveat to the masses. But Mr. Bones is no French poodle, and *Timbuktu*, a meditation on the thinker as canine rambler, could change its author's fortunes, again. We're not dogs, after all, and thoughtful humans can covet a smart tale.

Chronology

1947	Paul Auster is born in Newark, New Jersey on February 3 to Samuel and Queenie Auster.
1969	Graduates with a B.A. in English and comparative literature from Columbia University.
1970	Receives M.A. in Renaissance literature from Columbia.
1971	Moves to France and lives with girlfriend Lydia Davis, a writer.
1974	Auster and Davis return to New York and are married on October 6. Three years later they have a son. Publishes *Unearth*.
1975	Receives grant from the Ingram Merrill Foundation.
1976	Publishes *Wall Writing*.
1979	Davis and Auster divorce. Auster wins fellowship from National Endowment for the Arts in poetry.
1980	Publishes *White Spaces* and *Facing the Music*.
1981	Marries the writer Siri Hustvedt. They later have a daughter.
1982	Publishes *The Invention of Solitude* and *The Art of Hunger*. Also publishes *The Random House Book of Twentieth-Century French Poetry* (edited and translated by Auster).
1985	Publishes *City of Glass*.
1986	Publishes *Ghosts* and *The Locked Room*. Becomes a lecturer at Princeton University until 1990.

1987	Publishes the three novels, *City of Glass*, *Ghosts*, and *The Locked Room* as *The New York Trilogy*. Also publishes *In The Country of Last Things*.
1988	Publishes *Disappearances: Selected Poems*.
1989	Publishes *Moon Palace*.
1990	Publishes *The Music of Chance* (nominated for the PEN/Faulkner Award) and *Ground Work: Selected Poems and Essays 1970–1979*. Receives the Morton Dauwen Zabel Award from the American Academy and Institute of Arts and Letters.
1992	Publishes *Leviathan* and *Squeeze Play*, an early mystery novel he wrote under the pseudonym Paul Benjamin.
1993	Awarded the Prix Medicis Étranger for *Leviathan*. *The Music of Chance* adapted into a film. Publishes *Autobiography of the Eye*.
1994	Publishes *Mr. Vertigo*.
1995	Films *Smoke* and *Blue in the Face* released. Auster wrote the screenplays for both, and co-directed *Blue in the Face* with Wayne Wang. *Smoke* awarded the Silver Bear, Special Jury Prize; the International Film Critics Circle Award; and the audience Award for Best Film at the Berlin Film Festival.
1996	Leaves longtime publisher Viking Penguin to sign a three-book deal with Henry Holt.
1997	Publishes *Hand to Mouth: A Chronicle of Early Failure*.
1998	Publishes *Timbuktu*.
1999	Film *Lulú on the Bridge* released (written and directed by Auster) .
2002	Publishes *The Book of Illusions: A Novel*; *I Thought My Father Was God: And Other True Tales from NPR's National Story Project* (editor); *The Red Notebook: True Stories*; and *The Story of My Typewriter* (co-authored with artist Sam Messer).

Contributors

HAROLD BLOOM is Sterling Professor of the Humanities at Yale University and Henry W. and Albert A. Berg Professor of English at the New York University Graduate School. He is the author of over 20 books, including *Shelley's Mythmaking* (1959), *The Visionary Company* (1961), *Blake's Apocalypse* (1963), *Yeats* (1970), *A Map of Misreading* (1975), *Kabbalah and Criticism* (1975), *Agon: Toward a Theory of Revisionism* (1982), *The American Religion* (1992), *The Western Canon* (1994), and *Omens of Millennium: The Gnosis of Angels, Dreams, and Resurrection* (1996). *The Anxiety of Influence* (1973) sets forth Professor Bloom's provocative theory of the literary relationships between the great writers and their predecessors. His most recent books include *Shakespeare: The Invention of the Human* (1998), a 1998 National Book Award finalist, *How to Read and Why* (2000), *Genius: A Mosaic of One Hundred Exemplary Creative Minds* (2002), and *Hamlet: Poem Unlimited* (2003). In 1999, Professor Bloom received the prestigious American Academy of Arts and Letters Gold Medal for Criticism, and in 2002 he received the Catalonia International Prize.

CHARLES BAXTER is the author of three novels, including *The Feast of Love* (2000), four collections of short stores, three collections of poems, and a collection of essays on fiction called *Burning Down the House* (1997). He teaches at the MFA program at the University of Michigan-Ann Arbor.

STEPHEN FREDMAN is a Professor at the University of Notre Dame. He is the author of *A Menorah for Athena: Charles Reznikoff and Jewish Dilemmas of Objectivist Poetry* (2000).

PASCAL BRUCKNER is an acclaimed French essayist and novelist, who was awarded the prestigious Académie Française Prix 2000 and Medici Prize 1995.

WILLIAM DOW teaches at the American University of Paris. He has published articles in such journals as *Publications of the Modern Language Association*, *The Emily Dickinson Journal*, *Twentieth-Century Literature*, and *ESQ: A Journal of the American Renaissance*.

JOHN ZILCOSKY is an Assistant Professor of German at the University of Toronto. He is the author of *Kafka's Travels: Exoticism, Colonialism, and the Traffic of Writing* (2002).

WILLIAM LAVENDER is Coordinator of the Low Residency MFA Program at the University of New Orleans, and the founding editor of Lavender Ink Press. His essays have appeared journals including *Contemporary Literature* and *Poetics Today*. He has published two chapbooks of poems, *Guest Chain* and *Heart's Sentence*, a collection of poems, *look the universe is dreaming* (2003), and is the editor of *Another South: Experimental Writing in the South* (2002).

ALISON RUSSELL is an Assistant Professor at Xavier University. She is the author of *Crossing Boundaries: Postmodern Travel Literature* (2000).

STEVEN E. ALFORD teaches humanities at Nova Southeastern University in Fort Lauderdale, Florida. He has published two other articles on Paul Auster that investigate the issues of identity and space in Auster's work.

TIM WOODS is a Senior Lecturer at the University of Wales, Aberystwyth. In addition to his numerous essays, he books include *Beginning Postmodernism* (1999), and several volumes on which he served as editor.

PADGETT POWELL has taught writing at University of Florida since 1984. He has published four novels and two collections of short stories, and his latest novel is *Mrs. Hollingsworth's Men* (2002). He is also winner of the Prix de Rome and a Whiting Writers Award.

KATHARINE WASHBURN authored the novel, *The Pearl Test* (2001), and co-edited, with Clifton Fadiman and John S. Major, *World Poetry: An Anthology of Verse from Antiquity to Our Time* (1998).

STEVEN WEISENBURGER is an Associate Professor of English at the University of Kentucky. His most recent books are *A Southern Horror: Race, Sex, and the 1898 Wilmington Massacre* (2003) and *The Modern Medea: A Story of Slavery and Child-Murder from the Old South* (1998).

BRUCE BAWER is the author of *Diminishing Fictions* (1998) and *Prophets and Professors* (1995). He also authored *A Place at the Table: The Gay Individual in American Society* (1994) and *Stealing Jesus: How Fundamentalism Betrays Christianity* (1998).

ALIKI VARVOGLI teaches at University of Dundee's School of American Studies in Scotland. He has published essays on Saul Bellow, E. Annie Proulx and Raymond Carver.

LINDA L. FLECK is the translator of *The Anthropology of Anger: Civil Society and Democracy in Africa* (1996), written by Celestin Monga.

STEVEN G. KELLMAN teaches at the University of Texas at San Antonio. He has an extensive list of publications on a variety of subjects, including modern American and British literature, nineteenth-century American writers, the European novel, literary theory, film and film theory.

Bibliography

Adams, Timothy Dow. "Photography and Ventriloquy in Paul Auster's *The Invention of Solitude.*" *True Relations: Essays on Autobiography and the Postmodern.* Eds: Thomas G. Counser and Joseph Fichtelberg (introd). Westport, CT: Greenwood, 1998: 11–22.

Alford, Steven E. "Spaced Out: Signification and Space in Paul Auster's *The New York Trilogy.*" *Contemporary Literature* 36, no. 4 (Winter 1995): 613–32.

———. "Mirrors of Madness: Paul Auster's *The New York Trilogy.*" *Critique: Studies in Contemporary Fiction* 37, no.1 (Fall 1995): 17–23.

Andrews, Corey. "The Subject and the City: The Case of the Vanishing Private Eye in Paul Auster's *City of Glass.*" *Henry Street: A Graduate Review of Literary Studies* 6, no.1 (Spring 1997): 61–72.

Barone, Dennis, Ed. *Beyond the Red Notebook: Essays on Paul Auster.* Philadelphia: University of Pennsylvania Press, 1995.

———. "Auster's Memory." *The Review of Contemporary Fiction* 14, no. 1 (Spring 1994): 32–34.

Brault, Pascale-Anne. "Translating the Impossible Debt: Paul Auster's *City of Glass.*" *Critique: Studies in Contemporary Fiction* 39, no. 3 (Spring 1998): 228–238.

Benedetti, David. "An Interview with Paul Auster." *American Poetry* 8 (Fall 1990): 188–92.

Birkerts, Sven. *American Energies: Essays on Fiction.* New York: William Morrow, 1992.

Bradbury, Malcolm. *The Modern American Novel: New Edition.* New York: Viking, 1993.

Chapman, Siobhan and Christopher Routledge. "The Pragmatics of Detection: Paul Auster's *City of Glass*." *Language and Literature: Journal of the Poetics and Linguistics Association* 8, no. 3 (October 1999): 241–53.

Cohen, Josh. "Desertions: Paul Auster, Edmond Jabes, and the Writing of Auschwitz." *Journal of the Midwest Modern Language Association* 33–34, no. 3–1 (Fall 2000–Winter 2001): 94–107.

De Lost Santos, Oscar. "Auster vs. Chandler: Or, Cracking the Case of the Postmodern Mystery." *Connecticut Review* 16, no. 1 (Spring 1994): 75–80.

Dotan, Eyal. "The Game of Late Capitalism: Gambling and Ideology in *The Music of Chance*." *Mosaic: A Journal for the Interdisciplinary Study of Literature* 33, no. 1 (March 2000): 161–176.

Drenttel, William, ed. *Paul Auster: A Comprehensive Bibliographic Checklist of Published Works 1968–1994*. New York: William Drenttel New York, 1994.

Finkelstein, Norman. "In the Realm of the Naked Eye: The Poetry of Paul Auster." *American Poetry* 8 (Fall 1990): 175–187.

Ford, Mark. "Inventions of Solitude: Thoreau and Auster." *Journal of the American Studies* 33, no. 2 (August 1999): 201–219.

Herzogenrath, Bernd. *An Art of Desire: Reading Paul Auster*. Amsterdam, Netherlands: Rodopi, 1999.

Irwin, Mark. "Memory's Escape: Inventing *The Music of Chance*—A Conversation with Paul Auster." *Denver Quarterly* 28, no. 3 (Winter 1994): 111–122.

Little, William. "Nothing to Go On: Paul Auster's *City of Glass*." *Contemporary Literature* 38:1 (Spring 1997): 133–63.

Mallia, Joseph. "Paul Auster Interview." *Bomb* 23 (Spring 1988): 24.

Malmgren, Carl D. "Detecting/Writing the Real: Paul Auster's *City of Glass*." *Narrative Turns and Minor Genres in Postmodernism*. Eds. Theo D'haen and Hans Bertons. Amsterdam: Rodopi, 1995.

Marling, William. "Paul Auster and the American Romantics." *Literature* 7, no. 4 (March 1997): 301–10.

McCaffery, Larry and Sinda Gregory. "An Interview with Paul Auster." *Mississippi Review* 20, no. 1–2 (1991) 49–62.

———. "An Interview with Paul Auster." *Contemporary Literature* 33, no. 1 (Spring 1992): 1–12.

Nealon, Jeffrey T. "Work of the Detective, Work of the Writer: Paul Auster's *City of Glass*." *Modern Fiction Studies* 42. 1 (1996): 91–110.

Rohr, Susanne. "The World as 'Ordinary Miracle' in William Dean Howells's *A Hazard of New Fortunes* and Paul Auster's *Moon Palace*."

REAL: The Yearbook of Research in English and American Literature 15 (1999): 93:110.

Rowen, Norma. "The Detective in Search of the Lost Tongue of Adam: Paul Auster's *City of Glass*." *Critique: Studies in Contemporary Fiction* 32, no. 4 (Summer 1991): 105–114.

Rubenstein, Roberta. "Doubling, Intertextuality, and the Postmodern Uncanny: Paul Auster's *New York Trilogy*." *LIT: Literature Interpretation Theory* 9, no. 3 (December 1988): 254–62.

Sarmento, Clara. "Paul Auster's *The New York Trilogy*: The Linguistic Construction of an Imaginary Universe." *Interdisciplinary Literary Studies: A Journal of Criticism and Theory* 3, no. 2 (Spring 2002): 82–101.

Segal, Alex. "Paul Auster's *The Locked Room*." *Critique: Studies in Contemporary Fiction* 39, no. 3 (Spring 1998): 239–257.

Szabo, Anna T. "The Self-Consuming Narrative: Paul Auster's *New York Trilogy*." *AnaChronist* (1996): 266–79.

Shiloh, Ilana. *Paul Auster and Postmodern Quest: On the Road to Nowhere*. New York: Peter Lang, 2002.

Varvogli, Aliki. *The World That is the Book: Paul Auster's Fiction*. Liverpool: Liverpool University Press, 2002.

Wesseling, Elizabeth. "*In the Country of Last Things*: Paul Auster's Parable of the Apocalypse." *Neophilogus* 75, no 4 (1991): 496–504.

Acknowledgments

"The Bureau of Missing Persons: Notes on Paul Auster's Fiction," by Charles Baxter. From *The Review of Contemporary Fiction* 14, no. 1 (Spring 1994): 40–43. © 1994 by Charles Baxter. Reprinted by permission.

"'How to Get Out of the Room That Is the Book?' Paul Auster and the Consequences of Confinement," by Stephen Fredman. From *Postmodern Culture* 6, no. 3 (May 1996). © 1996 by Stephen Fredman. Reprinted by permission.

"Paul Auster, or The Heir Intestate," by Pascal Bruckner. From *Beyond the Red Notebook: Essays on Paul Auster*, edited by Dennis Barone. © 1995 by the University of Pennsylvania Press. Reprinted by permission of the University of Pennsylvania Press.

"Paul Auster's *The Invention of Solitude*: Glimmers in a Reach to Authenticity," by William Dow. From *Critique: Studies in Contemporary Fiction* 39, no. 3 (Spring 1998): 272–81. Reprinted with permission of the Helen Dwight Reid Educational Foundation. Published by Heldref Publications, 1319 Eighteenth St., NW, Washington, DC 20036–1802. Copyright © 1998.

"The Revenge of the Author: Paul Auster's Challenge to Theory," by John Zilcosky. From *Critique: Studies in Contemporary Fiction* 39, no. 3 (Spring 1998): 195–206. Reprinted with permission of the Helen Dwight Reid Educational Foundation. Published by Heldref Publications, 1319 Eighteenth St., NW, Washington, DC 20036–1802. Copyright © 1998.

"The Novel of Critical Engagement: Paul Auster's *City of Glass*" by William Lavender. From *Contemporary Literature* 34, no. 2 (Summer, 1993): 219–239. © 1993 by the Board of Regents of the University of Wisconsin System. Reprinted by permission of the University of Wisconsin Press.

"Deconstructing *The New York Trilogy*: Paul Auster's Anti-Detective Fiction" by Alison Russell. From *Critique: Studies in Contemporary Fiction* 31, no. 2 (Winter 1990): 71–84. Reprinted with permission of the Helen Dwight Reid Educational Foundation. Published by Heldref Publications, 1319 Eighteenth St., NW, Washington, DC 20036–1802. Copyright © 1990.

"Chance in Contemporary Narrative: The Example of Paul Auster" by Steven E. Alford. From *LIT: Literature Interpretation Theory* 11, no. 1 (July 2000): 59–82. © 2000 by OPA (Overseas Publishers Association). Reprinted by permission of the Taylor & Francis Group.

"'Looking for Signs in the Air': Urban Space and the Postmodern in *In the Country of Last Things*," by Tim Woods. From *Beyond the Red Notebook: Essays on Paul Auster*, edited by Dennis Barone. © 1995 by the University of Pennsylvania Press. Reprinted by permission of the University of Pennsylvania Press.

"'The End Is Only Imaginary,'" by Padgett Powell. From *New York Times Book Review* (May 17, 1987): 11–12. © 1987 by Padgett Powell. Reprinted by permission.

"A Book at the End of the World: Paul Auster's *In the Country of Last Things*," by Katharine Washburn. From *The Review of Contemporary Fiction*, 14, no. 1 (Spring 1994): 62–65. © 1994 by *The Review of Contemporary Fiction*. Reprinted by permission.

"Inside *Moon Palace*," by Steven Weisenburger. From *The Review of Contemporary Fiction*, 14, no. 1 (Spring 1994): 70–79. © 1994 by Steven Weisenburger. Reprinted by permission.

"Doubles and more doubles," by Bruce Bawer. From *The New Criterion* 7, no. 8 (April 1989): 67–74. © 1989 by Bruce Bawer. Reprinted by permission.

"Exploding Fictions," by Aliki Varvogli. From *The World That is the Book: Paul Auster's Fiction*. © 2002 by Aliki Varvogli. Reprinted by permission.

"From Metonymy to Metaphor: Paul Auster's *Leviathan*," by Linda L. Fleck. From *Critique: Studies in Contemporary Fiction* 39, no. 3 (Spring 1998): 258–270. Reprinted with permission of the Helen Dwight Reid Educational Foundation. Published by Heldref Publications, 1319 Eighteenth St., NW, Washington, DC 20036–1802. Copyright © 1998.

"Austerity Measures: Paul Auster Goes to the Dogs," by Steven G. Kellman. From *Hollins Critic* 37, no. 4 (October 2000): 1–13. © 2000 by Hollins University. Reprinted by permission.

Index

Affective space, 138
Alford, Steven E., 113
American identities, 4–5
Anna Blume (*In the Country of Last Things*)
  broken recollections of, 149–51
  calamities of, 168–9
  death and, 153–5
  name of, 169
  urban space and, 139, 140–1, 142–5
Anti-detective fiction, 97
Art, representational, 178–80
Art of Hunger, The (Hamsun), 150
Art of Hunger (Auster), 2, 227–8, 229
Auster, Paul
  appearances in his fiction, 2, 65, 67–8, 73, 229–30
  on chance, 114–9
  chronology of events in life of, 228, 233–4
  father's death, 21–3
  literary similarities to, 1
  parallels with Quinn (*City of Glass*), 93–4
  relationship with his father, 43–4
  translations by, 232
Austin, Jacqueline, 57
Author
  authority of, 68
  destruction of (*City of Glass*), 65–7
  disappearance of (*City of Glass*), 66–7
  disappearance of (*Ghosts*), 68–9
  postmodernist devices, 65

  search for identity of (*City of Glass*), 94
  self-examination of, 69
  solitude and, 70
  See also Narrator

Bakhtin, M.M., 95
Barth, John, 78
Barthes, Roland, 64, 65, 89
Baseball, 218
Bauman, Zygmunt, 60
Bawer, Bruce, 183
Baxter, Charles, 3
Beckett, Samuel, 78
Benjamin, Paul (pseudonym), 228, 230
Benjamin Sachs (*Leviathan*), 191–2
  affinity with Don DeLillo's character, 194–5
  death of, 202
  fall of, 211, 215
  fiction by, 197, 212–4
  guilt and redemption of, 200–1
  as mirror image of Peter Aaron, 215
  resolving identity of, 207–8
  Statue of Liberty and, 198–9, 201–2
  tragedy in, 210–1, 218–9
  withdrawal and isolation of, 199–200
Black (*Ghosts*), 8, 9–10, 20, 105–6
Blakelock, Ralph Albert, 179–80
Blue (*Ghosts*)
  death of, 9–10
  quest for truth, 104

"the room of the book" and, 8–9, 11
solitude and, 20
trapped in hermetic world of text,
104–5
violent hierarchy with Black, 105–6
Blue in the Face (film), 231
Book of Job, 219
"The Book of Memory" (Auster)
masculine self-generative creativity in,
21–9
meaninglessness in, 22–3
memory and, 36–8
post-Holocaust imagery and, 29–32,
36
postmodern typology in, 57–9
"the room of the book" theme and,
17–20
spatiality and, 138
urban space in, 141–2
wordplay in, 149
See also *Invention of Solitude, The*
(Auster)
Book of Questions, The (Jabés), 14–6, 17
Boris Stepanovich (*In the Country of Last
Things*), 149
Brooks, Peter, 77, 88, 89
Bruckner, Pascal, 43
Bruno, Giordano, 54
Bulgakov, Mikhail, 224–5
Butor, Michel, 63, 77

Chance
Auster on, 114–9
as coincidence reflecting lived
experience, 120
contradictions on, 130–1
as culturally pervasive, 113–4
fate and, 124–7
inheritance and, 45–6
in *Leviathan*, 193–4, 207–9
manifested in Auster's fiction, 119
meaninglessness and, 22–3, 122–3
as metaphysical synchronity, 120–1
in *Moon Palace*, 177, 178
as reflections of the universe's

structure, 123–4
time and, 127–30
writerly practice and, 74
See also Coincidence
Chatman, Seymour, 79, 82
Christopher Smart Award, 227
City of Glass (Auster)
Auster's appearance in, 2
criticism of itself within, 94–5
as deconstruction of detective novel,
77–8
destruction of author in, 65–7
discovering true author of, 67–8
Don Quixote and, 100–1
ironic turn at end of, 93
isolation in, 155
notion of characters in, 83–8
plotting, 88–93
"private eye" metaphor in, 98–9
Quinn's identity crisis in, 99–100
title, 98
See also *New York Trilogy* (Auster)
Codrescu, Andrei, 171–2
Coincidence
Auster's personal experiences with,
225
in *The Invention of Solitude*, 56
meaninglessness and, 22–3
as metaphysical correspondence,
121–2
in *Moon Palace*, 188
repetition in, 117
in *Smoke*, 225
See also Chance
Comedy and tragedy, 210–1
Confinement theme, 44–5
Couser, Thomas, 51

Daniel Quinn. See Quinn (*City of Glass*)
David Antin (*Ghosts*), 11
Death
as an aesthetic action, 153
release and transcendence through,
153–5
writing and, 71–3

De Certeau, Michel, 139
"Decisive Moment, The" (Auster), 139–40
Deconstruction, 15, 77-78, 97-8
DeLillo, Don, 194–5
Derrida, Jacques, 103, 105
Detective genre
  Auster's challenge to, 64–5
  City of Glass as deconstruction of, 77–8
  deconstructing conventional elements of, 97–8
  as end-dominated, 99
  "oedipal", 62
  postwar, 62–3
  Romance and, 110
Dickinson, Emily, 27
Don Quixote (Cervantes), 100–1, 224
Dow, William, 51
Dwight McCartin (*Leviathan*), 218

Effing. *See* Thomas Effing (*Moon Palace*)
Emily Fogg (*Moon Palace*), 173, 176
Ermarth, Elizabeth, 175

The Fall theme, 199–200
Fanshawe
  naming power of, 108
  paternal message of, 109
  search for fugitive author and, 69
Fate, 124–6, 126–7
Father/son relationship
  between Auster and his father, 28-30, 3–4
  constructing identity of father ("Portrait of an Invisible Man"), 53–5, 57
  Leviathan's autobiographical elements and, 217–8
  regeneration of father through the son (The Book of Memory), 28–30, 32–6
Ferdinand (*In the Country of Last Things*), 154–5, 162–3

Ferrara, Fernando, 83, 87–8
Figural narration, 80
Fleck, Linda L., 207
Fogg (*Moon Palace*)
  coincidences and, 121–2
  inheritance of, 176
  name of, 185
  quest of, 172–4
  temporality and, 177
Forster, E.M., 82
Foucault, Michel, 66, 139
Four-Gated City, The (Lessing), 165
Frank, Anne, 29–30, 30–2
Fredman, Stephen, 7
French poets, 14–7
Frye, Northrop, 109–10, 211

Gass, William H., 82–3, 86, 87–8
Genealogical narrative, 174–6
Ghosts (Auster)
  disappearance of author in, 68–9
  logocentric quest for origin in, 102–3, 104
  narrator, 68, 69
  physicality of writing theme in, 14
  "the room of the book" theme in, 18
  self-mirroring in, 104
  title, 103
  See also New York Trilogy (Auster)
Gide, Andre, 212
Gregory, Linda, 114

Hamsun, Knut, 150, 229
Hand to Mouth: A Chronicle of Early Failure (Auster), 227
Hassan, Ihab, 52
Havel, Vaclav, 205
Heart of a Dog, The (Bulgakov), 224–5
Henry Chow (*Timbuktu*), 224
Henry Dark (*City of Glass*), 86
Hermeneutic code, 91–3
Humes, H.L., 230
Hunger (Hamsun), 229
"The Hunger Artist" (Kafka), 1–2

Identity. *See* Self-identity
Inheritance
    by Auster, 43–4, 45–6
    chance and, 45–6
    of Fogg (*Moon Palace*), 176
Inter-textuality, 94
In the Country of Last Things (Auster)
    Anna's calamities in, 168–9
    bag people in, 162–3
    death in, 153–5
    erasure of history and information in,
        150, 151–2
    food in, 167–8
    hellish present in, 166–7
    imaginary end in, 164
    isolation in, 156
    lost-and-found personalities in, 6
    naming of characters in, 169
    plotting, 165–6
    the Runners in, 161–2
    setting, 162
    urban spatiality in, 138–9, 140–1,
        142–5, 151, 156–8
Invention of Solitude, The (Auster), 227
    chance in, 56, 114–5
    combining the tragic and optimistic
        in, 56–7
    confinement theme in, 44–5
    diaristic and anecdotal structure in,
        54–5
    father/son relationship in, 28-30,
        43–4
    isolation in, 155
    lost identity theme in, 5–6
    narrator in, 71
    postmodernist devices, 55–6
    questioning of postmodern typologies
        in, 51–4
    responsibility of aesthetic self theme
        in, 59–60
    uncertainty of self theme in, 47–8
    See also "Book of Memory, The"
        (Auster); "Portrait of an Invisible
        Man" (Auster)
Isolation, 155–6, 199–200

Jabés, Edmond, 14–7
James, Henry, 82
Jameson, Frederic, 59, 137, 151, 213,
    214
Jencks, Charles, 52
Jewish writers, 19
Jews
    memory and, 36, 37–8
    post-Holocaust imagery and, 29–32
    The Book of Questions (Jabés), 14-16
Jim Nashe (*In the Country of Last
    Things*), 6
Julian Barber (*Moon Palace*), 186
    See also Thomas Effing (*Moon Palace*)

Kafka, Franz, 1–2
Kellman, Steven G., 222
Kermode, Frank, 63
Kitty Wu (*Moon Palace*), 173, 186

Language
    by Auster's father, 54–5
    "authentic", 54
    challenging inadequacy of, 226–7
    disintegration of memory and,
        149–52
    materiality of, 148–9
    monadology, 24–5, 26
    narrator's surrender to, 72–3
    poetic element in, 11–2
    spatiality and, 145–6
    wordplay, 149
Lavender, William, 77
Lefebvre, Henri, 137–8
Lessing, Doris, 165
Leviathan (Auster)
    asking why? in, 212
    autobiographical elements in, 193,
        217–8
    books within, 196–7, 212–4
    chance events in, 193-94, 207–8
    distinction between the real and the
        textual in, 205–6
    extratextual elements in, 216

the Fall theme in, 199–200
imagining self as other theme in,
    203–5
The Locked Room and, 192
metonymy in, 208–9, 220–1
mirror images in, 215
Peter Aaron's fiction creation in,
    202–3
political elements in, 194–6, 215
quest for meaning in, 195–6
realistic narrative in, 191–2
retribution in, 219
Statue of Liberty in, 198–9
tragedy and comedy in, 210–1
Literary theory
    attack on detective genre, 77–8
    Auster's challenge to detective, 64–5
    post-war detective, 63–4
Locked Room, The (Auster)
    chance in, 122–3
    Leviathan and, 192
    logocentric quest in, 106–8
    questioning authority of author in, 69
    title, 106
    See also New York Trilogy (Auster)
Logocentrism, 98, 100, 106–8
Lost in the Funhouse (Barth), 78
Luck (Rescher), 123–4
Lulu on the Bridge (film), 231–2
Lyotard, Jean-Francois, 52, 53

McCaffery, Larry, 12, 114
Mallarmé, Stéphane, 14, 15
Mallia, Joseph, 116
Malmgren, Carl D., 94
Mao II (DeLillo), 194–5
Marco Fogg. *See* Fogg (*Moon Palace*)
Masculinist fantasy of self-generative
    creativity, 21–9
Max Work (*City of Glass*), 66, 78, 79
Meaninglessness
    in "The Book of Memory", 22–3
    chance and, 22–3, 115–6, 122–3
    scientific account of nature and, 118
Memory
    as a course of political resistance and

autonomy, 152–3
    illusion of time and, 116–8
    language and disintegration of,
        149–52
    quest of self and, 48
    writing and, 18-21, 36–9
Metaphor, 209, 220–1
Metonymy, 208–9, 211–2, 220–1
Monadology, 24–5
Monk, Leland, 124
Moonlight (Auster), 179
Moonlight (Blakelock), 179–80
Moon Palace (Auster)
    chance/coincidence in, 120–2, 178,
        188
    compared with *New York Trilogy*,
        186–7
    genealogical narrative in, 174–6, 180
    hero's quest in, 172-4, 185–6
    isolation in, 155
    moon references in, 187–9
    references to the 1960's in, 172
    representational art in, 178–80
    representational discourse in, 180–1
Morality, 58–9
Mr. Bones (*Timbuktu*), 222–3, 225,
    226–7, 230
Mr. Vertigo (Rawley), 228–9, 230
"The Musgrave Ritual" (Brooks), 89
Music of Chance, The (Auster), 6, 120,
    123, 228

Narrative
    chance events and, 128–31
    deconstruction of (*City of Glass*),
        78–82
    genealogical, 174–6
    as a political tool, 152
    as straying from a linear progression
        (*In the Country of Last Things*),
        149–50
    temporal sequences and, 128, 130
    See also Narrator
Narrator
    access to counterpart's physical
        presence (*The Locked Room*), 106–7

as author, 68
  death and, 71–3
  in *Leviathan* vs. *The Locked Room*, 192
  questioning authority of author (*The
    Locked Room*), 69
  search for origin (*The Locked Room*),
    107–8
  as a self-undermining linguistic agent
    (*City of Glass*), 101–2
  as a self-undermining linguistic agent
    (*The Locked Room*), 108
  See also Author; Narrative
New York Trilogy (Auster)
  Auster's appearances in, 229–30
  compared with *Moon Palace*, 186–7
  deconstructive principles in, 97–8
  denial of closure in, 99
  fate theme in, 125–6
  interlinking of texts within, 106
  Leviathan and, 192–3
  lost identity theme in, 6
  naming in, 183–4
  parodies of Romance in, 109–10
  plot coincidences in, 120
  publication of, 73
  recurring elements in, 184–5
  as a travel narrative, 110–1
  See also City of Glass (Auster); *Ghosts*
    (Auster); *Locked Room, The* (Auster)
Nisbet, Robert, 175
Nomadism theme, 45, 46

Overdetermination, 91

Passing Time (Butor), 77
Paternal authority, 100, 109
Penguin (publisher), 73
Peter Aaron (*Leviathan*), 191
  fairy tale of, 209–10
  fiction created by, 202-3,
  linked with Sachs, 204-5, 210, 215
  resolving Sachs' identity and, 207–8
Peter Stillman Jr. (*City of Glass*), 83–4,
    91, 100

Peter Stillman Sr. (*City of Glass*), 84–7
  disappearance of, 90–1, 102
  mapping course of, 88-90
  overdetermination of, 91
Pinocchio story, 24, 29, 34-6
Plot coincidences, 120
Poe, Edgar Allan, 63
Poetry
  Auster on, 227
  Auster's attempts at writing, 12–3
  encounter between prose and, 12,
    13–4
Poets
  French, 14–7
  modern, 11
Point of view, 78, 80
  See also Narrator
"Portrait of an Invisible Man" (Auster),
    53–4, 57, 215-6
  See also Invention of Solitude, The
    (Auster)
Post-Holocaust imagery, 29–32, 36
Postmodern author, 65
Postmodernism
  "The Book of Memory" and, 57–9
  devices in *The Invention of Solitude*,
    55–6
  questioned in *The Invention of Solitude*,
    51–4
  responsibility of aesthetic self and,
    59–60
  spatiality and, 137–8
Post-structuralists, 52–3
Powell, Padgett, 161
Prigogine, Ilya, 177
Production of Space, The (Lefebvre),
    137–8

Quinn (*City of Glass*)
  death and, 71–2
  detective quest of, 65–6
  hermeneutic coding of, 91–3
  identity crisis of, 99–100, 183–4
  layers of identities in, 78–82
  madness of, 70

mapping Stillman's course, 88–90
meeting with Peter Stillman, 85–7
parallels with Paul Auster, 93–4
search for ultimate authority, 100–1
three personalities of, 66

Racevskis, Karlis, 52, 58
Rawley, Walt, 228–9, 230
Reed Dimagio (*Leviathan*), 201, 218–20
Rescher, Nicholas, 123–4
Reznikoff, Charles, 139–40
Rhyming words, 22
Robbe-Grillet, Alain, 63–4
Romance, 109–10
"the room of the book" theme
    The Book of Questions (Jabés) and, 14–6
    death/meaninglessness and, 21–3
    frameworks of, 7–8
    in *Ghosts*, 8–11
    masculinist self-generation and, 23–9,
        32–6
    memory and, 36–9
    poetry and, 11–4
    post-Holocaust imagery and, 29–32
    writing the book in "The Book of
        Memory", 17–20
Roth, Philip, 196
Rowen, Norma, 93
Russell, Alison, 82, 97

Sachs. *See* Benjamin Sachs (*Moon Palace*)
Samuel Farr (*In the Country of Last
    Things*), 168
Self, the
    imagining as the other, 203–5
    quest for, 48–9
    recreation of, 46–7
    uncertainty of, 46–8
    wandering and, 46
Self-identity
    double, 9–10
    layers of (*City of Glass*), 78–82
    lost and found, 3–6
    Quinn's crisis with, 99–100, 183–4

Self-preoccupation, 46–7
Setting
    In the Country of Last Things, 162
    Smoke (film), 225
Sol Barber (*Moon Palace*), 176
Solitude
    of author, 70
    connections with others through, 58
    imagery, 18
    "the room of the book" and, 18-9,
        20–1
"Solitude" (Holiday), 27
Solomon Barber (*Moon Palace*), 173
Son/father relationship. *See* Father/son
    relationship
Spatiality
    in Auster's fiction, 138
    economic production and, 137–8
    language and, 145–9
    social consciousness and, 144–5
    urban space (*In the Country of Last
        Things*), 138–9, 140–1, 151, 156–8
    urban space (*The Book of Memory*),
        141–2
Squeeze Play (Benjamin/Auster), 228,
    230
Statue of Liberty (*Moon Palace*), 198–9,
    201–2, 214
Stengers, Isabelle, 177
Stillman (*City of Glass*). *See* Peter
    Stillman Jr., Peter Stillman Sr.
Structuralists, 52–3
Structure
    diaristic and anecdotal, 54–5
    tragedy and comedy, 210–1
Sun and Moon (publisher), 73

Temporality
    chance and, 127-30
    illusion of time and, 116–8
    rhythms of events, 176–8
    spatiality vs., 149–51
Temporal sequence, 127–8
Thomas Effing (*Moon Palace*), 173, 176,
    178-9, 186

Timbuktu (Auster), 222–3, 226–7, 228, 230–1
Timbuktu (Auster), 225
Tobin, Patricia, 175
Todorov, Tzetan, 88
Tower of Babel, 88–90
Tragedy, 210–1, 218–9
Travel theme, 110–1
Tsvetaeva, Marina, 140
Turner, Maria, 201, 203–4, 210

Ungaretti, Giuseppe, 227
Urban space, 138–49, 150–1, 156–8

Van Dine, S.S., 63
Varvogli, Aliki, 191
Violent hierarchy, 105–6, 108

Walden (Thoreau), 104
Wandering, 45, 46

Wang, Wayne, 231
Washburn, Katharine, 165
Watt (Beckett), 78
Weisenburger, Steven, 171
White (*Ghosts*), 8
White Spaces (Auster), 13-14, 225
Willy G. Christmas (*Timbuktu*), 222–3, 228, 229, 231
Wittgenstein, Ludwig, 145, 146
Woods, Tim, 137
Woolf, Virginia, 82
Writing
    death and, 71–3
    memory and, 36–9
    physicality of, 14
    responsibility of aesthetic self and, 59-60
    See also "the room of the book" theme

Zilcosky, John, 63